The Women *of* Shakespeare's PLAYS

Analysis of the Role of the Women in Selected Plays
with
Plot Synopses and Selected One Act Plays

Courtni Crump Wright

UNIVERSITY
PRESS OF
AMERICA

Lanham • New York • London

Copyright © 1993 by
University Press of America®, Inc.
4720 Boston Way
Lanham, Maryland 20706

3 Henrietta Street
London WC2E 8LU England

Library of Congress Cataloging-in-Publication Data
Wright, Courtni Crump.
The women of Shakespeare's plays : analysis of the role of the women
in selected plays : with plot synopses and selected one-act plays / by
Courtni Crump Wright.
p.   cm.
Includes bibliographical references and index.
1. Shakespeare, William, 1564–1616—Characters—Women.
2. Shakespeare, William, 1564–1616—Adaptations.
3. Shakespeare, William, 1564–1616—Plots.   4. Women in literature.
5. Women—Drama. I. Title.
PR2991.W75   1992   822.3'3—dc20   92–2411 CIP

ISBN 0–8191–8825–5 (cloth : alk. paper)
ISBN 0–8191–8826–3 (pbk. : alk. paper)

The paper used in this publication meets the minimum requirements of
American National Standard for Information Sciences—Permanence
of Paper for Printed Library Materials, ANSI Z39.48–1984.

To

My family; National Cathedral School class of
1997; and friends.

St. James Palace residence of Queen Mother, formerly used by Henry VIII, home of the Court of St. James

CONTENTS

PREFACE

Have you ever traveled backward in time to another epoch, to another way of life? Have you ever experienced the joy and awe of walking where a favorite person from history or literature has walked? Perhaps you have watched the fog envelop the keep of a castle while listening to the soft whispers of the castle's former residents, or perhaps you have heard the voices of the historical greats as they try to tell about their time periods.

As a Council for Basic Education Fellow for the summer of 1990, extensive study was spent reading about Shakespeare and the influence of the politics of his time on his decision to dramatize certain events and portray certain people. Readings covered the life of Henry VIII and his impact on society and literature, Elizabeth I and her struggles to restore and maintain the advances made by her father while still remaining unmarried and on the throne, and James I who had the unenviable task of following these two strong personalities.

The National Cathedral School (Wash., D.C.) Katherine Lee 1991 Summer Study Fellowship allowed me to actually visit memorable sites heretofore only studied. Places such as Stratford-upon-Avon, Hampton Court, Dover Castle, Westminster Cathedral, Edinborough, the Tower of London, Canterbury Cathedral, and many more were finally a reality, not the topics of textbooks. With the assistance of the Katherine Lee Fellowship, a visit to the palatial estate of Henry VIII and attendance at lectures which discussed the effect of his break with the Roman Catholic Church on the social, political, and religious aspects of his times were made a reality. At the Tower of London, it was possible to stand on the site on which the block awaited Anne Boleyn, the second of Henry VIII's six wives and mother of Elizabeth I, approximately three hundred years ago. In Westminster Cathedral, tears blurred the vision as the irony of the relationship of the two sisters, Mary I and Elizabeth I was very dramatically depicted as the elaborate coffin of Elizabeth lay over the burial site of Mary. Two sisters born of different mothers, one Roman Catholic and the other Anglican, one

PREFACE

despised and misunderstood by many of her countrymen because she set aside all of the cultural contributions of her illustrious father and restored the Roman Catholic Church; the other loved because she returned England to the glory that was Henry VIII's reign and tolerated religious differences, united in a cathedral which was originally a Roman Catholic abbey and finally an Anglican cathedral. A visit to the birth place in Edinborough of James VI of Scotland who became James I of England on a cold, torrentially rainy July first brought home the hardship of life during the Renaissance. The picturesque houses of Stratford-upon-Avon with their thatched roofs, slanting wooden floors, and abundant gardens will long live in memory. And at Canterbury Cathedral, the heart froze as the docent vividly discussed the murder of Thomas Becket, an archbishop and chancellor of England, who chose the love of the church over the love of his king.

The impact of all of these experiences and many more will, hopefully, be shared by you as a reader of this analysis of the importance of the contribution of the women of Shakespeare's times and recent history on the meaning of his plays. Shakespeare created women who lived and breathed on the page and the stage. The women possessed personalities, wit, candor, ambition, and love. They suffered from disappointments and heartache as well as reveled in successes. They were drawn from history and every-day life, and as such reflected the times in which they lived and voiced the hopes for equality and respect desired by all women then and now.

1. WILLIAM SHAKESPEARE: HIS ART, LIFE, and TIMES

Born in April of 1564 in a little village northwest of London by the name of Stratford-upon-Avon and christened on April 26th, William Shakespeare was to become one of the greatest and most disputed playwrights of his time or any other. Although Shakespeare was destined to become one of the premier authors of the modern theater and the originator of many words and expressions, the exact date of his birth remains unknown with his birthday being celebrated on April 23rd, the feast day of St. George, the patron saint of England. Ironically, the 23rd of April is the actual date of Shakespeare's death. Shakespeare's destiny for success began with the marriage of his father into a socially prominent family and continued as he gained favor with the theater going people of London.

In 1557 Shakespeare's father, John Shakespeare, married into the well-respected, land owning family of the Ardens of Park Hall by marrying Mary Arden. John Shakespeare, although a politically active, financially comfortable member of the middle class, worked all of his life with one goal in mind, that of being referred to as a "gentleman." He was a glove maker by trade and fortunate enough to be the master of his own shop by profession, and the Bailiff of Stratford-upon-Avon by political choice. However, financial difficulties and the inability to pay his church tithe ended his dream of acquiring a coat-of-arms and the appellation of "gentleman" to which he was entitled by virtue of his title as Bailiff and his marriage into the Arden family.

John Shakespeare did, however, educate his son William as was appropriate for the son of a prominent citizen. Shakespeare attended school taught by well-paid graduates of Oxford University from the time he was seven years old. His school day consisted of nine hours of instruction daily the year round with three brief holiday breaks. The curriculum centered around Latin, reading, writing, grammar, and recitation. Shakespeare also engaged in playing the popular games of his time such as "St. George and the Dragon" and "Robin

Hood." As he grew older, Shakespeare was exposed to the world of the theater by viewing plays enacted by traveling troupes of actors who produced the early morality plays which were designed to teach the citizenry the ethical, religious, and proper ways of life.

Shakespeare was eighteen years old when he married Anne Hathaway, a woman eight years his senior in November of 1582, without posting the customary marriage banns. The marriage banns were usually read in church each of three Sundays prior to the marriage. Shakespeare's family, however, requested a waiver of this policy. Shakespeare's daughter, Susanna, was born approximately six months later on May 26, 1583, and on February 2, 1585, the twins Hamnet and Judeth were born.

For Shakespeare, theater life and London were exciting and intellectually stimulating in comparison to the quiet world of Stratford-upon-Avon as London resounded with the hustle and bustle of merchants trading their wares to an ever expanding population. The streets were clogged with people, sights, sounds, and smells from all parts of the world as the Renaissance brought different cultures together. The Thames, with its changeable tides which sometimes stranded travellers or cancelled trips altogether when too high, was the main route of travel. The Tower of London stood as a memory of Henry VIII, who sent three wives and many dissenters to reside and die behind those walls. Anne Boleyn and Mary I were fresh memories, for their recent roles in shaping English history, to the London which Shakespeare was to explore. Shakespeare must have marveled, also, at the wealth of literature, not only in Latin but French and Italian, flowing from the bookstalls and making the theaters come alive with words and feelings. Authors such as Thomas Nash, Christopher Marlowe, Ben Jonson, John Donne, Thomas Kidd, Edmund Spenser, and many others were flourishing under the new liberal thinking and the increasing freedom of creativity brought about by the return of Protestantism after the death of Queen Mary I. This was the time of Queen Elizabeth I, great benefactress of the stage and English literature, who reigned from 1558 to 1603.

The theater of Shakespeare and Elizabeth I was undergoing a change from the morality plays of the Middle Ages to the more secular plays of the Renaissance, and Shakespeare as a Renaissance man took full advantage of the opportunity to entertain the audience as well as to instruct it. In writing the history plays, Shakespeare drew heavily from *The Third Chronicles ed. 1587* by Holinshed. This volume was considered the most authoritative work on history of its time. Often early works of other playwrights were used as the starting point for Shakespeare's works. *The Taming of the Shrew* was believed to have been based on a work entitled *The Shrew*. Other plays such as the three Henry plays,

Henry IV parts one and two and *Henry V*, were based on Hall's *The Union of the Two Novel and Illustre Families of Lancaster and York 1548* edition.

Shakespeare, being a sensitive and politically astute writer, was very careful not to chronicle the life of any living English monarch in his plays. He was quite aware from the experiences of other writers that it was not financially or politically prudent to point out the shortcomings of the nobility for the ridicule of the populous at-large. The theater was growing in popularity as a source of entertainment but had not obtained the freedom of speech which it was to enjoy in future years. The Henry VIII of the play by the same name was a kinder, gentler man than the actual king who was known for imprisoning or beheading those who opposed his will. This softening of the king's character is thought to have cloaked and, perhaps, weakened the message of the play. In fact, only one play, *The Merry Wives of Windsor*, concerned itself with life in England during Shakespeare's lifetime. The plot of *The Merry Wives of Windsor* revolved around the folly of a tarnished knight in his pursuit of the wives of Windsor. It is thought that this play was commissioned by Elizabeth I because of the immense popularity of Falstaff, a somewhat tarnished but very humorous knight, who first appeared in the first and second *Henry IV* plays.

The everyday man who enjoyed Shakespeare's plays required only one thing of the playwright--entertainment. The plays were held during the day in the warm months since the theaters were neither lighted nor heated. The majority of the audience stood in the open with only the well-to-do being able to afford the covered seats. Therefore, foul weather and winter cold brought the theater season to a halt. Since the theaters were not built in the major cities, being considered unsuitable tenants of respectable neighborhoods, the theater-goer had to travel considerable distances into the countryside in order to view a production. To satisfy the hungry traveler food, such as turkey legs and beef-on-a-stick, was sold in the theater before the play began and during intermission.

The actors of Shakespeare's times, always men and boys since no respectable woman would subject herself to such cramped and dirty living conditions, were forced to bear many hardships and censorships. They were considered to be unruly, drunken, loud people. The living conditions were poor, often only a barn for accommodations, as they traveled from one theater to another. It was only after Shakespeare had acquired a reputation as a playwright and after the financial success of the Globe Theater that Shakespeare's company could establish itself at one theater and not travel as often. Even with the relative comfort of a theater, Shakespeare's company was obliged to perform the plays in the homes of the paying patrons.

The theatrical company and its playwright also needed the support, both political and financial, of the patron who would support them against the municipal authorities who disliked the performers as riffraff and the stage as a financial wasteland which lost more money than it made. Also, the theater was subjected to considerable artistic criticism by both the patron, local authorities, and theatergoers themselves. Shakespeare, upon first establishing himself as an actor, aligned himself with the Lord Chamberlain's Men, one of the major troupes in operation between 1594 and 1613. This troupe was renamed the King's Men under the rule of James I as soon as the king assumed responsibility for its support. Often the troupe would be commissioned to write a play in tribute to a special person or for a special event, such as the birthday of the Queen in whose presence the play would first be presented. These play commissions were considered an honor to write and were rewarded by generous compensation from the patron. Later the play would be presented to a public audience for a few pennies admission to the theater.

The majority of the revenue generated by the troupe came from performances before public audiences. The profit and expenses were shared equally by all members of the company. Stardom was shared as well by the actors with each taking a turn staring in the type of play for which he was best suited. The staging of the plays was also a shared responsibility with each actor being responsible for props, costumes, and other necessities. Later, as in the case of Shakespeare's troupe, the actors controlled the management of the playhouses in which they performed with the obvious advantage of controlling all of the profits.

The ordinary theater-goer of the time of Elizabeth I demanded considerable energy from the actor. Plays were expected to contain gory scenes of battle, fancy duels, and bloody deaths. The action of the scenes had to be larger than life, for the average theater-goer could see dueling and death as common-place events in London streets; theater had to take the normal life of London to the extreme. To accommodate the tastes of the audience, the troupe of actors used real swords and practiced carefully choreographed duels. When blood was required, the actor would place a poultry blood-filled ox bladder under his shirt. This bladder would be pierced by the point of the sword of the opponent in the next dueling scene. More than one actor was seriously wounded or killed in attempts at reality as an overly zealous co-star thrust strongly through the shirt, woolen undervest worn for added protection, and the blood-filled ox bladder of his opponent. The upper classes, however, claimed to be more impressed with the strength of Shakespeare's words than with the force of the duels. For those theater-goers, who were largely supporting patrons of the arts, Shakespeare developed many new theatrical techniques, perfected many old techniques such as the play-within-a-play, and coined many new words and phrases.

Shakespeare's plays followed the Elizabethan practice of reflecting life as it was rather than as the church wanted it to be, as in the morality plays of the Middle Ages and followed the five act format of the ancient Greek and Roman plays. The playwright often wrote using the play-within-a-play theatrical device which allowed the dramatist to create the fragile world of the stage reflecting life apart from the main play being watched by the audience. The audience was treated to the character's actions in the main play and the characters' feeling and inner thoughts in the secondary play. The frailties of man were displayed for the audience to consider and experience. In addition to the play-within-a-play device for showing the inner emotions of the characters, Shakespeare used the soliloquy which allowed the character to stand on the stage and talk through his troubles aloud but alone. The audience benefited from additional knowledge of the character's motivations without having to watch additional, lengthy action.

The structure of the stage was also important to the understanding of the play. The stage was usually bare of scenery or curtains. The loft above the stage was called "heaven," and the area below the stage floor was "hell." Actors ascended to "heaven" via a rope which pulled them up into the loft, and a sinner descended into the bowels of "hell" via a trap door in the stage floor. Angels could float onto the stage from above and evils spirits and ghosts, the extreme ends of the strong teachings of the church and very important during the Elizabethan times, could rise from below. The area in between the loft and the stage floor was the world of everyday life.

Shakespeare was a prolific playwright producing approximately two plays every year for a total of thirty-six plays of which there were twelve comedies, nine histories, eleven tragedies, and four romances. Challenges continue to be made regarding his authorship of these plays with the names of Sir Walter Raleigh, Sir Francis Bacon, and many others being offered as the true author of the works ascribed to Shakespeare. However, not even the most recent computer-generated test of the rhythm, wording, and phrasing of Shakespeare's work against the work of the other noted writers of his time could discredit Shakespeare as the true author of the plays bearing his name.

Engraved upon his monument in Holy Trinity Church in Stratford-upon-Avon is a sample of his wit as well as the date of his death, April 23, 1616. This message was composed in the hopes of stopping the custom of transferring the bones from the inside of the church to the cemetery after the crypts inside were filled. The engraving remains surrounded by flowers but in clear view of sightseers and worshippers today.

Good frend for Iesvs sake forebeare,
To digg the dvst, encloased heare!
Blest be ye man yt spares thes stones,
And Cvst be he yt moves my bones.

Shakespeare will always be the immortal Bard and his lines, wit, words, and observations on mankind will be enjoyed and studied "So long as men can breathe or eyes can see, / So long lives this, and this gives life to thee." (Sonnet 18)

2. THE WOMEN of SHAKESPEARE'S PLAYS: AN OVERVIEW

The women of Shakespeare's plays exemplify both the traditional role of the women of the Middle Ages and the changing role of the women of the Elizabethan Age of Renaissance England. This duality in the personalities of the women in the plays mirrors the changing role of women in the times in which Shakespeare lived as they struggled with their strengths, weaknesses, and the expectations of their societies.

The women of the Middle Ages, as dictated by the Catholic Church, were expected to be more concerned with their families than with themselves, were fairly naive and uneducated, had read few if any books, and received little if any education in anything other than the art of needlework and housewifery. Their spouses were selected for them and were often total strangers to whom the women would owe total allegiance and obedience. As they entered into an arranged dowry-bearing marriages, the women were aware that their duty was to marry the man found suitable by their fathers: love, if they were lucky, would come later.

The women of the Middle Ages were firm believers in the church, the devil, and punishment for the wages of sin. They led their families in devotions to God and presented pious, God-fearing faces to the world. Usually, if of the middle and upper classes, they were escorted to the market area by a male member of the family; women never would have thought of venturing forth unprotected from the eyes and attentions of rude men. The women of the Middle Ages were protected, respected, and treated quite chivalrously as was appropriate for a time when the rules of knighthood continued to influence behavior. However, the same sort of treatment would have been afforded to any expensive household commodity. The women of the Middle Ages were property, owned by their husbands, without any rights of their own.

The Renaissance women of Elizabeth I's reign benefited from many of the chivalric codes of the Middle Ages. They, too, were often escorted to the market for protection. These women, too, were the mainstay of religion in the home and feared the wrath of God and the forces of the Devil with equal vigor. However, the women of the Renaissance and the Elizabethan Age were changing and broadening their control over their own lives.

The rise to power of Mary I and Elizabeth I provided the women with positive, aggressive, self-confident female role models who ruled Renaissance England with determination and, sometimes, an iron hand. The strength of these two monarchs encouraged the women to become more aware of the growing freedoms which awaited them, although they continued to remain under the authority of their husbands.

The Renaissance and Elizabethan Age women were somewhat better educated than the women of the Middle Ages and a bit more outspoken. Their husbands might not have been willing to provide education for them, however, the times dictated that if women could be queens, then all women should have the opportunity to study with a tutor who would instruct them in reading and writing which enabled them to be able to read the sonnets of Shakespeare and the other writers of the time as well as the popular volume of history by Holinshed.

The women attended the theater, although they still could not act in any performances and often found themselves the butt of theatrical jokes about shrewish housewives. These women continued to be commodities to the men of their families, but they were becoming a bit more outspoken on matters of importance such as marriage. Often, the women of the Elizabethan Age would select their own spouses from among the suitors who would write sonnets to them in the style of Shakespeare or John Donne. This liberty, of course, was taken with the approval of their fathers.

However, the women of the Renaissance and the Elizabethan Age were not as yet modern women. They were not independent, were not allowed to work outside the home if members of the upper classes, and were not as well educated as men. The influence of the Catholic Church, which had controlled the lives of the women of the Middle Ages, still influenced their lives as Protestantism was restored to England. Yet, the women of the Elizabethan Age found a way to show their taste in clothing and hairstyles. Further, they believed that women were not inferior to men as illustrated by the out-spoken Mistress Page of *The Merry Wives of Windsor* who outsmarted Falstaff at every turn.

The women of Shakespeare's England emulated the colorful court of Elizabeth I, the daughter of Henry VIII and Anne Boleyn, in their choice of clothing styles and colors. Elizabeth I was fond of showing off her fair skin and wore rather low cut, revealing bodices on her gowns. The women of her court and of the upper classes followed her example by wearing low cut bodices with skirts which accentuated the hips.

The women also followed the fashion of the court which preferred fair skin and fair hair. In order to accomplish this lightening of the skin and hair, a make-up composed of a lead-based, fairly corrosive agent was applied to the skin. Over time, this make-up caused pocking of the skin and the loss of eyebrows which were then penciled in making thin eyebrows a fashion statement. The bleaching solution used to lighten the hair unfortunately produced baldness with repeated applications. This baldness resulted in the use of ornate, jeweled wigs, often made from the hair sold by peasant girls.

After the skin and hair were lightened, the women faced another problem of teeth which appeared discolored since brushing of the teeth was not a common practice and fluorinated water was unknown. To brighten the teeth the women began brushing with a compound which initially lightened the teeth but, unfortunately, caused the teeth to turn dark and sometimes to become knobby with repeated applications. The women of the peasant classes were too busy working the farm plots, selling their wares in the markets, making clothing, cooking meals, and raising children to be preoccupied with cosmetic and fashion trends. Inadequate food, hygiene, and dangerous child-birth practices were even more constant enemies of the lower classes.

The women of Shakespeare's plays mirrored the traditions of the times in which the plays were written and the time periods about which they were written. Shakespeare was an astute writer who knew that a play containing very liberated women would be insulting, shocking, and unpopular with the majority of the theater-goers. Therefore, his libertine was Kate, whose very actions were wild, shocking, and shrewish. Shakespeare seized the opportunity to highlight the teachings of society which would dictate that the elder daughter must be married first before the younger, while not saying that these traditions were incorrect. He commented on a society which would treat its women like chattel and expect total obedience while giving little respect or consideration. Shakespeare also portrayed a society which would cherish a fair skinned daughter over a brunette to the point of contributing to the girl's abhorrent behavior. Actually, Shakespeare must have found dark women intriguing since he wrote one hundred fifty-four sonnets to his "Dark Lady," a woman believed to have been a dark-haired beauty of Italian heritage.

Shakespeare mirrored a society that would foster a meaningless feud between families which resulted in the deaths of many of its young members by writing about the ill-fated love between Juliet and Romeo in a very sensitive manner. In this play, Shakespeare gave Juliet the courage to love someone definitely not of her father's selection, knowing that at the very least she would cause her father's anger. Juliet was willing to risk everything, including ostracism and death, in the hopes that a marriage between feuding families would unite them in peace.

However, Shakespeare also showed the weakness of the women of his plays and his society when he allowed Ophelia to be driven mad by the circumstances of her life and the manipulations of others over which she had little or no control. Ophelia was, perhaps, one of the more pitiable examples of the effects of an oppressive society which would use a woman as a pawn without consideration for the psychological effects on the woman.

Perhaps Shakespeare was trying to mirror the courage of Elizabeth I who refused to marry anyone for fear that any marital relationship would diminish her authority over the government of her country and purloin the love of her psubjects. Elizabeth I was definitely a unique, free-thinking woman when she responded to the many attempts by Parliament to marry her to suitable prospects by saying that she was married to her country.

Elizabeth I was constantly dodging the attempts of her advisors to arrange marriages of political and financial convenience for England. She was repeatedly courted by the sons of kings and the kings themselves. Only her strong will and her sovereign power saved her from being a pawn in the political circles of which she was a member. Had she been a princess or a commoner, her fate would have undoubtedly been different, just as the fates of countless women of nobility had been different, including the fate of her own mother whose out-spoken nature alienated many influential advisors of King Henry VIII.

Shakespeare as a writer during the Elizabethan Age had witnessed the consequences of speaking out against the customs of the time. He had seen other writers fall on hard times after criticizing the nobility. However, like the other writers of the times, he could not resist the new freedom fostered by Elizabeth's love of literature. Under the Catholicism of Mary I, the church was restored with a death blow being delivered to literature, art, and the theater. Mary I was a devout Catholic who believed that music, art, and literature should all be to the glory of God rather than for the entertainment of people. Her strong beliefs all but killed the flowering of literature, music, and art encouraged by her father, Henry VIII. However, with her death and the ascension of Elizabeth I to the throne, the arts began to thrive once more. Poets, playwrights, songwriters, and artists prospered under the support and encouragement of this patron and benefactress of the arts.

Knowing that women were still not treated as equals by the men in the society of the time despite the many changes brought about by Elizabeth I, Shakespeare cagily depicted strong women as the heroines in his plays. He portrayed women such as Cleopatra in *Antony and Cleopatra* and Juliet in *Romeo* and *Juliet* as the medium to illustrate his views on the need for change in society's opinion of the role of women. A woman like Calpurnia in *Julius Caesar* was used as the conscience of her husband as she tried to assist him in achieving greater heights and rising above the jealousy of others. Shakespeare also employed women like Kate in *The Taming of the Shrew* as statements against the folly of society which would favor one woman over another based on appearance.

Shakespeare was a mirror of the struggles of the women of his times from Elizabeth I to the lowliest of peasant women as they struggled to gain more freedoms, rights, education, and respect.

The Women of Shakespeare's Plays: One Act Play

Approximate running time: twenty -five minutes

DRAMATIS PERSONAE
LADY MACBETH
KATE
JULIET
PORTIA
CLEOPATRA
JULIA
GERTRUDE

OPHELIA
CALPHURNIA
VIOLA
BEATRICE
ADRIANA
DESDEMONA
HELENA

As the play begins, the women are assembled on stage for a tea party. They are clustered in groups of three with the narrator free to visit each group. The women are very agitated and in pantomimed involvement in their conversations.

NARRATOR: The women of several of Shakespeare's plays have summoned you here today to be witness to their varied experiences at the hands of their betrothed, lovers, or husbands. They have endured much, nagged seldom, suffered in silence often, and learned the ways of men and the world in which they live. Joining the tea party today are Adriana, the long suffering wife of Antipholus of Ephesus; Ophelia, the lover of Hamlet; Portia, the wife of Brutus; Calphurnia, the helpmate of Caesar; the ambitious Lady Macbeth; lovely Juliet; Katherine, the curst; Viola and Julia, much wronged by love; Helena, caught in a love triangle; Desdemona, unwitting cause of her husband's downfall; Mistress Page, defeater of Falstaff; Beatrice of *Much Ado About Nothing*; and Cleopatra, famed queen of the Nile. Each has her unique story to tell, her own frustrations to voice. However unique, these are the tales of the lives

of every woman and of the Women of Shakespeare. *[sits stage right]*
ADRIANA: *[Steps forward to center stage to address the audience--the other women freeze and look slightly toward her as she begins to speak.]*
His company must do his minions grace, whilst I at home starve for a merry look. Hath homely age th'alluring beauty took from my poor cheek? Then he hath wasted it. Are my discourse dull? Barren my wit? If voluble and sharp discourse be marred, unkindness blunts it more than marble hard. Do their gay vestments his affections bait? That's not my fault: he's master of my state. What ruins are in me that can be found by him not ruined? Then he is the ground of my defeatures. My decayed fair a sunny look of his would soon repair. But, too unruly deer, he breaks the pale and feeds from home; poor I am but his stale. *[Returns to her place in the group--conversation resumes animatedly]*
OPHELIA: *[Steps forward to center stage to address the audience--the other women freeze and look slightly toward her as she begins to speak.]*
You must sing 'A-down a-down, and you call him a-down-a. 'O, how the wheel becomes it! It is the false steward, that stole his master's daughter. There's rosemary, that's for remembrance. Pray you, love, remember. And there is pansies, that's for thoughts. There's fennel

for you, and columbines. There's rue for you, and here's some for me. We may call it herb of grace o' Sundays. O, you must wear your rue with a difference. There's a daisy. I would give you some violets, but they withered all when my father died. They say 'a made a good end.
        Song
And will'a not come again?
And will'a not come again?
No, no, he is dead;
Go to thy deathbed;
He never will come again.
His beard was as white as snow,
All flaxen was his poll.
He is gone, he is gone,
And we cast away moan.
God 'a' mercy on his soul! *[Returns to her place in the group--conversation resumes animatedly]*
CALPHURNIA: *[steps forward to center stage to address the audience--the other women freeze and look slightly toward her as she begins to speak.]*
Caesar, I never stood on ceremonies, Yet now they fright me. There is one within, besides the things that we have heard and seen, recounts most horrid sights seen by the watch. A lioness hath whelped in the streets, and graves have yawned and yielded up their dead. Fierce fiery warriors fought upon the clouds in ranks and squadrons and right form of war, which drizzled blood upon the Capitol. The noise of battle hurtled in the air, horses did neigh, and dying

men did groan, and ghosts did shriek and squeal about the streets. O Caesar, these things are beyond all use, and I do fear them. When beggars die there are no comets seen; the heavens themselves blaze forth the death of princes. *[Returns to her place in the group--conversation resumes animatedly]*

LADY MACBETH: *[steps forward to center stage to address the audience--the other women freeze and look slightly toward her as she begins to speak.]*
Out, damned spot. Out I say! One-two-why then 'tis time to do't. Hell is murky. Fie, my lord, fie! a soldier and afeard? What need we fear who knows it, when none can call our power to accompt? Yet who would have thought the old man to have had so much blood in him? The Thane of Fife had a wife. Where is she now? What, will these hands ne'er be clean? No more o' that, my lord, no more o' that! You mar all with this starting. Hear's the smell of blood still. All the perfumes of Arabia will not sweeten this little hand. Oh, oh, oh! Wash your hands, put on your nightgown, look not so pale! I tell you yet again, Banquo's buried. He cannot come out on's grave. To bed, to bed! There's a knocking at the gate. Come, come, come, come, give me your hand! What's done cannot be undone. To bed, to bed, to bed! *[Returns to her place in the group--conversation resumes animatedly]*

JULIET: *[steps forward to center stage to address the audience--the other women freeze and look slightly toward her as she begins to speak.]*
Dost thou love me? I know thou wilt say 'Ay'; and I will take thy word. Yet, if thou swear'st, thou mayst prove false. At lovers' perjuries, they say Jove laughs. O gentle Romeo, if thou dost love, pronounce it faithfully. Or if thou thinkest I am too quickly won, I'll frown and be perverse and say thee nay, so thou wilt woo; but else, not for the world. In truth fair Montague, I am too fond, And therefore thou mayst think my havior light; but trust me, gentleman, I'll prove more true than those that have more cunning to be strange. I should have been more strange, I must confess, but that thou overheard'st, ere I was ware, my true-love passion. Therefore pardon me, and not impute this yielding to light love, which the dark night hath so discovered. *[Returns to her place in the group--conversation resumes animatedly]*

KATE: *[steps forward to center stage to address the audience--the other women freeze and look slightly toward her as she begins to speak.]*
Fie, fie, unknit that threat'ning unkind brow and dart not scornful glances from those eyes to wound thy lord, thy king, thy governor. It blots thy beauty as frosts do bite the meads, confounds thy fame as whirlwinds shake fair buds, and in no

sense is meet or amiable. Thy husband is thy lord, thy life, thy keeper, thy head, thy sovereign; one that cares for thee and for thy maintenance; commits his body to painful labor both by sea and land, to watch the night in storms, the day in cold, whilst thou li'st warm at home, secure and safe; and craves no other tribute at thy hands but love, fair looks, and true obedience-too little payment for so great a debt. I am ashamed that women are so simple to offer war where they should kneel for peace, or seek for rule, supremacy, and sway, when they are bound to serve, love, and obey. In token of which duty, if he please, my hand is ready, may it do him ease.*[Returns to her place in the group--conversation resumes animatedly]*

VIOLA:*[steps forward to center stage to address the audience--the other women freeze and look slightly toward her as she begins to speak.]*
I left no ring with her. What means this lady? Fortune forbid my outside have not charmed her. She made good view of me; indeed, so much That methought, her eyes had lost their tongue, for she did speak in starts distractedly. She loves me sure; the cunning of her passion invites me in this churlish messenger. None of my lord's ring? Why, he sent her none. I am the man. If it be so, as 'tis, poor lady, she were better love a dream. Disguise, I see

thou art a wickedness wherein the pregnant enemy does much. How easy is it for the proper false in women's waxen hearts to set their forms! Alas, our frailty is the cause not we, for such as we are made of, such we be.
[Returns to her place in thegroup--conversation resumes animatedly]
PORTIA: *[steps forward to center stage to address the audience--the other women freeze and look slightly toward her as she begins to speak.]*
Is Brutus sick, and is it physical to walk unbraced and suck up the humors of the dank morning? What, is Brutus sick, and will he steal out of his wholesome bed to dare the vile contagion of the night, and tempt the rheumy and unpurged air, to add unto his sickness? No, my Brutus. You have some sick offense within your mind, which by the right and virtue of my place I ought to know of; and upon my knees I charm you, by my once commended beauty, by all your vows of love, and that great vow which did incorporate and make us one,...I grant I am a woman; but withal a woman that Lord Brutus took to wife. I grant I am a woman; but withal a woman well-repute Cato's daughter. Think you I am no stronger than my sex, being so fathered and so husbanded? Tell me your counsels; I will not disclose 'em. I have made strong proof of my constancy, giving myself a voluntary

wound here, in the thigh. Can I bear that with patience, and not my husband's secrets?

[Returns to her place in the group-- conversation resumes animatedly]

JULIA: *[steps forward to center stage to address the audience--the other women freeze and look slightly toward her as she begins to speak.]*

Nay, would I were so ang'red with the same! O hateful hands, to tear such loving words! Injurious wasps, to feed on such sweet honey, and kill the bees that yield it with your stings! I'll kiss each several paper for amends. Look, here is writ 'Kind Julia,' Unkind Julia! As in revenge of thy ingratitude, I will throw thy name against the bruising stones, trampling contemptuously on thy disdain. And here is writ 'Love-wounded Proteus.' Poor wounded name! My bosom as a bed shall lodge thee til thy wound be thoroughly healed, and thus I search it with a sovereign kiss. But twice or thrice was 'Proteus' written down-Becalm good wind, blow not a word away til I have found each letter in the letter.

[Returns to her place in the group-- conversation resumes animatedly]

HELENA: *[steps forward to center stage to address the audience--the other women   freeze and look slightly toward her as she begins to speak.]*

How happy some o'er other some can be! Through Athens I am thought as fair as she. But what of that? Demetrius thinks not so; he will not know what all but he do know. And as he errs, doting on Hermia's eyes, So I, admiring of his qualities. Things base and vile, holding no quantity, love can transpose to form and dignity. Love looks not with the eyes, but with the mind, and therefore is winged Cupid painted blind. Nor hath Love's mind of any judgement taste; wings, and not eyes, figure unheedy haste. And therefore is Love said to be a child, because in choice he is so oft beguiled. I will go tell him of fair Hermia's flight. Then to the wood will he to-morrow night pursue her; and for this intelligence if I have thanks, it is a dear expense. But herein mean I to enrich my pain, to have his sight thither and back again.

[Returns to her place in the group-- conversation resumes animatedly]

DESDEMONA: *[steps forward to center stage to address the audience--the other women freeze and look slightly toward her as she begins to speak.]*

My mother had a maid called Barbary. She was in love, and he she loved proved mad and did foresake her. She had a song of "Willow"; and old thing 'twas; but it expressed her fortune, and she died singing it. That song to-night will not go from my mind; I have much to do but to go hang my head all at one side and sing it like poor Barbary. Prithee dispatch.

Singing

'The poor soul sat sighing by a sycamore tree,

Sing all a green willow;

Her hand on her bosom, her head on her knee,

Sing willow, willow, willow;

The fresh streams ran by her and murmured her moans;

Sing willow, willow, willow;

Her salt tears fell from her, and soft'ned the stones-

Sing willow, willow, willow;

Sing all a green willow must be my garland. Let nobody blame him; his scorn I approve-'

[Returns to her place in the group--conversation resumes animatedly]

BEATRICE: *[steps forward to center stage to address the audience--the other women freeze and look slightly toward her as she begins to speak.]*

What fire is in mine eyes? Can this be true? Stand I condemned for pride and scorn so much? Contempt, farewell! and maiden pride, adieu! No glory lives behind the back of such, and, Benedick, love on; I will requite thee, taming my wild heart to thy loving hand, if thou dost love, my kindness shall incite thee to bind our loves up in a holy band; for others say thou dost deserve, and I believe it better than reportedly.

[Returns to her place in the group--conversation resumes animatedly]

GERTRUDE, the QUEEN of DENMARK: *[steps forward to center stage to address the audience--the other women freeze and look slightly toward her as she begins to speak.]*

O Hamlet, speak no more. Thou turn'st mine eyes into my very soul, And there I see such black and grained spots as will not leave their tinct. O, speak to me no more. These words like daggers enter into mine ears. No more, sweet Hamlet. No more.

[Returns to her place in the group--conversation resumes animatedly]

MISTRESS PAGE: *[steps forward to center stage to address the audience--the other women freeze and look slightly toward her as she begins to speak.]*

That likewise have we thought upon, and thus Nan Page my daughter, and my little son, and three or four more of their growth, we'll dress like urchins, ouphs, and fairies, green and white, with rounds of waxen tapers on their heads, and rattle in their hands. Upon a sudden, as Falstaff, she and I are newly met, let them from forth a sawpit rush at once with some diffused song. Upon their sight, we two in great amazedness will fly. Then let them all encircle him about, and, fairy-like, to pinch the unclean knight.

[Returns to her place in the group--conversation resumes animatedly]

CLEOPATRA: *[steps forward to center stage to address the audience- -the other women freeze and look slightly toward her as she begins to speak.]*
Sir, I will eat no meat, I'll not drink, sir--If idle talk will once be necessary--I'll not sleep neither. This mortal house I'll ruin, do Caesar what he can. Know, sir, that I will not wait pinioned at your master's court nor once be chastised with the sober eye of dull Octavia. Shall they hoist me up and show me to the shouting varletry of censuring Rome? Rather a ditch in Egypt be gentle grave unto me! Rather on Nilus' mud lay me stark-nak'd and let the waterflies blow me into abhorring! Rather make my country's high pyramids my gibbet and hang me up in chains!
[Returns to her place in the group-- conversation resumes animatedly]
NARRATOR: The afternoon is complete with shared biscuits, tea, and conversation. You have shared their strengths, fears, doubts, and frustrations, and now the women take their leave quoting Puck from *A Midsummer Night's Dream*:

If we shadows have offended,
Think but this, and all is mended-
That you have but slumbered here
While these visions did appear.

3.THE COMEDY OF ERRORS

The Play

In *The Comedy of Errors*, a play of mistaken identity, two sets of long separated twins are reunited. The humor in this early and crudely simplistic Shakespearean comedy arises from not only the mistaken identity but the interaction between the improperly paired masters and servants and the masters with the women in their lives.

Egeon of Syracuse, father of twin sons, survives a shipwreck which separates him from one of his sons and his wife approximately twenty years before the action of the play begins. He has arrived in Ephesus to search for not only the long missing family members, but for the son who has recently set out in search of his twin brother and has failed to return. Unfortunately, there is a rule in Ephesus which states that no one from Syracuse may enter Ephesus upon fear of death without paying a fine of one thousand marks for his life. Poor Egeon is penniless and cannot pay. However, he is pitied by the Duke of Ephesus who gives him one day to acquire the money or face death.

During the course of the day, the twin sons of Egeon, both of whom are named Antipholus and their twin man-servants named Dromio inadvertently trade places assuming that each is the other. Much chaos and confusion ensue as the Antipholuses think that they have given instructions to their man-servants, only to have spoken instead to the servant of the unknown twin.

Adriana, wife of Antipholus of Ephesus, mistakes her husband's twin for him as she summons him to lunch. In actuality, she has summoned his twin who, knowing himself to be unmarried, does not respond. Becoming furious with her often philandering husband, Adriana locks the house to him. The real Antipholus of Ephesus arrives home and becomes incensed that his house is locked. He does not understand his wife's irritation, thinking her merely jealous due to one too many rendezvous. He leaves, angry and hungry, to seek comfort and lunch elsewhere.

More confusion arises as the goldsmith and the lady-friend mistake Antipholus of Syracuse for his twin brother, Antipholus of Ephesus. The goldsmith demands payment for a gold chain given to Antipholus of Syracuse in error, and the lady-friend demands her promised token of affection also from the wrong twin. Antipholus of Syracuse is totally confused and denies any knowledge of having ordered the chain which he feels was given to him as a welcoming gift by the very friendly people of Ephesus. He confides in his man-servant who, being Dromio of Ephesus not Dromio of Syracuse, thinks his master to be losing his wits and becoming deranged. Actually, everyone including the servants, knows that Antipholus has ordered a chain as a token of affection for his wife and in a fit of anger has decided to give the token to his more deserving lady-friend.

In the mean time, Adriana is told by her husband's lady-friend that he has promised her a gold chain, and that he has failed to deliver it. Adriana knows that the chain is to have been a gift from her husband to herself, and that the goldsmith is demanding payment. Adriana believes that her husband must be mad to so openly give a gift to another woman, deny his actions, and refuse to pay for the gift thereby causing a public scandal. To further add insult, Antipholus has even denied that he has a wife. Adriana, fearing for her husband's health and fuming with anger, has Antipholus confined in a small cell for his own good. Antipholus is dragged away vehemently denying all of the charges against him.

While Antipholus of Ephesus is undergoing great discomfort, Antipholus of Syracuse, the bearer of the gold chain, is confused as to his good fortune as a stranger in the town. However, the good fortune does not last long, for as Antipholus of Syracuse and the mismatched Dromio are surveying the town, the goldsmith accosts him for payment and Adriana accuses him of being her deranged husband escaped from confinement. Antipholus of Syracuse and Dromio of Ephesus take cover in the abbey fearing that all of the people have gone insane, and that they will be murdered.

All is not quiet as the still angry Adriana demands the release of her husband from the abbey claiming that he is mad and in need of treatment, and that he has wronged her by his relationship with another woman. The Abbess blames Adriana for her husband's ill health saying that constant nagging has caused him to lose his sanity. Adriana reluctantly repents for her conduct and promises to be a better wife.

Suddenly another Antipholus and another Dromio appear further confusing the Abbess and Adriana who believe that Antipholus and Dromio are safely inside the abbey which is conveniently near the place where the scheduled execution of Egeon of Syracuse is to take place. A relieved Egeon sees his son and is overjoyed knowing that his son will pay the fine required to save his father's life. However, Antipholus of Ephesus denies all knowledge of this man since he is not the son raised by Egeon but the long lost son who has not seen his father since the shipwreck. Fortunately, the confusion is resolved as Antipholus and Dromio of Ephesus and Antipholus and Dromio of Syracuse recognize each other as their own mirror images. Very soon Adriana's confusion and that of Egeon is made clear. The Abbess acknowledges that she is the former and long, lost wife of Egeon, the mother of the Antipholuses, and the mistress of the Dromios.

All live happily ever after in Ephesus as Antipholus of Syracuse marries Luciana, the sister of Adriana; Egeon lives with his wife, the former Abbess; Antipholus of Ephesus begins to understand that philandering eventually causes pain and confusion; and Adriana learns to never be jealous or doubtful of her husband again.

Adriana

Although *The Comedy of Errors* is a simplistic play which laughs at the confusion of life, a lesson is also taught to the theater audience by the conversion of Adriana into a trusting wife and Antipholus of Ephesus into a more caring husband. Throughout the play, Adriana has doubted her husband's loyalty and love. She has been provided with evidence of his infidelity by a woman claiming the right to a love token from him. Adriana admits to the Abbess that, on occasion, she has scolded her husband for tardiness to dinner and for noticing other women but does not accept his madness as the result of her efforts. The older, more conservative Abbess refuses to allow Adriana to escape that which is considered during the time period of this play to be the duty of the wife; namely, the physical and emotional well-being of her husband. Adriana is reprimanded for not being more gentle, loving, and forgiving of her husband's ill-humors, tardiness, and slightly wandering eye. Adriana's submission to both the instruction of the Abbess and the expectations of the times helps to restore her husband to health; however, Adriana, unlike her sister who thinks that a woman must accommodate the troubles of life and the wanderings of a husband, feels that she has a right to complain about her fate.

However, Antipholus of Ephesus is not without blame in this comedy of confusion. He has given Adriana reason to doubt his fidelity by being known for having a wandering eye and by seeking solace in the arms of another woman, the town courtesan. Antipholus learns from his brief imprisonment and the constant scolding of his wife that perhaps he should mend this ways and be more attentive at home.

Shakespeare, in an otherwise light-hearted entertainment, has taken a brief moment in the person of Adriana to remind the women of his time of the consequences of their suspicious natures and argumentative ways as Adriana is blamed for having driven her husband mad. However, Adriana, while being expected to adhere to the tenants of the times, has asserted herself by locking the house to her husband and having him imprisoned for his own good. She is assuming some of the more liberal freedoms and rights of the Renaissance woman as she takes charge of the situations which affect her life. Adriana is a bit drastic in her actions perhaps, but the desired effect is accomplished; Antipholus of Ephesus is made aware of the consequences of his actions in a manner which leaves little doubt about her dissatisfaction with his behavior. Perhaps Shakespeare has also reminded the husbands of the Renaissance to make a more concerted effort to honor their wives in order to reduce suspicion, criticism, and marital discord.

This passage taken from Act II, scene i depicts Adriana's frustration at her husband's dalliances and her position in life, a position over which she feels helpless.

> His company must do his minions grace,
> Whilst I at home starve for a merry look.
> Hath homely age th'alluring beauty took
> From my poor cheek? Then he hath wasted it.
> Are my discourse dull? Barren my wit?
> If voluble and sharp discourse be marred,
> Unkindness blunts it more than marble hard.
> Do their gay vestments his affections bait?
> That's not my fault: he's master of my state.
> What ruins are in me that can be found
> By him not ruined? Then he is the ground
> Of my defeatures. My decayed fair
> A sunny look of his would soon repair.
> But, too unruly deer, he breaks the pale
> And feeds from home; poor I am but his stale.

Adriana, similar to other women of the Renaissance, voices her frustration at being little more that personal property to be used and ignored by her husband as suits his fancy. However, Adriana does not remain frustrated and hopeless.

She soon takes matters into her own hands and encourages Antipholus of Ephesus to acknowledge the errors of his ways and to see her as a person who can and will exercise at least the right to respect and fair treatment.

The Comedy of Errors: One Act Play

Approximate running time twenty minutes

DRAMATIS PERSONAE
ANTIPHOLUS OF EPHESUS
DROMIO OF EPHESUS
ADRIANA
LUCIANA
FIRST MERCHANT,
friend of Antipholus of Syracuse,
a creditor of Angelo.
A COURTESAN

ANTIPHOLUS OF SYRACUSE
DROMIO OF SYRACUSE
EGEON
DUKE OF EPHESUS
JAILER
SECOND MERCHANT,
ABBESS, Emilia; wife of Egeon;
mother of the two Antipholuses.

[Outside the Duke's palace]
[Enter Duke, Egeon, Jailer walking to center stage]
DUKE OF EPHESUS: Merchant of Syracusa, plead no more; I am not partial to infringe our laws. It hath been decreed, both by the Syracusians and ourselves, to admit no traffic to our adverse towns. Nay, more, if any born at Ephesus be seen at Syracusian marts and fairs; again, if any Syracusian born come to the bay of Ephesus, he dies, unless a thousand marks be levied, to quit the penalty and to ransom him. Thy substance, valued at the highest rate, cannot amount unto a hundred marks; therefore by law thou art condemn'd to die. Well, Syracusian, say, in brief, the cause why thou departed'st from thy native home, and for what cause thou camest to Ephesus.
EGEON: *[Slowly and with deliberation]* In Syracusa was I born and wed unto a woman. With her I lived in joy; our wealth increased by prosperous voyages I often made to Epidamnum: From whom my absence was not six months old, before herself had made provision for her following me, and soon and

safe arrived where I was. There had she not been long but she became a joyful mother of two goodly sons; The one so like the other as could not be distinguish'd but by names. That very hour, and in the self-same inn, a meaner woman was delivered of such a burden, male twins, both alike. Those, for their parents were exceeding poor, I bought, and brought up to attend my sons. My wife, not meanly proud of two such boys, made daily motions for our home return: Unwilling I agreed. Alas, too soon we came aboard! A league from Epidamnum had we sail'd, before the always-wind-obeying deep gave any tragic instance of our harm. My wife, more careful for the latter-born, had fasten'd him unto a small spare mast, to him one of the other twins was bound, whilst I had been like heedful of the other. The children thus disposed, my wife and I, fasten'd ourselves at either end the mast; and floating straight, obedient to the stream, was carried towards Corinth, as we thought. Two ships from far making amain to us, of Corinth that, of Epidaurus this. Ere the ships could meet by twice five leagues, we were encounter'd by a mighty rock; which being violently borne upon, our helpful ship was splitted in the midst; so that, in this unjust divorce of us. Fortune had left to both of us alike what to delight in, what to sorrow for. Her part, was carried with more speed before the wind; and in our sight they three were taken up by fishermen of Corinth. At length, another ship had seized on us; And, knowing whom it was their hap to save, gave healthful welcome to their shipwrackt guests;

DUKE OF EPHESUS: What have befall'n of them and thee till now?

EGEON: My youngest boy, and yet my eldest care, at eighteen years became inquisitive after his brother; and importuned me that his attendant might bear him company in the quest of him; five summers have I spent in furthest Greece, roaming clear through the bounds of Asia, and, coasting homeward, came to Ephesus.

DUKE OF EPHESUS: Hapless Egeon, whom the fates have markt to bear the extremity of dire mishap! Now, trust me, were it not against our laws, against my crown, my oath, my dignity, my soul should sue as advocate for thee. But, though thou art adjudged to the death, and passed sentence may not be recall'd. Yet will I favour thee in what I can. Therefore, merchant, I'll limit thee this day to seek thy life by beneficial help. Try all the friends thou hast in Ephesus; Beg thou, or borrow, to make up the sum, and live; if no, then thou art doom'd to die. *Enter Antipholus and Dromio of Syracuse as others leave stage]*

ANTIPHOLUS OF SYRACUSE: Go bear it to the Centaur, where we

host, and stay there, Dromio, till I come to thee.

DROMIO OF SYRACUSE: Many a man would take you at your word, and go indeed, having so good a mean. *[Exit.]*

ANTIPHOLUS OF SYRACUSE: I to the world am like a drop of water, that in the ocean seeks another drop; so I, to find a mother and a brother, in quest of them, unhappy, lose myself. Here comes the almanack of my true date. *[Enter Dromio of Ephesus]* What now? how chance thou art return'd so soon?

DROMIO OF EPHESUS: Return'd so soon! rather approach'd too late: the capon burns, the pig falls from the spit; the clock hath strucken twelve upon the bell. My mistress made it one upon my cheek: she is so hot, because the meat is cold; the meat is cold, because you come not home; you come not home, because you have no stomach; you have no stomach, having broke your fast; but we, that know what 'tis to fast and pray, are penitent for your default to-day.

ANTIPHOLUS OF SYRACUSE: Stop in your wind, sir: tell me this, I pray, where have you left the money that I gave you?

DROMIO OF EPHESUS: O, sixpence, that I had o' Wednesday last to pay the saddler for my mistress' crupper. The saddler had it, sir; I kept it not.

ANTIPHOLUS OF SYRACUSE: I am not in a sportive humour now. Tell me, and dally not, where is the money? Come, Dromio, come, these jests are out of season; Where is the gold I gave in charge to thee?

DROMIO OF EPHESUS: To me, sir! Why, you gave no gold to me.

ANTIPHOLUS OF SYRACUSE: Come on, sir knave, have done your foolishness, and tell me how thou hast disposed thy charge.

DROMIO OF EPHESUS: My charge was but to fetch you from the mart. Home to your house, the Phoenix, sir, to dinner:

ANTIPHOLUS OF SYRACUSE: In what safe place have you bestow'd my money; or I shall break that merry sconce of yours.

DROMIO OF EPHESUS: I have some marks of yours upon my pate, some of my mistress' marks upon my shoulders; but not a thousand marks between you both.

ANTIPHOLUS OF SYRACUSE: Thy mistress' marks! what mistress, slave, hast thou?

DROMIO OF EPHESUS: Your worship's wife, she that doth fast till you come home to dinner, and prays that you will hie you home to dinner.

ANTIPHOLUS OF SYRACUSE: What, wilt thou flout me thus unto my face, being forbid? There, take you that, sir knave. *[Beating him.]*

DROMIO OF EPHESUS: What mean you, sir? for God's sake, hold

your hands! Nay, an you will not, sir, I'll take my heels. *[Exit]*
ANTIPHOLUS OF SYRACUSE: Upon my life, by some device or other the villain is o'er-raught of all my money. *[Exit] [Enter Adriana and Luciana]*
ADRIANA: Neither my husband nor the slave return'd, that in such haste I sent to seek his master! Sure, Luciana, it is two o'clock.
LUCIANA: Good sister, let us dine, and never fret: A man is master of his liberty: Time is their master; and when they see time, they'll go or come: if so, be patient, sister.
ADRIANA: Why should their liberty than ours be more?
LUCIANA: Because their business still lies out o' door. The beasts, the fishes, and the winged fowls, are their males' subjects and at their controls are masters to their females and their lords: Then let your will attend on their accords.
ADRIANA: This servitude makes you to keep unwed. But, were you wedded, you would bear some sway.
   LUCIANA: Ere I learn love, I'll practice to obey.
ADRIANA: How if your husband start some other where?
LUCIANA: Till he come home again, I would forbear.
ADRIANA: Patience unmoved! no marvel though she pause; they can be meek that have no other cause.
[Enter Dromio of Syracuse]

ADRIANA: Say, is your tardy master now at hand?
DROMIO OF EPHESUS: Nay, he's at two hands with me, and that my two ears can witness.
ADRIANA: Say, didst thou speak with him? Know'st thou his mind?
DROMIO OF EPHESUS: Ay, ay, he told his mind upon mine ear:
LUCIANA: Spake he so doubtfully, thou couldst not feel his meaning?
DROMIO OF EPHESUS: Nay, he struck so plainly, I could too well feel his blows; and withal so doubtfully, that I could scarce understand them.
ADRIANA: But say, I prithee, is he coming home?
DROMIO OF EPHESUS: When I desired him to come home to dinner, he ask'd me for a thousand marks in gold: "Tis dinner-time," quoth I. "My gold,"quoth he. "Your meat doth burn," quoth I. "My gold,"quoth he. "Will you come home?" quoth I. "My gold," quoth he. "Where is the thousand marks I gave thee, villain?" "The pig," quoth I, "is burn'd." "My gold,"quoth he. "My mistress, sir," quoth I. "Hang up thy mistress! I know not thy mistress; out on thy mistress! I know," quoth he, "no house, no wife, no mistress."
ADRIANA: Go back again, thou slave, and fetch him home.
DROMIO OF EPHESUS: Go back again, and be new beaten home! For God's sake, send some other messenger.

ADRIANA: Back, slave, or I will break thy pate across.

DROMIO OF EPHESUS: And he will bless that cross with other beating: Between you I shall have a holy head. Am I so round with you as you with me, that like a football you do spurn me thus? You spurn me hence, and he will spurn me hither: If I last in this service, you must case me in leather. *[Exit]*

ADRIANA: His company must do his minions grace, whilst I at home starve for a merry look. Hath homely age th'alluring beauty took from my poor cheek? Then he hath wasted it. Are my discourses dull? Barren my wit? If voluble and sharp discourse be marr'd, unkindness blunts it more than marble hard. Do their gay vestments his affections bait? That's not my fault, he's master of my state. What ruins are in me that can be found by him not ruin'd? Then is he the ground of my defeatures. My decayed fair a sunny look of his would soon repair. But, too unruly deer, he breaks the pale, and feeds from home; poor I am but his stale. *[Exit] [Enter Antipholus and Dromio of Syracuse]*

ANTIPHOLUS: How now, sir! is your merry humour alter'd? As you love strokes, so jest with me again. You know no Centaur? You received no gold? Your mistress sent to have me home to dinner? My house was at the Phoenix? Wast thou mad, that thus so madly thou didst answer me?

DROMIO OF SYRACUSE: What answer, sir? When spake I such a word?

ANTIPHOLUS OF SYRACUSE: Even now, even here, not half an hour since.

DROMIO OF SYRACUSE: I did not see you since you sent me hence, home to the Centaur, with the gold you gave me.

ANTIPHOLUS OF SYRACUSE: Villain, thou didst deny the gold's receipt, and told'st me of a mistress and a dinner.

DROMIO OF SYRACUSE: What means this jest? I pray you, master, tell me.

ANTIPHOLUS: Yea, dost thou jeer and flout me in the teeth? Think'st thou I jest? Hold, take thou that, and that. *[Beats Dromio]*

DROMIO OF SYRACUSE: Hold, sir, for God's sake! Now your jest is earnest: Upon what bargain do you give it me?

DROMIO OF SYRACUSE: But, I pray, sir, why am I beaten?

ANTIPHOLUS OF SYRACUSE: Dost thou not know?

DROMIO OF SYRACUSE: Nothing, sir, but that I am beaten.

ANTIPHOLUS OF SYRACUSE: Shall I tell you why?

DROMIO OF SYRACUSE: Ay, sir, and wherefore; for they say every why hath a wherefore.

ANTIPHOLUS OF SYRACUSE: Why, first, for flouting me; and then, wherefore, for urging it the second time to me.

DROMIO OF SYRACUSE: Was there ever any man thus beaten out of season, when in the why and the wherefore is neither rime nor reason? Well, sir, I thank you.

ANTIPHOLUS OF SYRACUSE: Thank me, sir! for what?

DROMIO OF SYRACUSE: Marry, sir, for this something that you gave me for nothing.

ANTIPHOLUS OF SYRACUSE: I'll make you amends next, to give you nothing for something. *[Enter Adriana and Luciana]*

ADRIANA: How comes it now, my husband. O, how comes it, that thou art then estranged from thyself? Thyself I call it, being strange to me, that, undividable, incorporate, am better than thy dear self's better part. Ah, do not tear away thyself from me!

ANTIPHOLUS OF SYRACUSE: Plead you to me, fair dame? I know you not, in Ephesus I am but two hours old.

LUCIANA: Fie, brother! How the world is changed with you! When were you wont to use my sister thus? She sent for you by Dromio home to dinner.

ANTIPHOLUS OF SYRACUSE: By Dromio!

DROMIO OF SYRACUSE: By me!

ADRIANA: By thee; and this thou didst return from him. That he did

buffet thee, and, in his blows, denied my house for his, me for his wife.

ANTIPHOLUS OF SYRACUSE: Did you converse, sir, with this gentlewoman? What is the course and drift of your compact?

DROMIO OF SYRACUSE: I, sir! I never saw her till this time.

ANTIPHOLUS OF SYRACUSE: Villain, thou liest; for even her very words didst thou deliver to me on the mart.

DROMIO OF SYRACUSE: I never spake with her in all my life. *[stepping back]*

ANTIPHOLUS OF SYRACUSE: *[aside]* How can she thus, then, call us by our names, unless it be by inspiration?

LUCIANA: Dromio, go bid the servants spread for dinner.

DROMIO OF SYRACUSE: O, for my beads! I cross me for a sinner. This is the fairy land! O spite of spites! We talk with goblins, owls, and elvish sprites. If we obey them not, this will ensue, they'll suck our breath, or pinch us black and blue.

ADRIANA: Come, come, no longer will I be a fool, to put the finger in the eye and weep, whilst man and master laugh my woes to scorn. Come, sir, to dinner. Dromio, keep the gate. Husband, I'll dine above with you to-day. Come, sister. Dromio, play the porter well.

ANTIPHOLUS OF SYRACUSE: *[aside]* Am I in earth, in heaven, or in hell? Sleeping or waking? mad or well-advised? Known unto these, and to myself disguised! I'll say as they say, and persever so, and in this mist at all adventures go.

DROMIO OF SYRACUSE: Master, shall I be porter at the gate?

ADRIANA: Ay; and let none enter, lest I break your pate.

LUCIANA:Come, come, Antipholus, we dine too late.*[Exeunt] [Enter Second Merchant, Angelo, and an Officer]*

SECOND MERCHANT: You know since Pentecost the sum is due, and since I have not much importuned you; nor now I had not, but that I am bound to Persia, and want guilders for my voyage:

ANGELO: Even just the sum that I do owe to you is growing to me by Antipholus; and in the instant that I met with you he had of me a chain: at five o'clock I shall receive the money for the same. Pleaseth you walk with me down to his house, I will discharge my bond, and thank you too.

MERCHANT: That labour may you save: see where he comes.*[Enter Antipholus and Dromio of Ephesus]*

ANTIPHOLUS OF EPHESUS: While I go to the goldsmith's house, go thou and buy a rope's-end: that will I bestow among my wife and her confederates for locking me out of my doors by day. But, soft! I see the goldsmith. Get thee gone; Buy thou a rope, and bring it home to me.

DROMIO OF EPHESUS: I buy a thousand pound a year! I buy a rope! *[Exit]*

ANTIPHOLUS OF EPHESUS: *[Greets merchant]* Good signior, take the stranger to my house, and with you take the chain, and bid my wife disburse the sum on the receipt thereof. Perchance I will be there as soon as you.

ANGELO: Then you will bring the chain to her yourself?

ANTIPHOLUS OF EPHESUS: No; bear it with you, lest I come not time enough.

ANGELO: Well, sir, I will. Have you the chain about you?

ANTIPHOLUS OF EPHESUS: If I have not, sir, I hope you have; or else you may return without your money.

ANGELO: Nay, come, I pray you, sir, give me the chain: You hear how he importunes me; the chain!

ANTIPHOLUS OF EPHESUS: Why, give it to my wife, and fetch your money.

ANGELO: Come, come, you know I gave it you even now. Either send the chain, or send me by some token.

ANTIPHOLUS OF EPHESUS: I owe you none till I receive the chain.

ANGELO: You know I gave it you half an hour since.

ANTIPHOLUS OF EPHESUS: You gave me none: you wrong me much to say so.

ANGELO: Arrest him officer. I would not spare my brother in this case, if he should scorn me so

apparently. *[Enter Dromio of Syracuse from the Bay]*
DROMIO OF SYRACUSE: Master, there's a bark of Epidamnum that stays but till her owner comes aboard,
and then she bears away.
ANTIPHOLUS OF EPHESUS: How now! a madman! Why, thou peevish sheep, what ship of Epidamnum stays for me?
DROMIO OF SYRACUSE: A ship you sent me to, to hire waftage.
ANTIPHOLUS OF EPHESUS: Thou drunken slave, I sent thee for a rope, and told thee to what purpose and what end.
DROMIO OF SYRACUSE: You sent me for a rope's-end as soon. You sent me to the bay, sir, for a bark.
ANTIPHOLUS OF EPHESUS: *[frustrated and angry]* To Adriana, villain, hie thee straight: Give her this key, and tell her, in the desk that's cover'd o'er with Turkish tapestry there is a purse of ducats; let her send it. Tell her I am arrested in the street,
And that shall bail me: hie thee, slave, be gone. On, officer, to prison till it come.*[Exeunt Second Merchant, Angelo, Officer, and Antipholus of Ephesus]*

[Outside the house of Antipholus of Ephesus. [Enter Adriana and Luciana from stage right and Dromio of Syracuse from stage left]

DROMIO OF SYRACUSE: *[running]* Here, go; the desk, the purse! sweet, now, make haste.
ADRIANA: Where is thy master, Dromio? Is he well? Why, man, what is the matter?
DROMIO OF SYRACUSE: I do not know the matter. He is 'rested on the case.
ADRIANA: What, is he arrested? tell me at whose suit.
DROMIO OF SYRACUSE: I know not at whose suit he is arrested well; but is in a suit of buff which 'rested him, that can I tell. Will you send him, mistress, redemption, the money in his desk?
ADRIANA: Go fetch it, sister. This I wonder at that he, unknown to me, should be in debt.*[Exit Luciana]* Tell me, was he arrested on a band?
DROMIO OF SYRACUSE: Not on a band, but on a stronger thing, a chain, a chain. *[Enter Luciana with the purse.]*
ADRIANA: Go, Dromio; there's the money, bear it straight and bring thy master home immediately. *[Exeunt]*

[The Mart]
[Enter Antipholus and Dromio of Syracuse from opposite sides of the stage]
ANTIPHOLUS OF SYRACUSE: Is there any ship that puts forth to-night? May we be gone?
DROMIO OF SYRACUSE: Why, sir, I brought you word an hour

since, that the bark Expedition put forth to-night.

ANTIPHOLUS OF SYRACUSE: The fellow is distract, and so am I; and here we wander in illusions: Some blessed power deliver us from hence! *[Enter a Courtesan]*

COURTESAN: Give me the ring of mine you had at dinner, or, for my diamond, the chain you promised; And I'll be gone, sir, and not trouble you. I pray you, sir, my ring, or else the chain: I hope you do not mean to cheat me so.

ANTIPHOLUS OF SYRACUSE: Avaunt, thou witch! Come, Dromio, let us go.   *[Exit running]*

COURTESAN: My way is now to hie home to his house, and tell his wife that, being lunatic, he rush'd into my house, and took perforce my ring away. This course I fittest choose. *[Exit] [Enter Antipholus of Ephesus and the Officer]*

ANTIPHOLUS OF EPHESUS: Here comes my man; I think he brings the money. *[Enter Dromio of Ephesus with a rope's-end.]* How now, sir! have you that I sent you for?

DROMIO OF EPHESUS: Here's that, I warrant you, will pay them all.

ANTIPHOLUS OF EPHESUS: But where's the money?

DROMIO OF EPHESUS: Why, sir, I gave the money for the rope.

ANTIPHOLUS OF EPHESUS: Five hundred ducats, villain, for a rope? To what end did I bid thee hie thee home?

DROMIO OF EPHESUS: To a rope's-end, sir; and to that end am I return'd.

ANTIPHOLUS OF EPHESUS: And to that end, sir, I will welcome you. *[Beating him.]*

DROMIO OF EPHESUS: I would I were senseless, sir, that I might not feel your blows.

ANTIPHOLUS OF EPHESUS: Thou art sensible in nothing but blows, and so is an ass.

DROMIO OF EPHESUS: I am an ass, indeed; you may prove it by my long ears. *[Enter Adriana, Luciana, and courtesan and a schoolmaster called Pinch]*

DROMIO OF EPHESUS: Mistress, 'respice finem', respect your end; or rather, the prophecy like the parrot, "Beware the rope's-end."

ANTIPHOLUS OF EPHESUS: Wilt thou still talk?   *[Beating him]*

ADRIANA: Good Doctor Pinch, you are a conjurer; Establish him in his true sense again, and I will please you what you will demand.

PINCH: I charge thee, Satan, housed within this man, to yield possession to my holy prayers, and to thy state of darkness hie thee straight; I conjure thee by all the saints in heaven!

ANTIPHOLUS OF EPHESUS: Peace, doting wizard, peace! I am not mad. Did this companion with the saffron face revel and feast at my house to-day, whilst upon me the guilty door were shut and I denied to enter in my house?

ADRIANA: O husband, God doth know you dined at home;

ANTIPHOLUS OF EPHESUS: Dined at home! Thou villain, what sayest thou?

DROMIO OF EPHESUS: Sir, sooth to say, you did not dine at home.

ANTIPHOLUS OF EPHESUS: Were not my doors lock'd up, and I shut out?

DROMIO OF EPHESUS: Perdy, your doors were lock'd, and you shut out.

ANTIPHOLUS OF EPHESUS: And did not she herself revile me there?

DROMIO OF EPHESUS: Sans fable, she herself reviled you there.

ANTIPHOLUS OF EPHESUS: Did not her kitchen-maid rail, taunt, and scorn me?

DROMIO OF EPHESUS: Certes, she did; the kitchen-vestal scorn'd ye.

ANTIPHOLUS OF EPHESUS: And did not I in rage depart from thence?

DROMIO OF EPHESUS: In verity you did.

ANTIPHOLUS OF EPHESUS: Thou hast suborn'd the goldsmith to arrest me.

ADRIANA: Alas, I sent you money to redeem you, by Dromio here, who came in haste for it.

DROMIO OF EPHESUS: Money by me! heart and good-will you might; but surely, master, not a rag of money.

ADRIANA: [to Pinch] O, bind him, bind him!

ANTIPHOLUS OF EPHESUS: What, will you murder me? Thou, jailer, thou, I am thy prisoner: wilt thou suffer them to make a rescue?

OFFICER: Masters, let him go. He is my prisoner, and you shall not have him.

PINCH: Go bind this man, for he is frantic too. [They bind Dromio of Ephesus]

ADRIANA: Go bear him hence. Sister, go you with me. [Exeunt Pinch and Assistants, with Antipholus and Dromio of Ephesus stage right] [Enter Antipholus of Syracuse with his rapier drawn, and Dromio of Syracuse stage left]

LUCIANA: God, for thy mercy! they are loose again.

ADRIANA: And come with naked swords. Let's call more help, to have them bound again.

OFFICER: Away! they'll kill us. [Exeunt Adriana and others fearfully, stage right]

ANTIPHOLUS OF SYRACUSE: I see these witches are afraid of swords. Come to the Centaur; fetch our stuff from thence: I long that we were safe and sound aboard. [Enter Adriana, Luciana, the Courtesan, and others from stage right and Dromio of Syracuse and Antipholus of Syracuse from stage left]

ADRIANA: Hold, hurt him not, for God's sake! he is mad. Some get within him, take his sword away:

Bind Dromio too, and bear them to my house.

DROMIO OF SYRACUSE: Run, master, run; for God's sake, take a house! This is some priory: in, or we are spoil'd. *[Exeunt Antipholus and Dromio of Syracuse to the abbey][Enter Abbess]*

ABBESS: Be quiet, people. Wherefore throng you hither?

ADRIANA: To fetch my poor distracted husband hence. Let us come in, that we may bind him fast, and bear him home for his recovery.

ABBESS: How long hath this possession held the man?

ADRIANA: This week he hath been heavy, sour, sad, and much different from the man he was; but till this afternoon his passion ne'er brake into extremity of rage.

ABBESS: Hath he not lost much wealth by wrack of sea? Buried some dear friend? Hath not else his eye stray'd his affection in unlawful love, a sin prevailing much in youthful men, who give their eyes the liberty of gazing? Which of these sorrows is he subject to?

ADRIANA: To none of these, except it be the last; namely, some love that drew him oft from home.

ABBESS: You should for that have reprehended him.

ADRIANA: Why, so I did.

ABBESS: Ay, but not rough enough.

ADRIANA: As roughly as my modesty would let me.

ABBESS: Haply, in private.

ADRIANA: And in assemblies too.

ABBESS: Ay, but not enough.

ADRIANA: It was the copy of our conference: In bed, he slept not for my urging it; at board, he fed not for my urging it; alone, it was the subject of my theme; in company I often glanced it; still did I tell him it was vile and bad.

ABBESS: And thereof came it that the man was mad: The venom-clamours of a jealous woman poisons more deadly than a mad-dog's tooth. It seems his sleeps were hinder'd by thy railing. And thereof comes it that his head is light. Thou say'st his meat was sauced with thy upbraidings. Unquiet meals make ill digestions, thereof the raging fire of fever bred.*[Adriana hangs head in shame]*

LUCIANA: She never reprehended him but mildly, when he demean'd himself rough-rude and wildly. *[to Adriana]* Why bear you these rebukes, and answer not?

ADRIANA: She did betray me to my own reproof. Good people, enter, and lay hold on him.

ABBESS: No, not a creature enters in my house.

ADRIANA: Then let your servants bring my husband forth.

ABBESS: Neither: he took this place for sanctuary, and it shall privilege him from your hands till I have brought him to his wits again, or lose my labour in assaying it.

ADRIANA: I will attend my husband, be his nurse, and therefore let me have him home with me.

ABBESS: Be patient; for I will not let him stir till I have used the approved means I have, with wholesome syrups, drugs, and holy prayers, to make of him a formal man again. Therefore depart, and leave him here with me.

ADRIANA: I will not hence, and leave my husband here. And ill it doth beseem your holiness to separate the husband and the wife.

ABBESS: Be quiet, and depart: thou shalt not have him. *[Exit]* *[Enter Duke of Ephesus and Egeon bareheaded]*

ADRIANA: Justice, most sacred duke, against the abbess!

DUKE OF EPHESUS: She is a virtuous and a reverend lady. It cannot be that she hath done thee wrong.

ADRIANA: May it please your grace, Antipholus my husband, a most outrageous fit of madness took him. Desp'rately he hurried through the street, with him his bondman, doing displeasure to the citizens by rushing in their houses, we came again to bind them. Then they fled into this abbey, whither we pursued them, and here the abbess shuts the gates on us, and will not suffer us to fetch him out, nor send him forth, that we may bear him hence. Therefore, most gracious duke, with

thy command. Let him be brought forth, and borne hence for help.

DUKE OF EPHESUS: Go, some of you, knock at the abbey-gate, and bid the lady abbess come to me. I will determine this before I stir. *[Enter a Servant]*

DUKE OF EPHESUS: Come, stand by me; fear nothing.

ADRIANA: Ay me, it is my husband! *[Enter Antipholus and Dromio of Ephesus]*

ANTIPHOLUS OF EPHESUS: Justice, most gracious duke, O, grant me justice!

EGEON: *[aside]* Unless the fear of death doth make me dote, I see my son Antipholus and Dromio.

ANTIPHOLUS OF EPHESUS: Justice, sweet prince, against that woman there!

EGEON: Most mighty duke, vouchsafe me speak a word. Haply I see a friend will save my life, and pay the sum that may deliver me.

DUKE OF EPHESUS: Speak freely, Syracusian, what thou wilt.

EGEON: Is not your name, sir, call'd Antipholus? And is not that your bondman Dromio? Why look you strange on me? you know me well.

ANTIPHOLUS OF EPHESUS: I never saw you in my life till now.

EGEON: Tell me thou art my son Antipholus.

ANTIPHOLUS OF EPHESUS: I never saw my father in my life.

EGEON: But seven years since in Syracusa, boy. Thou know'st we parted:

ANTIPHOLUS OF EPHESUS: The duke, and all that know me in the city, can witness with me that it is not so. I ne'er saw Syracusa in my life.

DUKE OF EPHESUS: I tell thee, Syracusian, twenty years have I been patron to Antipholus. During which time he ne'er saw Syracusa. *[Enter Abbess, with Antipholus and Dromio of Syracuse.]*

ABBESS: Most mighty duke, behold a man much wrong'd.

ADRIANA: *[in disbelief]* I see two husbands, or mine eyes deceive me.

DUKE OF EPHESUS: One of these men is Genius to the other;

DROMIO OF SYRACUSE: I, sir, am Dromio. Command him away.

DROMIO OF EPHESUS: I, sir, am Dromio. Pray, let me stay.

ANTIPHOLUS OF SYRACUSE: Egeon art thou not? or else his ghost?

DROMIO OF SYRACUSE: O, my old master! who hath bound him here?

ABBESS: Whoever bound him, I will loose his bonds, and gain a husband by his liberty. Speak, old Egeon, if thou be'st the man that hadst a wife once call'd Emilia, that bore thee at a burden two fair sons: O, if thou be'st the same Egeon, speak, and speak unto the same Emilia!

EGEON: If I dream not, thou art Emilia: If thou art she, tell me where is that son that floated with thee on the fatal raft?

ABBESS: By men of Epidamnum he and I and the twin Dromio all were taken up. But by and by rude fishermen of Corinth by force took Dromio and my son from them, and me they left with those of Epidamnum. What then became of them I cannot tell; I to this fortune that you see me in.

DUKE OF EPHESUS: Why, here begins his morning story right: These two Antipholus', these two so like, and these two Dromios, one in semblance. These are the parents to these children, which accidentally are met together. Antipholus, thou camest from Corinth first?

ANTIPHOLUS OF SYRACUSE: No, sir, not I; I came from Syracuse.

DUKE OF EPHESUS: *[confusedly]* Stay, stand apart; I know not which is which.

ANTIPHOLUS OF EPHESUS: I came from Corinth, my most gracious lord.

DROMIO OF EPHESUS: And I with him.

ADRIANA: Which of you two did dine with me to-day?

ANTIPHOLUS OF SYRACUSE: I, gentle mistress.

ADRIANA: And are not you my husband?

ANTIPHOLUS OF EPHESUS: *[going to Adriana's side]* No; I say nay to that.

ANTIPHOLUS OF SYRACUSE: And so do I; yet did she call me so: And this fair gentlewoman, her sister here, did call me brother.

ANTIPHOLUS OF SYRACUSE: I see we still did meet each other's man; And I was ta'en for him, and he for me; And thereupon these errors are arose.

ABBESS: Renowned duke vouchsafe to take the pains to go with us into the abbey here, and hear at large discoursed all our fortunes; and all that are assembled in this place, that by this sympathized one day's error have suffer'd wrong, go keep us company, and we shall make full satisfaction.

DUKE OF EPHESUS: With all my heart, I'll gossip at this feast. *[Exeunt Duke, Abbess, Egeon, and attendants--Dromios alone on stage]*

DROMIO OF EPHESUS: Methinks you are my glass, and not my brother: I see by you I am a sweet-faced youth. Will you walk in to see their gossiping?

DROMIO OF SYRACUSE: Not I, sir; you are my elder.

DROMIO OF EPHESUS: That's a question: how shall we try it?

DROMIO OF SYRACUSE: We'll draw cuts for the senior: till then lead thou first.

DROMIO OF EPHESUS: Nay, then, thus: We came into the world like brother and brother, and now let's go hand in hand, not one before another. *[Exeunt]*

White Tower of Tower of London; used as royal residence by Henry VIII

4. HAMLET, PRINCE OF DENMARK

The play

    Hamlet, Prince of Denmark is a complicated play of deceit, intrigue, and the supernatural, as well as the interaction between people in which the main character Hamlet must develop a new and deeper understanding of himself and others as he searches for truth.

    Two months after being widowed Gertrude, Queen of Denmark and mother of Hamlet, marries Claudius, the brother of her deceased husband. Hamlet is sorely distressed by his mother's lack of feeling, especially since a rumor is circulating that King Claudius actually killed Hamlet's napping father by pouring poison in his ear.

    Hamlet's grief is heightened by the appearance of a ghost claiming to be his murdered father and asking for revenge. Hamlet is tormented by his internal debate as to the legitimacy of this ghost. Could his mother have been a party to the murder of his father, or is this an evil, lying ghost set on destroying Hamlet's soul? Finally, Hamlet is convinced to "wipe away all trivial fond records,.../... thy commandment all alone shall live/Within the book and volume of my brain." He will avenge his father's murder at great cost to himself.

    Hamlet decides to "put an antic disposition on" and to pretend madness in order to uncover the past doings of the king and queen and to plot his course of action. His actions convince Ophelia and her father, Polonius, of his madness. However, they think that Hamlet has been made mad by his unrequited love for Ophelia, who is not of his social class.

    The king and queen, learning of the changes in Hamlet's personality, summon Hamlet's former friends Rosencrantz and Guildenstern to spy on him. They are convinced that it is not only the love of the fair Ophelia which has driven Hamlet mad but the hasty remarriage of the queen to her late husband's brother. The king, queen, and Polonius plan to allow Hamlet to conveniently have a private meeting with Ophelia in order to really test his sanity while they eaves-drop.

Hamlet, suspecting that he is being tested, convinces Polonius that he is truly mad as he uncovers from the unsuspecting Rosencrantz and Guildenstern that they have not come merely to visit but have been summoned by the king to spy on Hamlet. Hamlet also learns from his former friends that actors are approaching the palace and begins to formulate the plan of using these actors to produce a theatrical extravaganza which will mirror the death of his father at the hands of his uncle saying, "the play's the thing/Wherein I'll catch the conscience of the king."

The king, queen, and Polonius continue their plan of uncovering the reason for Hamlet's madness by using Ophelia as a decoy as they eaves-drop on a conversation between Hamlet and Ophelia. They decide that although Hamlet may have spoken harshly to Ophelia, he is not driven made by love but by something else troubling his soul. Claudius agrees that Hamlet should be watched since "Madness in great ones must not unwatched go."

When Hamlet's mother, Gertrude, summons him to her rooms with the hopes of uncovering the cause of his sorrow, it is Hamlet who leads the discussion by accusing his mother of a lack of loyalty towards his late father. As he speaks, Hamlet hears someone behind the drapes. Thinking the presence that of the treacherous king, Hamlet lunges and kills the eaves-dropping Polonius. The queen and Hamlet are distressed at the murder of the meddling but harmless Polonius. To compound Hamlet's distress, the ghost of his father appears to scold Hamlet for the rough treatment given to his mother. Hamlet warns his mother not to tell Claudius that his madness is merely an act as he exits her rooms dragging the body of Polonius. The king, fearing the further mad actions of Hamlet, has Hamlet taken by Rosencrantz and Gildenstern to England where Hamlet is to be killed. However, Hamlet outsmarts his captors and returns to Denmark.

While Hamlet is away, Laertes, the brother of Ophelia, returns to find his father murdered and Ophelia driven mad by grief. The king plays on Laertes' despair and gains his agreement to avenge his father's murder and Ophelia's madness by killing Hamlet with a poisoned sword and cup of poisoned wine.

Hamlet soon has the opportunity to observe Claudius' actions as the actors stage their play within this Shakespearean play. The actors' play parallels the murder of Hamlet's father and the betrayal by his mother.

After the play, a "friendly" duel or display of swordsmanship between Hamlet and Laertes begins. The match appears to be progressing in Hamlet's favor causing the unsuspecting Gertrude to drink a toast to him from the poisoned cup of wine. In their struggles with the poisoned sword, both Hamlet and Laertes are wounded. As the queen dies, she belatedly warns Hamlet of the poison. Dying, Laertes confesses that the king is to blame for the poison. Hamlet finally gets his revenge by mortally wounding the king but, unfortunately, does not live to claim his rightful throne.

The play ends with Hamlet's death and Horatio telling the emissaries from England of the treacheries and misfortunes of this royal house of Denmark.

Ophelia

Ophelia in many ways is a pawn in this play. She is used by the king and her father in order to uncover the reason for Hamlet's madness. She is again used by Hamlet to prove to the eaves-droppers that he is mad. She is also manipulated by a social custom which will allow a man of superior position to woo a woman from a lesser station while forcing her to remain respectfully distant. Ophelia's brother, Laertes, warns her that Hamlet's interest is "Forward, not permanent, sweet, not lasting,/The perfume and suppliance of a minute,/No more." Ophelia must always remember that Hamlet's position probably will not allow him to marry as he would like but, rather, as the state chooses. Polonius warns her in the first act that Hamlet's vows of love are momentary "Giving more light than heat...," and commands her not to speak with Hamlet. However, this order is quickly overridden when it is necessary for Ophelia to play another role, that of a spy on Hamlet's madness.

Ophelia is also betrayed by her own feelings for Hamlet and the natural desire to believe that she is loved by him. She is confused by Hamlet's words and actions saying that Hamlet has "importuned me with love/In honorable fashion." She wants to believe that his affections are real even after hearing the advice of her family.

Later, when Ophelia is being used to uncover Hamlet's madness, Hamlet denies ever giving her trinkets of affection. She scolds him saying, "Take these again, for the novel mind/Rich gifts wax poor when givers prove unkind." Hamlet confesses that once he did love Ophelia and then promptly scolds her for having believed him and orders her to a nunnery asking why she would wish to be "a breeder of sinners." Further, Hamlet claims that women also are inconstant and unworthy of love; they "jig, amble and lisp" and says that the changeable nature of people has made him mad.

Ophelia is left alone on stage to lament ever having seen the fall of the proud Prince of Denmark, assuming some of the responsibility for his downfall as one of the changeable people who has driven Hamlet mad because of her role in uncovering the cause of his madness and society's demands on a young woman. Small wonder Ophelia is driven mad herself in Act IV as she considers the duplicity of man and society.

Song
They bore him barefaced on the bier
[Hey non nony, nony, hey nony]
And in his grave rained many a tear-
Fare you well, my dove! You must sing 'A-down a-down, and you call
him a-down-a.' O, how the wheel becomes it! It is the false steward, that
stole his master's daughter. There's rosemary, that's for remembrance.
Pray you, love, remember. And there is pansies, that's for thoughts.
There's fennel for you, and columbines. There's rue for you, and here's
some for me. We may call it herb of grace o' Sundays. O, you must wear
your rue with a difference. There's a daisy. I would give some violets, but
they withered all when my father died.
[*Sings*]
And will'a not come again?
And will'a not come again?
No, no, he is dead;
Go to thy deathbed;
He never will come again.
His beard was as white as snow,
All flaxen was his poll.
He is gone, he is gone,
And we cast away moan.
God 'a' mercy on his soul!

Ophelia, who is all but forgotten by the end of the play by Hamlet in his
search for truth and the movement of the action of the play towards the resolution
of the triangle involving Hamlet, Gertrude, and Claudius, resides in the shadows
of the evils suggested by the deed of Claudius, the hasty marriage of Gertrude,
and the words of the murdered king's ghost.

Gertrude, the Queen

Gertrude, the Queen of Denmark, widow of Hamlet's father and wife of
Claudius, Hamlet's uncle, is a character who gives this play and her son Hamlet
motivation and direction. It is Gertrude's quick marriage to the brother of the
newly murdered king of Denmark which causes Hamlet to question reality and
truth. It is her rapid shift from dutiful wife and mother to sweetheart which
prompts Hamlet to begin his search for truth in love and life. Hamlet is tormented
by what he perceives as his mother's treasonous and unwomanly act of surrender
to her brother-in-law as their marriage follows too swiftly on her husband's death.

The king's death has not even been investigated, avenged, or mourned before Gertrude is wed to his brother, the new king. Hamlet does not have time to be sorrowful for the loss of his father before he must suffer the loss of his mother to another man and be expected to rejoice in his mother's new happiness.

If Gertrude intentionally means to show disrespect for her deceased husband, she succeeds. Her period of mourning would lead others to believe that she feels little or nothing for her dead husband. If she is afraid for her station in life as the queen rather than as the queen-mother should Hamlet take the throne, Gertrude removes any doubt that she will retain the title at any cost, even that of her honor. If Gertrude has incestuous feelings toward her brother-in-law which allow her to quickly put aside her dead husband, she surrenders to them with great abandon even appearing young again in the newness of love. Lastly, as has been speculated many times, if Gertrude has experienced incestuous thoughts toward her son, she suppresses them before they can overcome her by hastily marrying Claudius.

Gertrude is not faced by any of these questions until Hamlet confronts her in her room and forces her to see the effect of her actions on his life and her credibility in his eyes. It is then that Gertrude shrinks from her reflection in Hamlet's eyes and words and experiences the horror of her actions.

> O Hamlet, speak no more.
> Thou turn'st mine eyes into my very soul,
> And there I see such black and grained spots
> As will not leave their tinct.
> O, speak to me no more.
> These words like daggers enter into mine ears.
> No more, sweet Hamlet.
> No more.

Regardless of the reason for Gertrude's swift marriage to Hamlet's uncle and her brother-in-law, the deed relentlessly drives Hamlet in his search for truth and in his suspicion of all around him. It is not possible for Hamlet to believe the constancy of the heart of Ophelia when that of his mother seems so false. Gertrude's actions generate the drive for Hamlet's overwhelming thirst for the truth in relationships, love, and life, and ultimately lead to his death.

Hamlet: One Act Play

Approximate running time thirty-five minutes

DRAMATIS PERSONAE

HAMLET
OPHELIA
GERTRUDE
CLAUDIUS
GHOST
HORATIO

ROSENCRANTZ
GUILDENSTERN
POLONIUS
LAERTES
OSRIC

[Elsinore, a sentry post before the castle]
[Francisco and Bernardo on guard; enter Horatio and Marcellus, Francisco exits]
MARCELLUS: What, has this thing appear'd again to-night?
BERNARDO: I have seen nothing.
MARCELLUS: Horatio says 'tis but our fantasy, and will not let belief take hold of him. Therefore I have entreated him along with us to watch the minutes of this night. That, if again this apparition come, he may approve our eyes, and speak to it.
HORATIO: Tush, tush, 'twill not appear.
BERNARDO: Sit down awhile. Let us once again assail your ears, that are so fortified against our story, what we two nights have seen.
HORATIO: Well, sit we down, and let us hear Bernardo speak of this.
BERNARDO: Last night of all, when yond same star that's westward from the pole had made his course t'illume that part of heaven where now it burns...
MARCELLUS: Peace, break thee off; look, where it comes again!
[Enter Ghost]
BERNARDO: In the same figure, like the king that's dead.
MARCELLUS: Thou art a scholar, speak to it, Horatio.
BERNARDO: Looks it not like the king? Mark it, Horatio.
HORATIO: Most like, It harrows me with fear and wonder. What art thou, that usurp'st this time of night, together with that fair and warlike form in which the majesty of buried Denmark did sometimes march? By heaven I charge thee, speak!
MARCELLUS: It is offended.
BERNARDO: See, it stalks away!
HORATIO: Stay! speak, speak! I charge thee speak! *[Exit Ghost]*
MARCELLUS: 'Tis gone, and will not answer.

BERNARDO: How now, Horatio! you tremble, and look pale. Is not this something more than fantasy? What think you on't?

HORATIO: Before my God, I might not this believe without the sensible and true avouch of mine own eyes.

MARCELLUS: Is it not like the King?

HORATIO: As thou art to thyself: Such was the very armour he had on.

MARCELLUS: Thus twice before, and jump at this dead hour, with martial stalk hath he gone by our watch.

HORATIO: This bodes some strange eruption to our state. But, soft, behold! lo, where it comes again! *[Enter Ghost again]* I'll cross it, though it blast me. Stay, illusion! If thou hast any sound, or use of voice, speak to me. If there be any good thing to be done, that may to thee do ease, and grace to me, speak to me. If thou art privy to thy country's fate, which, happily, foreknowing may avoid, O, speak! Or if thou hast uphoarded in thy life extorted treasure in the womb of earth, for which, they say, you spirits oft walk in death,*[Cock crows]* speak of it:. Sstay, and speak! *[Exit Ghost]*

BERNARDO: It was about to speak when the cock crew.

HORATIO: And then it started like a guilty thing upon a fearful summons. Let us impart what we have seen to-night unto young Hamlet; for, upon my life, this spirit, dumb to us, will speak to him: Do you consent we shall acquaint him with it, as needful in our loves, fitting our duty?

MARCELLUS: Let's do't, I pray; and I this morning know where we shall find him most convenient. *[Exeunt]*

[A room of state in the castle. Enter the King, Queen, Hamlet, Polonius, Laertes]

KING: Though yet of Hamlet our dear brother's death the memory be green; Yet so far hath discretion fought with nature, that we with wisest sorrow think on him, together with remembrance of ourselves. Therefore our sometime sister, now our queen, th'imperial jointress of this warlike state, have we, as 'twere with a defeated joy, with one auspicious, and one dropping eye, with mirth in funeral, and with dirge in marriage, in equal scale weighing delight and dole, taken to wife. And now, Laertes, what's the news with you?

LAERTES: Dread my lord, your leave and favour to return to France.

KING: Have you your father's leave? What says Polonius?

POLONIUS: He hath, my lord, wrung from me my slow leave by laboursome petition.

KING: Take thy fair hour, Laertes; time be thine, and thy best graces spend it at thy will! But now, my cousin Hamlet, and my son,

HAMLET: *[aside]* A little more than kin, and less than kind.

KING: How is it that the clouds still hang on you?

HAMLET: Not so, my lord; I am too much i'th'sun.

QUEEN: Good Hamlet, cast thy nighted colour off, and let thine eye look like a friend on Denmark. Do not for ever with thy vailed lids seek for thy noble father in the dust.

KING: 'Tis sweet and commendable in your nature, Hamlet, to give these mourning duties to your father. But, you must know, your father lost a father; that father lost, lost his. We pray you, throw to earth this unprevailing woe; and think of us as of a father: for let the world take note, you are the most immediate to our throne; And with no less nobility of love than that which dearest father bears his son.

QUEEN: Let not thy mother lose her prayers, Hamlet: I pray thee, stay with us.

HAMLET: I shall in all my best obey you, madam.

KING: Why, 'tis a loving and a fair reply: Be as ourself in Denmark.- Madam, come. [*Exeunt all but Hamlet*]

HAMLET: O, that this too too solid flesh would melt, thaw, and resolve itself into a dew! Or that the Everlasting had not fix'd His canon 'gainst self-slaughter! O God! God! How weary, stale, flat, and unprofitable seem to me all the uses of this world! But two months dead! Must I remember? why, she would hang on him, as if increase of appetite had grown by what it fed on: and yet, within a month, let me not think on't. Frailty, thy name is woman! [*Enter Horatio, Marcellus, and Bernardo*]

HAMLET: But what is your affair in Elsinore? We'll teach you to drink deep ere you depart.

HORATIO: My lord, I came to see your father's funeral.

HAMLET: I pray thee, do not mock me, fellow-student; I think it was to see my mother's wedding. My father, methinks I see my father!

HORATIO: O, where, my lord?

HAMLET: In my mind's eye. He was a man, take him for all in all, I shall not look upon his like again.

HORATIO: My lord, I think I saw him yesternight.

HAMLET: Saw? who?

HORATIO: My lord, the king your father.

HAMLET: For God's love, let me hear.

HORATIO: A figure like your father, appears before them, and with solemn march goes slowly and stately by them. Thrice he walk'd whilst they stand dumb, and speak not to him. And I with them the third night kept the watch where, the apparition comes: I knew your father.

HAMLET: Did you not speak to it?

HORATIO: My lord, I did; but answer made it none: yet once methought it lifted up its head like as it would speak. But even then the morning cock crew loud; and at the sound it shrunk in haste away, and vanish'd from our sight. As I do live, my honour'd lord, 'tis true.

HAMLET: Indeed, indeed, sirs, but this troubles me. Hold you the watch to-night?

MARCELLUS AND BERNARDO: We do, my lord.

HAMLET: I will watch to-night. Perchance 'twill walk again. If it assume my noble father's person, I'll speak to it, though hell itself should gape, and bid me hold my peace. Give it an understanding, but no tongues: farewell./[*Exeunt all but Hamlet*] My father's spirit in arms! all is not well. I doubt some foul play: would the night were come! Till then sit still, my soul: foul deeds will rise, though all the earth o'erwhelm them, to men's eyes. [*Exit*]

[*A room in Polonius' house--Enter Laertes and Ophelia*]

LAERTES: My necessaries are embark'd. Farewell. And, sister, let me hear from you. For Hamlet, and the trifling of his favour, hold it a fashion. A violet in the youth of primy nature, forward, not permanent, sweet, not lasting, the perfume and suppliance of a minute; No more. Perhaps he loves you now;

and now no soil nor cautel doth besmirch the virtue of his will: but you must fear, his greatness weigh'd, his will is not his own; for he himself is subject to his birth. He may not, as unvalued persons do, carve for himself.

OPHELIA: But, good my brother, do not, as some ungracious pastors do, show me the steep and thorny way to heaven; whilst himself the primrose path of dalliance treads, and recks not his own rede.

LAERTES: O, fear me not. I stay too long. But here my father comes. *[Enter Polonius]*

POLONIUS: There, my blessing with thee! And these few precepts in thy memory see thou character. Give thy thoughts no tongue, nor any unproportion'd thought his act. Be thou familiar, but by no means vulgar. Beware of entrance to a quarrel; but being in, bear't, that th'opposed may beware of thee. Give every man thine ear, but few thy voice. Take each man's censure, but reserve thy judgement. Neither a borrower nor a lender be. For loan oft loses both itself and friend; and borrowing dulls the edge of husbandry. This above all, to thine own self be true; and it must follow, as the night the day, thou canst not then be false to any man. *[Exit Laertes]*

POLONIUS: What is't, Ophelia, he hath said to you?

OPHELIA: So please you, something touching the Lord Hamlet.

POLONIUS: 'Tis told me, he hath very oft of late given private time to you; and you yourself have of your audience been most free and bounteous. What is between you? Give me up the truth.

OPHELIA: He hath, my lord, of late made many tenders of his affection to me.

POLONIUS: Affection! pooh! you speak like a green girl, do you believe his tenders, as you call them?

OPHELIA: I do not know, my lord, what I should think.

POLONIUS: Marry, I'll teach you. Think yourself a baby; That you have ta'en these tenders for true pay, which are not sterling. Tender yourself more dearly.

OPHELIA: My lord, he hath importuned me with love in honourable fashion. And hath given countenance to his speech, my lord, with almost all the holy vows of heaven.

POLONIUS: Be somewhat scanter of your maiden presence; set your entreatments at a higher rate than a command to parley. Do not believe his vows.

OPHELIA: I shall obey, my lord. *[Exeunt.]*

[The sentry post before the castle]

HORATIO: Look, my lord, it comes!   *[Enter Ghost]*

HAMLET: Angels and ministers of grace defend us! *[Ghost beckons Hamlet]*

HORATIO: It beckons you to go away with it, as if it some impartment did desire to you alone.

HAMLET: It will not speak; then I will follow it. Why, what should be the fear? It waves me still. Go on; I'll follow thee.

MARCELLUS: You shall not go, my lord.

HAMLET: Hold off your hands. My fate cries out, still am I call'd: unhand me, gentlemen; I say, away! Go on; I'll follow thee. *[Exeunt Ghost and Hamlet]*

HORATIO: Have after.

MARCELLUS: Something is rotten in the state of Denmark. *[Exeunt]*
   [Enter Ghost and Hamlet]

HAMLET: Where wilt thou lead me? speak; I'll go no further.

GHOST: Mark me. My hour is almost come, when I to sulphurous and tormenting flames must render up myself. Pity me not, but lend thy serious hearing to what I shall unfold.

HAMLET: Speak; I am bound to hear.

GHOST: So art thou to revenge, when thou shalt hear. I am thy father's spirit; doom'd for a certain term to walk the night, and for the day confined to fast in fires, till the foul crimes done in my days of nature are burnt and purged away. Revenge his foul and most unnatural murder.

HAMLET: Murder!

GHOST: Murder most foul. Now, Hamlet, hear: 'Tis given out that, sleeping in my orchard, a serpent stung me; so the whole ear of Denmark is by a forged process of my death rankly abused. But know, thou noble youth, the serpent that did sting thy father's life now wears his crown.

HAMLET: O my prophetic soul! My uncle!

GHOST: Ay, that incestuous, that adulterate beast, won to his shameful lust the will of my most seeming-virtuous queen. But, soft! methinks I scent the morning air; brief let me be. Sleeping within my orchard, my custom always in the afternoon, upon my secure hour thy uncle stole, with juice of cursed hebenon in a vial, and in the porches of mine ears did pour the leperous distilment; whose effect holds such an enmity with blood of man, that, swift as quicksilver, it courses through the natural gates and alleys of the body; and, with a sudden vigour, it doth posset and curd, like eager droppings into milk, the thin and wholesome blood: so did it mine; and a most instant tetter bark'd about, most lazar-like, with vile and loathsome crust all my smooth body. Thus was I, sleeping, by a brother's hand of life, of crown, of queen, at once dispatch'd. Cut off even in the blossoms of my sin, no reckoning made, but sent to my account with all my imperfections on my head. But, howsoever thou pursuest this act, taint not thy mind, nor let thy soul contrive against thy mother aught. Leave her to heaven. Adieu, adieu, adieu! Remember me.   [Exit]

HAMLET: Remember thee! Yea, from the table of my memory I'll wipe away all trivial fond records, all saws of books, all forms, all pressures past, that youth and observation copied there; and thy commandment all alone shall live within the book and volume of my brain, unmix'd with baser matter.

HORATIO: What news, my lord? Good my lord, tell it.

HAMLET: No; you will reveal it.

HORATIO: Not I, my lord, by heaven.

MARCELLUS: Nor I, my lord.

HAMLET: It is an honest ghost, that let me tell you. And now, good friends, as you are friends, scholars, and soldiers, give me one poor request.

HORATIO: What is't, my lord? we will.

HAMLET: Never make known what you have seen to-night.

HORATIO and MARCELLUS: My lord, we will not.

HAMLET: Nay, but swear't.

HORATIO: In faith, my lord, not I.

MARCELLUS: Nor I, my lord, in faith.

HAMLET: Upon my sword.

GHOST: Swear.

HORATIO: Propose the oath, my lord.

HAMLET: Never to speak of this that you have seen, swear by my sword.

GHOST: Swear.

HAMLET: Come hither, gentlemen, and lay your hands again upon my sword. Never to speak of this that you have heard, swear by my sword.

GHOST: Swear.

HORATIO: O day and night, but this is wondrous strange!

HAMLET: And therefore as a stranger give it welcome. There are more things in heaven and earth, Horatio, than are dreamt of in your philosophy. As I, perchance, hereafter shall think meet to put an antic disposition on, that you, at such times seeing me, never shall, with arms encumber'd thus, or this head-shake, or by pronouncing of some doubtful phrase, or such ambiguous giving out, to note that you know aught of me. This not to do, so grace and mercy at your most need help you, swear.

GHOST: Swear.

HAMLET: Rest, rest, perturbed spirit! The time is out of joint: O cursed spite, that ever I was born to set it right!   *[Exeunt.]*

[Inside the castle] [Enter Polonius]

POLONIUS: How now, Ophelia! what's the matter?

OPHELIA: O, my lord, my lord, I have been so affrighted!

POLONIUS: With what, i'th'name of God?

OPHELIA: My lord, Lord Hamlet, with his doublet all unbraced; no hat upon his head; his stockings foul'd, ungarterd, and down-gyved to his ankle; pale as his shirt; his knees knocking each other; and with a look so piteous in purport as if he had been loosed out of hell to speak of horrors- he comes before me.

POLONIUS: Mad for thy love?

OPHELIA: My lord, I do not know; But, truly, I do fear it.

POLONIUS: What said he?

OPHELIA: He took me by the wrist, and held me hard; then goes he to the length of all his arm; and, with his other hand thus o'er his brow, he falls to such perusal of my face as he would draw it. Long stay'd he so; At last, a little shaking of mine arm, and thrice his head thus waving up and down, he raised a sigh so piteous and profound, that it did seem to shatter all his bulk, and end his being. That done, he lets me go; and, with his head over his shoulder turn'd, he seem'd to find his way without his eyes; ror out o' doors he went without their help, and, to the last, bended their light on me.

POLONIUS: Come, go with me: I will go seek the king. This is the very ecstasy of love whose violent property fordoes itself. What, have you given him any hard words of late?

OPHELIA: No, my good lord; but, as you did command, I did repel his letters, and denied his access to me.

POLONIUS: That hath made him mad. I am sorry that with better heed and judgement I had not quoted him. I fear'd he did but trifle, and meant to wrack thee; but, beshrew my jealousy! Come.   *[Exeunt]*

[A room in the castle]
[Enter King, Queen, and Polonius]

POLONIUS: I do think that I have found the very cause of Hamlet's lunacy.

KING: O, speak of that; that do I long to hear. He tells me, my dear Gertrude, he hath found the head and source of all your son's distemper.

QUEEN: I doubt it is no other but the main, his father's death, and our o'erhasty marriage.

POLONIUS: I will be brief. Your noble son is mad. That he is mad, 'tis true: 'tis true,'tis pity, and pity 'tis 'tis true. And now remains that we find out the cause of this effect, I have a daughter hath given me this: now gather, and surmise. "To the celestial and my soul's idol, the most beautified Ophelia."

QUEEN: Came this from Hamlet to her?

POLONIUS: Good madam, stay a while; I will be faithful. "Doubt thou the stars are fire; Doubt that the sun doth move; Doubt truth to be a liar; But never doubt I love. O dear Ophelia, I am ill at these numbers; I have not art to reckon my groans: but that I love thee best, O most best, believe it. Adieu.Thine evermore, most dear lady, whilst this machine is to him, Hamlet." This, in obedience, hath my daughter shown me.

KING: But how hath she receiv'd his love?

POLONIUS: I must tell you that, I prescripts gave her, that she should lock herself from his resort, admit no messengers, receive no tokens. Which done, she took the fruits of my advice; and he, repulsed, fell into a sadness; then into a fast; thence to a watch; thence into a weakness; into the madness wherein now he raves, and all we mourn for.

KING: Do you think 'tis this?

QUEEN: It may be, very like.

POLONIUS: [pointing to his head and shoulder] Take this from this, if this be otherwise: I will find where truth is hid.

KING: How may we try it further?

POLONIUS: You know, sometimes he walks four hours together here in the lobby. At such a time I'll loose my daughter to him: Be you and I behind an arras then; Mark the encounter. [Exeunt] [Enter Hamlet, Rosencrantz and Guildenstern]

GUILDENSTERN: My honour'd lord!

ROSENCRANTZ: My most dear lord!

HAMLET: My excellent good friends!How dost thou,Guildenstern? Ah, Rosencrantz! Good lads, how do ye both?

GUILDENSTERN: Happy, in that we are not overhappy; on Fortune's cap we are not the very button.

ROSENCRANTZ: None, my lord, but that the world's grown honest.

HAMLET: Then is doomsday near: but your news is not true. Let me question more in particular: what have you, my good friends, deserved at the hands of Fortune, that she sends you to prison hither? What make you at Elsinore?

ROSENCRANTZ: To visit you, my lord; no other occasion.

HAMLET: Were you not sent for? You were sent for; there is a kind of confession in your looks. I know the good king and queen have sent for you. If you love me, hold not off.

GUILDENSTERN: My lord, we were sent for.

HAMLET: I will tell you why. I have of late lost all my mirth, forgone all custom of exercises; and, indeed, it goes so heavily with my disposition that this goodly frame, the earth, seems to me a sterile promontory; man delights not me; no, nor woman neither. Why did you laugh, then, when I said "man delights not me"?

ROSENCRANTZ: If you delight not in man, what entertainment the players shall receive from you: we coted them on the way; and hither are they coming, to offer you service.

HAMLET: He that plays the king shall be welcome. [Flourish of trumpets within.]

GUILDENSTERN: There are the players.

HAMLET: Gentlemen, you are welcome to Elsinore. Masters, you are all welcome. Take them in.

POLONIUS: Come, sirs.

HAMLET: Follow him, friends: we'll hear a play to-morrow. *[Exeunt]* I have heard that guilty creatures sitting at a play have by the very cunning of the scene been struck so to the soul, that presently they have proclaim'd their malefactions. I'll have these players play something like the murder of my father before mine uncle. I'll observe his looks. The spirit that I have seen may be the devil: and the devil hath power t'assume a pleasing shape. I'll have grounds more relative than this: the play's the thing wherein I'll catch the conscience of the king.   *[Exit]*

[A room in the castle]
[Enter Polonius, King, and Ophelia]
POLONIUS: Ophelia, walk you here. Read on this book. I hear him coming: let's withdraw, my lord. *[Exeunt King and Polonius--enter Hamlet]*
HAMLET: To be, or not to be, that is the question. Whether 'tis nobler in the mind to suffer the slings and arrows of outrageous fortune, or to take arms against a sea of troubles, and by opposing end them? To die, to sleep, no more; and by a sleep to say we end the heart-ache, and the thousand natural shocks that flesh is heir to, 'tis a consummation devoutly to be wish'd. To die, to sleep, to sleep! perchance to dream: ay, there's the rub; For in that sleep of death what dreams may come, when we have shuffled off this mortal coil, must give us pause. Thus conscience does make cowards of us all. The fair Ophelia! Nymph, in thy orisons be all my sins remember'd.

OPHELIA: My lord, I have remembrances of yours, that I have longed long to re-deliver; I pray you, now receive them.

HAMLET: I never gave you aught.

OPHELIA: My honour'd lord, you know right well you did; take these again; for to the noble mind rich gifts wax poor when givers prove unkind. There, my lord.

HAMLET: I did love you once.

OPHELIA: Indeed, my lord, you made me believe so.

HAMLET: You should not have believed me. I loved you not. Get thee to a nunnery: why wouldst thou be a breeder of sinners? Go thy ways to a nunnery. Or, if thou wilt needs marry, marry a fool; for wise men know well enough what monsters you make of them. To a nunnery, go; and quickly too. Farewell. God has given you one face, and you make yourselves another: you jig, you amble, and you lisp, and nickname God's creatures, and make your wantonness your ignorance. To a nunnery, go.   *[Exit]*

OPHELIA: O, what a noble mind is here o'erthrown! And I, of ladies most deject and wretched, that suck'd the honey of his music vows, now see that noble and most sovereign reason, like sweet bells jangled, out of tune and harsh; that unmatch'd form and feature of blown youth blasted with ecstasy. O, woe is me t' have seen what I have seen, see what I see!*[Enter King and Polonius]*

KING: Love! his affections do not that way tend; There's something in his soul o'er which his melancholy sits on brood. He shall with speed to England, haply, the seas, and countries different, with variable objects, shall expel this something-settled matter in his heart. What think you on't?

POLONIUS: It shall do well: but yet do I believe the origin and commencement of his grief sprung from neglected love. How now, Ophelia! You need not tell us what Lord Hamlet said; We heard it all. My lord, let his queen mother all alone entreat him to show his grief. And I'll be placed, so please you, in the ear of all their conference.

KING: It shall be so. Madness in great ones must not unwatch'd go. *[Exeunt]*

[A hall in the castle] [Enter Hamlet and two or three of the players]

HAMLET: Speak the speech, I pray you, as I pronounced it to you, trippingly on the tongue./*Exeunt players] [Enter Polonius]* How now, my lord! Will the king hear this piece of work?

POLONIUS: And the queen too, and that presently.

HAMLET: Bid the players make haste. *[Exit Polonius] [Enter Horatio]*

There is a play to-night before the king; one scene of it comes near the circumstance which I have told thee of my father's death. I prithee, when thou seest that act a-foot, even with the very comment of thy soul observe my uncle. If his occulted guilt do not itself unkennel in one speech, it is a damned ghost that we have seen. I mine eyes will rivet to his face; and, after, we will both our judgements join in censure of his seeming.

HORATIO: Well, my lord. If he steal aught the whilst this play is playing, and scape detecting, I will pay the theft.

HAMLET: They're coming to the play; I must be idle. Get you a place.

[A flourish. Enter King, Queen, and others carrying torches.]

KING: How fares our cousin Hamlet?

HAMLET: Excellent, i'faith. Be the players ready?

ROSENCRANTZ: Ay, my lord; they stay upon your patience.

QUEEN: Come hither, my dear Hamlet, sit by me.

HAMLET: No, good mother; here's metal more attractive; for, look you, how cheerfully my mother looks, and my father died within's two hours.

OPHELIA: Nay, 'tis twice two months, my lord.

HAMLET: So long? Then there's hope a great man's memory may outlive his life half a year. Madam, how like you this play?

QUEEN: The lady doth protest too much, methinks.

KING: What do you call the play?

HAMLET: The Mouse-trap. This play is the image of a murder done in Vienna; Gonzago is the duke's name; his wife, Baptista. You shall see anon; 'tis a knavish piece of work. He poisons him i' th'garden for's estate. His name's Gonzago; you shall see anon how the murderer gets the love of Gonzago's wife.

OPHELIA: The king rises.

KING: Give me some light. Away!

[Exeunt all but Hamlet and Horatio]

HAMLET: O good Horatio, I'll take the ghost's word for a thousand pound. Didst perceive? Upon the talk of the poisoning,...

HORATIO: I did very well note him. *[Enter Rosencrantz and Guildenstern]*

GUILDENSTERN: The queen, your mother, in most great affliction of spirit, hath sent me to you.

ROSENCRANTZ: She desires to speak with you in her closet, ere you go to bed.

HAMLET: We shall obey, were she ten times our mother. *[Enter Polonius]*
POLONIUS: My lord, the queen would speak with you, and presently. *[Exit Polonius and others]* Soft! now to my mother. O heart, lose not thy nature! Let not ever the soul of Nero enter this firm bosom: let me be cruel, not unnatural. I will speak daggers to her, but use none; my tongue and soul in this be hypocrites, how in my words soever she be shent, to give them seals never, my soul, consent! *[Exit]*

[A room in the castle] [Enter King, Rosencrantz, and Guildenstern]
KING: I like him not; nor stands it safe with us to let his madness range. Therefore prepare you; I your commission will forthwith dispatch, and he to England shall along with you. Arm you, I pray you, to this speedy voyage.
ROSENCRANTZ and
　　GUILDENSTERN: We will haste us. *[Exeunt] [Enter Polonius]*
POLONIUS: My lord, he's going to his mother's closet. Behind the arras I'll convey myself, to hear the process; I'll warrant she'll tax him home.
KING: Thanks, dear my lord. *[Exit Polonius]* O, my offence is rank, it smells to heaven; it hath the primal eldest curse upon't, a brother's murder! Bow, stubborn knees; and, heart with strings of steel, be soft as sinews of the new-born babe! All may be well. *[Kneels] [Enter Hamlet]*
HAMLET: Now might I do it pat, now he is praying; and now I'll do't, and so he goes to heaven; and so am I revenged. A villain kills my father; and, for that, I, his sole son, do this same villain send to heaven. When he is drunk, asleep, or in his rage; or in th'incestuous pleasure of his bed; at gaming, swearing; or about some act that has no relish of salvation in't; then trip him, that his heels may kick at heaven; and that his soul may be as damn'd and black as hell, whereto it goes. *[Exit]*
KING: *[rising]* My words fly up, my thoughts remain below. Words without thoughts never to heaven go. *[Exit]*

[The Queen's closet. Enter Queen and Polonius]
POLONIUS: He will come straight. Look you lay home to him. Tell him his pranks have been too broad to bear with. Pray you, be round with him.
HAMLET: Mother, mother, mother!
QUEEN: I'll warrant you; fear me not:-withdraw, I hear him coming. *[Polonius goes behind the arras] [Enter Hamlet]*
HAMLET: Now, mother, what's the matter?
QUEEN: Hamlet, thou hast thy father much offended.
HAMLET: Mother, you have my father much offended. You are the queen, your husband's brother's wife; and- would it were not so!- you are my mother. Come, come, and sit you down; you shall not budge; you go not till I set you up a glass where you may see the inmost part of you.
QUEEN: What wilt thou do? thou wilt not murder me? Help, help!
POLONIUS: Help, help, help!
HAMLET: How now! a rat? Dead for a ducat, dead!
POLONIUS: O, I am slain! *[Dies]*
QUEEN: O me, what hast thou done?
HAMLET: Nay, I know not: is it the king?
QUEEN: O, what a rash and bloody deed is this!

HAMLET: A bloody deed! Almost as bad, good mother, as kill a king, and marry with his brother.
QUEEN: As kill a king!
HAMLET: Ay, lady, 'was my word. *[Opens curtain]* Thou wretched, rash, intruding fool, farewell! I took thee for thy better. Leave wringing of your hands: peace; sit you down, and let me wring your heart.
QUEEN: What have I done, that thou darest wag thy tongue in noise so rude against me?
HAMLET: Such an act that blurs the grace and blush of modesty; calls virtue hypocrite; takes off the rose from the fair forehead of an innocent love, and sets a blister there; makes marriage-vows as false as dicers' oaths.
QUEEN: Ay me, what act, that roars so loud, and thunders in the index?
HAMLET: Look here, upon this picture, and on this, the counterfeit presentment of two brothers. See, what a grace was seated on this brow; Hyperion's curls; the front of Jove himself; an eye like Mars, to threaten and command; a station like the herald Mercury new-lighted on a heaven-kissing hill; a combination and a form indeed, where every god did seem to set his seal, to give the world assurance of a man: This was your husband. Look you now, what follows. Here is your husband; like a mildew'd ear, blasting his wholesome brother. Have you eyes? Eyes without feeling, feeling without sight, ears without hands or eyes, smelling sans all.
QUEEN: O Hamlet, speak no more. Thou turn'st mine eyes into my very soul; and there I see such black and grained spots as will not leave their tinct.
HAMLET: Nay, but to live in the rank sweat of an enseamed bed.

QUEEN: O, speak to me no more; these words, like daggers, enter in mine ears; no more, sweet Hamlet!
HAMLET: *[Enter Ghost]* Save me, and hover o'er me with your wings, you heavenly guards! What would your gracious figure? Do you not come your tardy son to chide, that, lapsed in time and passion, lets go by th'important acting of your dread command?
GHOST: Do not forget. This visitation is but to whet thy almost blunted purpose. But, look, amazement on thy mother sits. O, step between her and her fighting soul, conceit in weakest bodies strongest works, speak to her, Hamlet.
HAMLET: How is it with you, lady?
QUEEN: Alas, how is't with you, that you do bend your eye on vacancy, and with th'incorporal air do hold discourse? Whereon do you look?
HAMLET: On him, on him! Look you, how pale he glares! Why, look you there! look, how it steals away! My father, in his habit as he lived! Look, where he goes, even now, out at the portal! *[Exit Ghost]*
QUEEN: This is the very coinage of your brain. O Hamlet, thou hast cleft my heart in twain.
HAMLET: O, throw away the worser part of it, and live the purer with the other half. Good night: but go not to my uncle's bed; assume a virtue, if you have it not. Refrain to-night; and that shall lend a kind of easiness to the next abstinence. *[Gesturing to Polonius]* I do repent: but heaven hath pleased it so, to punish me with this, and this with me, that I must be their scourge and minister. I will bestow him, and will answer well the death I gave him. So,

again, good night. *[Exit, dragging corpse]*

[A room in the castle] [Enter King, Queen, Rosencrantz, and Guildenstern]
KING: Now, Hamlet, where's Polonius?
HAMLET: At supper. Not where he eats, but where he is eaten. In heaven; send thither to see. If your messenger find him not there, seek him i' th'other place yourself. But, indeed, if you find him not within this month, you shall nose him as you go up the stairs into the lobby.
KING: Hamlet, this deed, for thine especial safety, must send thee hence. Therefore prepare thyself; the bark is ready, and every thing is bent for England. *[Exeunt]*

[A room in the castle. King, Queen and Horatio sit]
QUEEN: I will not speak with her.
HORATIO: She is importunate, indeed distract; her mood will needs be pitied. She speaks much of her father; says she hears there's tricks i' th'world. 'Twere good she were spoken with; for she may strew dangerous conjectures in ill-breeding minds.
QUEEN: Let her come in. *[Enter Ophelia distracted.]*
QUEEN: How now, Ophelia!
KING: How do you, pretty lady? How long hath she been thus? Follow her close; give her good watch. I pray you. *[Exit Horatio]* O, this is the poison of deep grief; it springs all from her father's death. *[Enter Laertes, armed]*
LAERTES: Where is this king? Sirs, stand you all without. I thank you:- keep the door. O thou vile king, Where is my father?
KING: Dead.
QUEEN: But not by him.

KING: Good Laertes, if you desire to know the certainty of your dear father's death, is't writ in your revenge.
OPHELIA:*[spesks dreamily]* You must sing, "Down a-down, an you call him a-down-a." O, how the wheel becomes it! It is the false steward, that stole his master's daughter. There's rosemary, that's for remembrance; pray you, love, remember: and there is pansies, that's for thoughts. There's fennel for you, and columbines:- there's rue for you; and here's some for me:-we may call it herb-grace o' Sundays:- O, you must wear your rue with a difference.- There's a daisy:- I would give you some violets, but they wither'd all when my father died:- they say he made a good end. *[sings]* For bonny sweet Robin is all my joy,- *[sings]*
And will a' not come again?
And will a' not come again?
No, no, he's dead:
Go to thy death-bed:
He never will come again.
His beard was as white as snow,
All flaxen was his poll:
He is gone, he is gone,
And we cast away moan:
God ha' mercy on his soul!
And of all Christian souls, I pray God.- God be wi'you. *[Exit]*
LAERTES: Dear maid, kind sister, sweet Ophelia! O heavens, is't possible a young maid's wits should be as mortal as an old man's life? Tell me why you proceeded not against these feats.
KING: O, for two special reasons; The queen his mother lives almost by his looks; and for myself, my virtue or my plague, be it either which, she's so conjunctive to my life and soul, that, as the star moves not but in his sphere, I could not but by her.

The other motive is the great love the general gender bear him.

LAERTES: And so have I a noble father lost; a sister driven into desperate terms, but my revenge will come.

KING: If it be so, Laertes, will you be ruled by me?

LAERTES: My lord, I will be ruled. The rather, if you could devise it so, that I might be the organ.

KING: Hamlet comes back: what would you undertake, to show yourself your father's son in deed more than in words?

LAERTES: To cut his throat i' th'church.

KING: Revenge should have no bounds. But, good Laertes, and set a double varnish on the fame the Frenchman gave you; bring you, in fine, together, and wager on your heads: he, being remiss, most generous, and free from all contriving, will not peruse the foils; so that, with ease, or with a little shuffling, you may choose a sword unbated, and, in a pass of practice, requite him for your father.

LAERTES: I will do't: And for that purpose I'll anoint my sword. I bought an unction of a mountebank, so mortal, that but dip a knife in it, where it draws blood no cataplasm so rare, collected from all simples that have virtue under the moon, can save the thing from death that is but scratch'd withal. I'll touch my point with this contagion, that, if I gall him slightly, it may be death.

KING: When in your motion you are hot and dry, and that he calls for drink, I'll have prepared him a chalice for the nonce; whereon but sipping, if he by chance escape your venom'd stuck, our purpose may hold there. *[Enter Queen]*

QUEEN: One woe doth tread upon another's heel, so fast they follow. Your sister's drown'd, Laertes.

LAERTES: Drown'd! Too much of water hast thou, poor Ophelia, and therefore I forbid my tears. Adieu, my lord. *[Exeunt]*

[A hall in the castle] [Enter Hamlet, Horatio, and Osric]

OSRIC: Your lordship is right welcome back to Denmark.

HAMLET: I humbly thank you, sir.

OSRIC: Sweet lord, if your lordship were at leisure, I should impart a thing to you from his majesty. My lord, his majesty bade me signify to you, that he has laid a great wager on your head: sir, this is the matter. Sir, here is newly come to court Laertes; believe me, an absolute gentleman, full of most excellent differences, of very soft society and great showing: indeed, to speak feelingly of him, he is the card or calendar of gentry, for you shall find in him the continent of what part a gentleman would see. You are not ignorant of what excellence Laertes is, I mean, sir, for his weapon.

HAMLET: What's his weapon?

OSRIC: Rapier and dagger. The king, sir, hath wager'd with him six Barbary horses. The king, sir, hath laid, that in a dozen passes between yourself and him, he shall not exceed you three hits: he hath laid on twelve for nine; and it would come to immediate trial, if your lordship would vouchsafe the answer.

HAMLET: I will win for him an I can; if not, I will gain nothing but my shame and the odd hits.

HORATIO: You will lose this wager, my lord.

HAMLET: I do not think so; since he went into France, I have been in continual practice; I shall win at the odds. But thou wouldst not think how ill all's here about my heart. But it is no matter. *[Enter King, Queen, Laertes, and others]*

KING: Come, Hamlet, come, and take this hand from me.

HAMLET: Give me your pardon, sir. I've done you wrong; but pardon't, as you are a gentleman. This presence knows, and you must needs have heard, how I am punish'd with sore distraction.

LAERTES: I am satisfied in nature, whose motive, in this case, should stir me most to my revenge. But in my terms of honour I stand aloof; and will no reconcilement till by some elder masters, of known honour, I have a voice and precedent of peace, to keep my name ungored. But till that time I do receive your offer'd love like love, and will not wrong it.

HAMLET: I embrace it freely; And will this brother's wager frankly play. Give us the foils.

LAERTES: Come, one for me.

KING: Give them the foils, young Osric. Cousin Hamlet, you know the wager?

HAMLET: Very well, my lord; Your Grace hath laid the odds o' th'weaker side.

LAERTES: This is too heavy, let me see another.

HAMLET: This likes me well. These foils have all a length?

KING: Set me the stoops of wine upon that table. If Hamlet give the first or second hit, or quit in answer of the third exchange, let all the battlements their ordnance fire; the king shall drink to Hamlet's better breath.

HAMLET: One.

LAERTES: No.

HAMLET: Judgement.

OSRIC: A hit, a very palpable hit.

KING: Stay; give me drink. Hamlet, this pearl is thine; here's to thy health. *[Trumpets sound, and shot goes off]*

QUEEN: Here, Hamlet, take my napkin, rub thy brows. The queen carouses to thy fortune, Hamlet.

KING: Gertrude, do not drink.

QUEEN: I will, my lord; I pray you, pardon me.

KING [aside]. It is the poison'd cup; it is too late.

LAERTES: My lord, I'll hit him now. And yet 'tis almost 'gainst my conscience. Have at you now! *[Laertes wounds Hamlet; then, in scuffling they change rapiers, and Hamlet wounds Laertes and the Queen falls.]*

HORATIO: They bleed on both sides. How is it, my lord?

OSRIC: How is't, Laertes.

LAERTES: Why, as a woodcock to mine own springe, Osric; I am justly kill'd with mine own treachery.

HAMLET: How does the queen?

KING: She swounds to see them bleed.

QUEEN: No, no, the drink, the drink, O my dear Hamlet, the drink, the drink! I am poison'd. *[Dies]*

HAMLET: O villainy! Ho! let the door be lock'd. Treachery! seek it out. *[Laertes falls]*

LAERTES: It is here, Hamlet. Hamlet, thou art slain; no medicine in the world can do thee good, in thee there is not half an hour of life; the treacherous instrument is in thy hand, unbated and envenom'd. The foul practice hath turn'd itself on me; lo, here I lie, never to rise again. Thy mother's poison'd. I can no more:- the king, the king's to blame.

HAMLET: The point envenom'd too! Then, venom, to thy work. *[Stabs the King]* Here, thou incestuous, murderous, damned Dane, drink off this potion. Is thy union here? Follow my mother. *[King dies]*

LAERTES: He is justly served. It is a poison temper'd by himself. Exchange forgiveness with me, noble Hamlet. Mine and my father's death come not upon thee. Nor thine on me!   [Dies]
HAMLET: Heaven make thee free of it! I follow thee. I am dead, Horatio. Wretched queen, adieu! Horatio, I am dead; Thou livest; report me and my cause aright to the unsatisfied.
O, I die, Horatio; the potent poison quite o'er-crows my spirit. The rest is silence.   [Dies]
HORATIO: Now cracks a noble heart. Good night, sweet prince; And flights of angels sing thee to thy rest!

5. *THE MERRY WIVES OF WINDSOR*

The play

The Merry Wives of Windsor is the only Shakespearean comedy set in England dealing with the trials and tribulations of the middle class. In this lighthearted comedy, Sir John Falstaff is seen in amorous pursuit of the women of the town of Windsor. However, the women do not return the affections of this aging, tarnished knight who once fought on the side of Henry IV and is now the subject of laughter as the women unite to teach Falstaff a lesson in humility.

As the play opens Shallow and Slender, a country justice and his cousin, and parson Evans are discussing Falstaff's lack of integrity and honesty as well as his knaves' thievery as they prepare to dine at the Garter, a popular neighborhood inn. Slender is infatuated with Anne Page, daughter of one of the families of Windsor and the love of a young, impoverished gentleman. Unfortunately, Slender is a bumbling suitor who is incapable of expressing himself clearly in a manner likely to win the heart of a young woman from a handsome but poor gentleman. Slender stumbles over his words just as he trips over his tall, awkward frame. Realizing that Slender is inept at wooing, parson Evans sends Slender's man-servant to engage the assistance of Mistress Quickly, an acquaintance of Mistress Page, in speaking for him.

However, Sir John Falstaff, who is lodging at the inn at which the gentlemen are planning to dine, does not suffer from a lack of words. No longer a man of means, having fallen on hard times, Falstaff must rely on his wit and vanity for sustenance. He envisions himself to be the source of desire for Mistress Page and longs to be equally appealing to Mistress Ford. Neither of the women is physically attracted to this vain, egotistical, aging knight. Nevertheless, Falstaff has convinced himself of their desire and hopes to win one or both of these well-to-do women as his benefactress being "out of heels" himself. Falstaff has written identical love letters to both women which he dispatches by one of his men. His plan is overheard by Pistol and Nym, two disgruntled former followers, who plan to tell Page and Ford of Falstaff's amorous and mercenary intentions toward their wives.

On behalf of his master Slender, Simple visits Mistress Quickly, the nurse of the French physician Caius, in his office where much confusion ensues. Simple hides in Caius' closet in an effort to avoid angering the physician who dislikes having company visit Mistress Quickly during working hours. However, Simple is discovered in the closet when the physician in a fractured English play-on-words looks for some "simples in my closet dat I vill not vor the vorld I shall leave behind." Caius soon understands that Mistress Quickly is being asked to not only speak for him to Anne Page but to be the go-between for Slender as well. The physician is incensed and composes a letter to the parson in which he challenges the parson to a duel for his interference with Anne Page on behalf of Slender. Little does he know that Mistress Quickly is also speaking to Anne Page for Fenton, the young, impoverished gentleman and Anne Page's preferred suitor. Ironically, Mistress Quickly, who prides herself on her knowledge of other people's affairs and especially those of Anne Page, does not realize that Anne loves Fenton.

Mistress Page and Mistress Ford, having each received a letter of amorous intention from Falstaff, meet and begin to plan a scheme whereby they will repay the wayward knight for his unsolicited advances. They are doubly insulted that Falstaff has sent the same letter to both of them, and that a knight who is so portly and sloppy has professed interest in them when neither of them has given him cause to take this liberty. Mistress Ford also worries that her often jealous husband will become aware of the letter and fly into a rage. Mistress Page, feeling that her husband is "as far from jealousy as I am from giving him cause," decides that the two women should plot against the "greasy knight."

As the women plot against Falstaff using Mistress Quickly as messenger, the husbands are informed by Pistol and Nym of Falstaff's interest in their wives. Page is not concerned, being a husband who totally trusts his wife's fidelity. However, Ford is suspicious of his wife's possible reaction to Falstaff and, as the men leave to witness the duel between the doctor and the pastor, he decides to disguise himself as a stranger named Brook in order to gain Falstaff's confidence and learn the truth of the relationship which exists between Falstaff and his wife.

Mistress Quickly shortly arrives at the inn to deliver the message that both women find Falstaff appealing, and that Mistress Ford will meet with him that day. As Falstaff gloats over his good fortune, Ford in the disguise of Brook, a gentleman who himself has designs on Mistress Ford, enters to uncover Falstaff's intentions toward his wife. His request of Falstaff is that the knight win the lady for him since his own efforts have been unsuccessful. Much to his surprise, Ford discovers that his wife has already invited Falstaff to come to her house for a rendezvous that day. Falstaff accepts the position of go-between and the offered purse, never intending to speak for Brook. However, he promises Ford that the match will not take long to make. A furious Ford is left doubting the loyalty of his wife and the wisdom of his own heart for having loved her.

While Ford waits for the opportunity to disclose his wife's true disloyal self, he encounters Page, Caius, Shallow, and Slender as they prepare for the dinner with Anne Page which will determine the man whom she will marry. Anne favors Fenton, Mistress Page prefers the doctor, and Page encourages Slender in the pursuit of his daughter's hand. They encounter Anne in conversation with Fenton who feels that he will never be able to gain her father's permission to marry her since he is from a financially ruined noble family.

Mistresses Ford and Page have successfully devised a plan in which to repay not only Falstaff but the jealous Ford after learning that Mistress Ford's husband has overheard Falstaff brag of his plans to visit her that day and has rushed home to interrupt what he imagines to be a romantic interlude. The women have contrived to fool Falstaff into believing that Ford is arriving home unexpectedly. They are pleasantly surprised when Ford actually appears saving them the effort of the charade. Falstaff, the portly knight, must escape with his life by hiding in a basket of dirty linen only to be dumped unceremoniously into the muddy Thames.

One dunking in the Thames is not enough for the conceited Falstaff who is an easy target for the women as they plan once more to turn his vanity against him. Falstaff is again invited to Mistress Ford's house while her husband is away. Not only does Falstaff agree to the visit Mistress Ford again, but he tells Ford as Brook of his intention to visit her on Brook's behalf. Once again the jealousy of Ford is aroused as he decides to interfere with his wife's plan in order to prove her a disloyal wife.

Once again the women lure Falstaff to Mistress Ford's home, and once again they pretend that Ford is about to break in on the tryst between Mistress Ford and Falstaff. This time Falstaff refuses to leave in the laundry basket causing the women to suggest that he dress as the aunt of Mistress Ford's maid in order to hide his true identity. As Falstaff is changing clothes, Ford arrives to again set upon the laundry basket being convinced that his wife's lover is hiding in it. All of the dirty clothes are removed from the basket only to reveal no one in hiding. Ford is beyond reason as he begins searching the house for Falstaff. This time he finds Falstaff in the guise of the maid's aunt, who as a suspected witch has been forbidden access to his home, and beats him as he hurriedly escapes with his life. After two successful attempts at punishing Falstaff for his boldness, Mistress Ford and Mistress Page agree that he has been soundly punished and plan to tell their husbands about the letters, Falstaff's visits, and their revenge. Upon hearing the story of the women's revenge on Falstaff, Ford promises his wife never to again question her loyalty as he and Page decide to publicly disgrace Falstaff for his attempts at seducing their wives by luring him to Herne's Oak, a place of enchantment. There Falstaff will encounter Anne Page and others dressed as fairies to bewitch and torment his mind just as the women have tormented his heart and ego.

Herne's Oak is also to be the site of Anne Page's elopement. Mistress Page has arranged for Anne to be spirited away by Caius; Page has contrived for Slender to steal her away; and Anne and Fenton have decided that Fenton will rescue her from the others in order to marry her.

The ever egotistical Falstaff feels that he has finally been justly rewarded for his pains in wooing Mistress Ford when both Mistress Ford and Mistress Page meet him in the park at Herne's Oak. Quickly, however, he learns to fear for his life as the women run away, and he is encircled by fairies who burn him with their candles. During the confusion of dance and song, Slender and the Caius steal away with "women" they believe to be Anne Page but who are actually young boys dressed as girls, while Anne and Fenton slip away together.

The assorted plots against Falstaff are disclosed as he finally realizes that the wives and husbands of Windsor have had their full revenge of him, leaving him to say, "This is enough to be the decay of lust and late-walking through the realm." As the plan against Falstaff is unfolded, so too unfolds the successful plan for the elopement of Anne Page. Mistress Page and Page discover that Anne has not married the suitors of their economic but loveless selection, but that Anne has married Fenton, her financially impoverished, true love. Ford reminds all involved that "In love the heavens do guide the state:/Money buys lands, and wives are sold by fate." Mistress Page and Page embrace their new son-in-law as they plan for all parties, including Falstaff, to laugh in good company at the past follies with Falstaff and to rejoice in the marriage of Anne Page to Fenton. All is forgiven of Falstaff with Ford saying that Falstaff has actually kept his promise to Brook since Ford is contentedly going home to be with his wife.

Mistress Page

As a woman of strong opinions, good marriage, and quick wits, Mistress Page is content within herself and her world. She knows that she is loved and trusted by her husband who considers her his partner rather that an ornament. She is aware of the security of their marriage, and she feels sorrow for her friend Mistress Ford whose husband is untrusting and jealous. As a strong female figure, Mistress Page is only too happy to help Mistress Ford rebuke Falstaff and conquer Ford's unfounded jealousy in one effort.

Also as a self-confident woman, Mistress Page is able to disagree with her husband as to the ideal spouse for her daughter. Although she has the same goal of marrying her daughter for wealth rather than for love, she disagrees on the appropriate man, seeking one of European flair rather than an Englishman. Mistress Page graciously accepts defeat as Anne marries the poor but noble man of her own selection.

Mistress Page is also the chief designer of the plot in the final episode of revenge against Falstaff. It is she, as a representative of every woman ever flirted with and wronged by a man, who plans the involvement of Anne and the younger children in the fairy story set to unfold at Herne's Oak, a place of enchantment.

> That likewise have we thought upon, and thus
> Nan Page my daughter, and my little son,
> And three or four more of their growth, we'll dress
> Like urchins, ouphs, and fairies, green and white,
> With rounds of waxen tapers on their heads,
> And rattle in their hands. Upon a sudden,
> As Falstaff, she and I are newly met,
> Let them from forth a sawpit rush at once
> With some diffused song. Upon their sight,
> We two in great amazedness will fly.
> Then let them all encircle him about,
> And, fairy-like, to pinch the unclean knight.

Not unlike Elizabeth I, who is believed to have commissioned this play and commanded that it be written and produced in fourteen days, Mistress Page is a determined leader who has earned the respect of her friends and, most importantly, her husband during a time in England in which women were newly exercising their rights to express themselves and to make choices. As Page said upon hearing of Falstaff's attentions toward his wife "If he should intend this voyage toward my wife, I would turn her loose to him; and what he gets more of her than sharp words, let it lie on my head." Mistress Page is a seasoned match for any man.

Hampton Court, estate of Henry VIII

6. *JULIUS CAESAR*

The play

Julius Caesar, one of Shakespeare's eleven tragedies, centers around the assassination of the emperor of ancient Rome on the Ides of March, 44 BC. Although a fairly straight-forward play, readers must decide whether Caesar is "the noblest man/That ever lived in the tide of times" or a manipulative, conniving tyrant. Further, the reader must decide whether Caesar's assassination was a senseless act committed by overly ambitious men or the justifiable release of the Roman people from the control of a power-hungry tyrant.

In the opening scene of the play, Julius Caesar is praised for his valor over the defeated Pompey. However, not all of Rome praises Caesar as he is three times offered and three times rejects the title of king. Marcus Brutus, Casca, Cassius, and five others fear that Caesar is acquiring too much power which will result in reduced governmental influence for them. These eight men unite to conspire to kill Caesar before he becomes too god-like in the eyes of the people. Cassius jealously points out that Caesar has a malady which makes him "as a sick girl" and surely not suitable to rule; Caesar is an epileptic. Cassius cannot comprehend why Caesar has been raised to such power and glory when he is more brave and, in fact, worthy of the same honor. Cassius convinces Brutus that he is worthy also of praise equal to that heaped on Caesar and that the reason for their lower status "is not in our stars,/But in ourselves" namely, their lack of ambition.

Cassius, Brutus, and the other conspirators meet to develop their plans; however, it is as if the gods are against them and favor Caesar. On the night of their meeting a terrible storm develops, and Caesar's wife Calpurnia recounts stories which tell of graves having "yawned and yielded up their dead." These omens, along with the prophesy of the soothsayer to "Beware the Ides of March," convince Calpurnia that Caesar is in danger. Caesar refuses to remain at home in safety saying "Cowards die many times before their deaths./The valiant never taste of death but once."

Caesar arrives at the Senate somewhat troubled by the prophesies and omens but determined to hear the appeals of the people for the return from banishment of the brother of a conspirator. However, Caesar refuses to amend his decision. Using Caesar's refusal as an excuse for murder, the assassins carry out the plan as each in turn stabs Caesar. Caesar dies, crying "Et tu, Bruté?" as his trusted associate Brutus also stabs him.

Marc Antony, loyal friend of Caesar, arrives shortly after Caesar's death. He is met by Brutus who tries to convince him that Caesar was evil and ambitious, thereby making his death necessary. After Marc Antony removes Caesar's body, Brutus addresses the people in order to convince them that Caesar's death has been for the good of Rome. Being weak, the people initially believe Brutus.

When it is Marc Antony's turn to speak, his words and the sight of the mutilated body of Caesar convince the people that Brutus and the other assassins have indeed killed a good and just man. The people immediately call for the death of these men who have gone into hiding.

Brutus begins to regret his role in the assassination of Caesar after twice being visited during the night by the ghost of Caesar. Although Brutus has an army of supporters, he knows that Marc Antony and the people have begun to hunt for Caesar's assassins and to demand their surrender. Knowing that he will never surrender and that the only other choice is death at the hands of Octavius Caesar and Marc Antony, Brutus falls on his sword and commits suicide.

The play ends with Marc Antony and Octavius Caesar paying homage to Brutus as the "noblest Roman of them all." They believe that Brutus became a conspirator, not out of envy, but because he believed that Julius Caesar's death and overthrow was for the good of all the people.

Calpurnia and Portia

The women of this play Calpurnia, wife of Julius Caesar, and Portia, wife of Brutus although secondary characters serve as the voice of reason to their husbands. Each tries to persuade her spouse to discuss troubling matters, share confidences, and find comfort in the oneness of marriage.

Portia

Portia, although supportive of Brutus in the manner expected of a wife, is not as strong a persona or help-mate as Calpurnia. It is not enough for her to remind Brutus of the oneness promised by marriage, she must also remind him of the gallantry of her father who fought bravely with Pompey against Caesar, and who killed himself rather than be captured and forced to abandon his beliefs. She feels that this kinship with a noble warrior who is both uncle and father-in-law to Brutus will give credence to her words. When Brutus is not swayed by these words, Portia inflicts a wound in her own thigh to prove her strength and ability to withstand pain and hardship. Finally, Brutus is moved to agree that his wife is indeed noble, and that he needs to become more receptive of her advice. Although a wise woman of noble birth, Portia realizes that in her husband's mind she is still not considered an equal. In this conversation, she voices her frustration after hearing Brutus in confidential discussion with his fellow male conspirators. She wants equal treatment, shared confidences, and the same level of trust.

Is Brutus sick, and is it physical
To walk unbraced and suck up the humors
Of the dank morning? What, is Brutus sick,
And will he steal out of his wholesome bed
To dare the vile contagion of the night,
And tempt the rheumy and unpurged air,
To add unto his sickness? No, my Brutus.
You have some sick offense within your mind,
Which by the right and virtue of my place
I ought to know of; and upon my knees
I charm you, by my once commended beauty,
By all your vows of love, and that great vow
Which did incorporate and make us one,
That you unfold to me, your self, your half,
Why you are heavy--and what men tonight
Have had resort to you; for here have been
Some six or seven, who did hide their faces
Even from darkness.
Within the bond of marriage, tell me, Brutus,
Is it excepted I should know no secrets
That appertain to you? Am I your self
But, as it were, in sort or limitation?
To keep with you at meals, comfort your bed,
And talk to you sometimes? Dwell I but in the suburbs
Of your good pleasure? If it be no more,
Portia is Brutus' harlot, not his wife.
If this were true, then should I know this secret.
I grant I am a woman; but withal
A woman that Lord Brutus took to wife.
I grant I am a woman; but withal
A woman well-repute, Cato's daughter.
Think you I am no stronger than my sex,

Being so fathered and so husbanded?
Tell me your counsels; I will not disclose 'em.
I have made strong proof of my constancy,
Giving myself a voluntary wound
Here, in the thigh. Can I bear that with patience,
And not my husband's secrets?

Calpurnia

Calpurnia, on the other hand, is treated more as a confidant and advisor by Caesar. She does not need to remind him of their vows of oneness or of her heritage. Calpurnia also does not have to inflict physical pain on herself to prove that she is capable of bearing Caesar's trust and burdens. She is able to approach her husband in Act II, sc ii and openly express her feelings, knowing that her fears will be considered worthy of consideration by this noble man.

Caesar, I never stood on ceremonies,
Yet now they fright me. There is one within,
Besides the things that we have heard and seen,
Recounts most horrid sights seen by the watch.
A lioness hath whelped in the streets,
And grave have yawned and yielded up their dead.
Fierce fiery warriors fought upon the clouds
In ranks and squadrons and right form of war,
Which drizzled blood upon the Capitol.
The noise of battle hurtled in the air,
Horses did neigh, and dying men did groan,
And ghosts did shriek and squeal about the streets.
O Caesar, these things are beyond all use,
And I do fear them.
When beggars die there are no comets seen;
The heavens themselves blaze forth the death of princes.
Alas, my lord,
Your wisdom is consumed in confidence!
Do not go forth to-day! Call it my fear
That keeps you in the house and not your own.
We'll send Marc Antony to the Senate House,
And he shall say you are not well to-day.

Calpurnia merely tells Caesar of the ill omens of which she has heard. Her words about death supplement those of the auger to momentarily convince Caesar to send a message to the Senate that he will not address them as planned. Unfortunately for Caesar, the promise of the crown, his ego, and the traitor Decius' interpretation of Calpurnia's dream into good omens change his mind. Caesar would have kept his promise to his wife had Decius not come between them. Calpurnia is no match for the overconfidence and foolhardy behavior of her husband and the false flattery of a traitor. Caesar meets his death at the hand of the assassins in the Senate. The unity of marriage is destroyed as Caesar ignores the good counsel of a person with only his best interests in mind.

Julius Caesar: One Act Play

Approximate running time forty minutes

DRAMATIS PERSONAE

BRUTUS	MARK ANTONY
CASSIUS	JULIUS CAESAR
MESSALA	CASCA
TITINIUS	OCTAVIUS CAESAR
DECIUS BRUTUS	PORTIA
METELLUS CIMBER	CLITO
CINNA	CALPURNIA
LUCIUS	A SOOTHSAYER
TREBONIUS	STRATO
DARDANIUS	VOLUMNIUS
YOUNG CATO	ARTEMIDORUS
MARULLUS	FLAVIUS
Tribune	PINDARUS
CINNA	Servant to Cassius
A poet	CICERO

SENATORS, CITIZENS, GUARDS, ATTENDANTS, etc.

[Rome]

[Enter Flavius, Marullus, and certain Commoners over the stage]

FLAVIUS: Hence! home, you idle creatures, get you home. Is this a holiday?

SECOND CITIZEN: But, indeed, sir, we make holiday, to see Caesar, and to rejoice in his triumph.

MARULLUS: Wherefore rejoice? What conquest brings he home? You blocks, you stones, you worse than senseless things! O you hard hearts, you cruel men of Rome, knew you not Pompey? And do you now put on your best attire? And do you now cull out a holiday? And do you now strew flowers in his way that comes in triumph over Pompey's blood? Be gone!

FLAVIUS: Go, go, good countrymen, and, for this fault, assemble all the poor men of your sort; draw them to Tiber banks, and weep your tears into the channel, till the lowest stream do kiss the most exalted shores of all. *[Exeunt all the Commoners]* Go you down that way towards the Capitol; this way will I: disrobe the images, if you do find them deck'd with ceremonies.

MARULLUS: May we do so? You know it is the feast of Lupercal.

FLAVIUS: It is no matter; let no images be hung with Caesar's trophies. *[Exeunt]*

[Rome, a public place] [Enter Caesar, Mark Antony, Calphurnia, Portia, Decius, Cicero, Brutus, Cassius, Casca a soothsayer]

SOOTHSAYER: Caesar!

JULIUS CAESAR: Ha! who calls? Who is it in the press that calls on me? I hear a tongue, shriller than all the music, cry "Caesar." Speak; Caesar is turn'd to hear.

SOOTHSAYER: Beware the ides of March.

JULIUS CAESAR: What man is that?

BRUTUS: A soothsayer bids you beware the ides of March.

JULIUS CAESAR: Set him before me; let me see his face.

CASSIUS: Fellow, come from the throng; look upon Caesar.

JULIUS CAESAR: What say'st thou to me now? Speak once again.

SOOTHSAYER: Beware the ides of March.

JULIUS CAESAR: He is a dreamer; let us leave him: pass. *[Exeunt all but Brutus and Cassius]*

CASSIUS: Brutus, I do observe you now of late: I have not from your eyes that gentleness and show of love as I was wont to have. You bear too stubborn and too strange a hand over your friend that loves you.

BRUTUS: Cassius, be not deceived: if I have veil'd my look, I turn the trouble of my countenance merely upon myself.

CASSIUS: Then, Brutus, I have much mistook your passion. Tell me, good Brutus, can you see your face?

BRUTUS: No, Cassius; for the eye sees not itself but by reflection from some other thing.

CASSIUS: 'Tis just: and it is very much lamented, Brutus, that you have no such mirrors as will turn your hidden worthiness into your eye, that you might see your shadow. I have heard, where many of the best respect in Rome, except immortal Caesar, speaking of Brutus, and groaning underneath this age's yoke, have wish'd that noble Brutus had his eyes.

BRUTUS: Into what dangers would you lead me, Cassius, that you would have me seek into myself for that which is not in me?

CASSIUS: Therefore, good Brutus, be prepared to hear. And, since you know you cannot see yourself so well as by reflection, I, your glass, will modestly discover to yourself that of yourself which you yet know not of. *[Flourish and shout]*

BRUTUS: What means this shouting? I do fear, the people choose Caesar for their king.

CASSIUS: Ay, do you fear it? Then must I think you would not have it so.

BRUTUS: I would not, Cassius; yet I love him well. What is it that you would impart to me?

CASSIUS: I know that virtue to be in you, Brutus, as well as I do know your outward favour. Well, honour is the subject of my story. We both have fed as well; and we can both endure the winter's cold as well as he. *[Flourish and shout]*

BRUTUS: Another general shout! I do believe that these applauses are for some new honours that are heap'd on Caesar.

CASSIUS: Why, man, he doth bestride the narrow world like a Colossus; and we petty men walk under his huge legs, and peep about to find ourselves dishonourable graves. Men at some time are masters of their fates: The fault, dear Brutus, is not in our stars, but in ourselves, that we are underlings. Brutus, and Caesar: what should be in that Caesar? Why should that name be sounded more than yours? Write them together, yours is as fair a name; sound them, it doth become the mouth as well; weigh them, it is as heavy; conjure with 'em, Brutus will start a spirit as soon as Caesar.

BRUTUS: Brutus had rather be a villager than to repute himself a son of Rome under these hard conditions as this time is like to lay upon us.

CASSIUS: I am glad that my weak words have struck but thus much show of fire from Brutus.

BRUTUS: The games are done, and Caesar is returning.

CASSIUS: As they pass by, pluck Casca by the sleeve; And he will, after his sour fashion, tell you what hath proceeded worthy note to-day. *[Enter Caesar and others]*

BRUTUS: I will do so. But, look you, Cassius, the angry spot doth glow on Caesar's brow.

CASSIUS: Casca will tell us what the matter is.

JULIUS CAESAR: Antony

ANTONY: Caesar?

JULIUS CAESAR: Let me have men about me that are fat; sleek-headed men, and such as sleep o' nights. Yond Cassius has a lean and hungry look; he thinks too much: such men are dangerous.

ANTONY: Fear him not, Caesar; he's not dangerous; he is a noble Roman, and well given.

JULIUS CAESAR: Such men as he be never at heart's ease whiles they behold a greater than themselves; and therefore are they very dangerous. Come on my right hand, for this ear is deaf, and tell me truly what thou think'st of him. *[Exeunt Caesar and all his train but Casca]*
CASCA: You pull'd me by the cloak; would you speak with me?
BRUTUS: Ay, Casca; tell us what hath chanced to-day, that Caesar looks so sad.
CASCA: Why, there was a crown offer'd him; and being offer'd him, he put it by with the back of his hand, thus; and then the people fell a-shouting.
BRUTUS: What was the second noise for?
CASCA: Why, for that too.
CASSIUS: They shouted thrice: what was the last cry for?
CASCA: Why, for that too.
BRUTUS: Was the crown offer'd him thrice?
CASCA: Ay, marry, was't, and he put it by thrice, every time gentler than other; and at every putting-by mine honest neighbours shouted.
CASSIUS: Who offer'd him the crown?
CASCA: Why, Antony.
BRUTUS: Tell us the manner of it, gentle Casca.
CASCA: Mark Antony offered him a crown and, as I told you, he put it by once: but, for all that, to my thinking, he would fain have had it.

Then he offer'd it to him again; then he put it by again: but, to my thinking, he was very loth to lay his fingers off it. And then he offer'd it the third time; he put it the third time by; and still as he refused it, the rabblement shouted, and clapp'd their chopp'd hands, and threw up their sweaty nightcaps, and utter'd such a deal of stinking breath because Caesar refused the crown, that it had almost choked Caesar; for he swounded, and fell down at it: and for my part, I durst not laugh, for fear of opening my lips and receiving the bad air.
CASSIUS: But, soft, I pray you: what, did Caesar swound?
CASCA: He fell down in the market-place, and foam'd at mouth, and   was speechless.
BRUTUS: 'Tis very like; he hath the falling-sickness. What said he when he came unto himself?
CASCA: When he came to himself again, he said, if he had done or said any thing amiss, he desired their worships to think it was his infirmity.
BRUTUS: And after that, he came, thus sad, away?
CASCA: Ay.
CASSIUS: Did Cicero say any thing?
CASCA: Ay, he spoke Greek.
CASSIUS: To what effect?
CASCA: It was Greek to me. I could tell you more news too. Marullus and Flavius, for pulling scarfs off Caesar's images, are put to silence.

Fare you well. There was more foolery yet, if I could remember it.

BRUTUS: And so it is. For this time I will leave you: To-morrow, if you please to speak with me, I will come home to you; or, if you will, come home to me, and I will wait for you.

CASSIUS: I will do so. Till then, think of the world. *[Exit Brutus]* Well Brutus, thou art noble; for who so firm that cannot be seduced? I will this night, in several hands, in at his windows throw, as if they came from several citizens, writings, all tending to the great opinion that Rome holds of his name; wherein obscurely Caesar's ambition shall be glanced at. And, after this, let Caesar seat him sure; for we will shake him, or worse days endure. *[Exit]*

[Rome. A street] [Thunder and lightning. Enter, from opposite sides, Casca, with his sword drawn, and Cicero]

CICERO: Good even, Casca: brought you Caesar home? Why are you breathless? and why stare you so?

CASCA: Are not you moved, when all the sway of earth shakes like a thing unfirm? O Cicero, I have seen tempests, when the scolding winds have rived the knotty oaks; and I have seen th'ambitious ocean swell and rage and foam, to be exalted with the threat'ning clouds. But never till to-night, never till now, did I go through a tempest dropping fire. Either there is a civil strife in heaven; or else the world, too saucy with the gods, incenses them to send destruction.

CICERO: Why, saw you any thing more wonderful?

CASCA: A common slave held up his left hand, which did flame and burn like twenty torches join'd; and yet his hand, not sensible of fire, remain'd unscorch'd. Besides, I ha' not since put up my sword, against the Capitol I met a lion, who glared upon me, and went surly by, without annoying me. And there were drawn upon a heap a hundred ghastly women, transformed with their fear; who swore they saw men, all in fire, walk up and down the streets. And yesterday the bird of night did sit even at noonday upon the market-place, hooting and shrieking. When these prodigies do so conjointly meet, let not men say, "These are their reasons, they are natural;" For, I believe, they are portentous things unto the climate that they point upon.

CICERO: Indeed, it is a strange-disposed time: But men may construe things after their fashion, glean from the purpose of the things themselves. Good night, then, Casca: this disturbed sky is not to walk in.

CASCA: Farewell, Cicero. *[Exit Cicero] [Enter Cassius]*

CASSIUS: Who's there?

CASCA: A Roman.

CASSIUS: Casca, by your voice.

CASCA: Your ear is good. Cassius, what night is this!

CASSIUS: A very pleasing night to honest men.

CASCA: Who ever knew the heavens menace so?

CASSIUS: Those that have known the earth so full of faults.

CASCA: But wherefore did you so much tempt the heavens?

CASSIUS: You are dull, Casca; and those sparks of life that should be in a Roman you do want, or else you use not. Now could I, Casca, name to thee a man most like this dreadful night, that thunders, lightens, opens graves, and roars as doth the lion in the Capitol, a man no mightier than thyself or me in personal action; yet prodigious grown, and fearful, as these strange eruptions are.

CASCA: 'Tis Caesar that you mean; is it not, Cassius?

CASSIUS: Let it be who it is.

CASCA: They say the senators to-morrow mean to establish Caesar as a king.

CASSIUS: I know where I will wear this dagger, then; Cassius from bondage will deliver Cassius.

CASCA: So can I. So every bondman in his own hand bears the power to cancel his captivity.

CASSIUS: There's a bargain made. Now know you, Casca, I have moved already some certain of the noblest-minded Romans to undergo with me an enterprise of honourable-dangerous consequence.

CASCA: Stand close awhile, for here comes one in haste.

CASSIUS: 'Tis Cinna, I do know him by his gait. He is a friend. *[Enter Cinna]* Cinna, where haste you so?

CINNA: To find out you. Who's that? Metellus Cimber?

CASSIUS: No, it is Casca; one incorporate to our attempts. Be you content: good Cinna, take this paper, and look you lay it in the praetor's chair, where Brutus may but find it; and throw this in at his window; set this up with wax.

CINNA: Well, I will hie, and so bestow these papers as you bade me.

CASSIUS: That done, repair to Pompey's theatre. *[Exit Cinna]* Come, Casca, you and I will yet, ere day, see Brutus at his house: three parts of him is ours already; and the man entire, upon the next encounter, yields him ours.

CASCA: O, he sits high in all the people's hearts: And that which would appear offence in us, his countenance, like richest alchemy, will change to virtue and to worthiness.

CASSIUS: Him, and his worth, and our great need of him, you have right well conceived. *[Exeunt]*

[Rome, enter Brutus in his orchard]
BRUTUS: What, Lucius, ho! I cannot, by the progress of the stars,

give guess how near to day.- Lucius,
I say! [Enter Lucius]
LUCIUS: Call'd you, my lord?
BRUTUS: Get me a taper in my
study, Lucius: When it is lighted,
come and call me here.
LUCIUS: I will, my lord. *[Exit]*
[Enter Lucius]
LUCIUS: The taper burneth in your
closet, sir. Searching the window for
a flint, I found this paper, thus seal'd
up; and, I am sure, it did not lie there
when I went to bed.
BRUTUS: Get you to bed again; it
is not day. Is not to-morrow, boy, the
ides of March?
LUCIUS: I know not, sir.
BRUTUS: Look in the calendar, and
bring me word.
LUCIUS: I will, sir. *[Exit]*
BRUTUS: The exhalations, whizzing
in the air, give so much light, that I
may read by them. *[Opens the letter
and reads]* "Brutus, thou sleep'st;
awake, and see thyself. Shall Rome,
etc. Speak, strike, redress!" "Brutus,
thou sleep'st: awake!" Such
instigations have been often dropp'd
where I have took them up.
"Shall Rome, etc." Thus must I piece
it out; Shall Rome stand under one
man's awe? What, Rome? My
ancestors did from the streets of
Rome the Tarquin drive, when he
was call'd a king. "Speak, strike,
redress!" Am I entreated to speak
and strike? O Rome, I make thee
promise, if the redress will follow,

thou receivest thy full petition at the
hand of Brutus! *[Enter Lucius]*
LUCIUS: Sir, March is wasted
fifteen days. *[Knock within]*
BRUTUS: 'Tis good. Go to the gate;
somebody knocks. *[Exit Lucius]*
Since Cassius first did whet me
against Caesar, I have not slept.
[Enter Lucius]
LUCIUS: Sir, 'tis your brother
Cassius at the door, who doth desire
to see you.
BRUTUS: Is he alone?
LUCIUS: No, sir, there are more
with him.
BRUTUS: Let 'em enter. *[Exit
Lucius]* O conspiracy, shamest thou
to show thy dangerous brow by
night, when evils are most free? O,
then, by day where wilt thou find a
cavern dark enough to mask thy
monstrous visage? *[Enter the
Conspirators, Cassius, Casca,
Decius, Cinna, Metellus Cimber, and
Trebonius]*
CASSIUS: I think we are too bold
upon your rest. Good morrow,
Brutus; do we trouble you?
BRUTUS: I have been up this hour;
awake all night. Know I these men
that come along with you?
CASSIUS: Yes, every man of them;
and no man here but honours you;
and every one doth wish you had but
that opinion of yourself which every
noble Roman bears of you.
BRUTUS: Give me your hands all
over, one by one.

CASSIUS: And let us swear our resolution.

BRUTUS: No, not an oath. So let high-sighted tyranny range on, till each man drop by lottery.

CASSIUS: But what of Cicero? shall we sound him? I think he will stand very strong with us.

CASCA: Let us not leave him out.

CINNA: No, by no means.

METELLUS CIMBER: O, let us have him; for his silver hairs will purchase us a good opinion, and buy men's voices to commend our deeds.

BRUTUS: O, name him not: let us not break with him; For he will never follow any thing that other men begin.

CASSIUS: Then leave him out.

DECIUS BRUTUS: Shall no man else be touch'd but only Caesar?

CASSIUS: Decius, well urged. I think it is not meet Mark Antony, so well beloved of Caesar, should outlive Caesar. We shall find of him a shrewd contriver; let Antony and Caesar fall together.

BRUTUS: Our course will seem too bloody, for Antony is but a limb of Caesar. Let's be sacrificers, but not butchers, Caius. For he can do no more than Caesar's arm when Caesar's head is off.

CASSIUS: Yet I fear him.

BRUTUS: Alas, good Cassius, do not think of him. If he love Caesar, all that he can do is to himself, take thought, and die for Caesar.

BRUTUS: Peace! count the clock.

CASSIUS: The clock hath stricken three.

CASSIUS: But it is doubtful yet, whether Caesar will come forth to-day or no; For he is superstitious grown of late; Quite from the main opinion he held once of fantasy, of dreams, and ceremonies.

DECIUS BRUTUS: Never fear that: if he be so resolved, I can o'ersway him. Let me work; for I can give his humour the true bent, and I will bring him to the Capitol.

CASSIUS: The morning comes upon's: we'll leave you, Brutus. And, friends, disperse yourselves; but all remember what you have said, and show yourselves true Romans.

BRUTUS: Good gentlemen, look fresh and merrily; let not our looks put on our purposes; but bear it as our Roman actors do, with untired spirits and formal constancy. And so, good morrow to you every one. *[Exeunt all but Brutus] [Enter Portia]*

PORTIA: Brutus, my lord!

BRUTUS: Portia, what mean you? Wherefore rise you now?

PORTIA: Y' have ungently, Brutus, stole from my bed: and yesternight, at supper, you suddenly arose, and walk'd about, musing and sighing, with your arms across; and when I ask'd you what the matter was, you stared upon me with ungentle looks.

BRUTUS: I am not well in health, and that is all.

PORTIA: Is Brutus sick, and is it physical to walk unbraced, and suck up the humours of the dank morning? What, is Brutus sick, and will he steal out of his wholesome bed, to dare the vile contagion of the night, and tempt the rheumy and unpurged air to add unto his sickness? No, my Brutus; you have some sick offence within your mind, which, by the right and virtue of my place, I ought to know of: and, upon my knees, I charm you, by my once-commended beauty, by all your vows of love, and that great vow which did incorporate and make us one, that you unfold to me, yourself, your half.

BRUTUS: Kneel not, gentle Portia.

PORTIA: Within the bond of marriage, tell me, Brutus, is it excepted I should know no secrets that appertain to you? Dwell I but in the suburbs of your good pleasure? If it be no more, Portia is Brutus' harlot, not his wife.

BRUTUS: You are my true and honourable wife; as dear to me as are the ruddy drops that visit my sad heart.

PORTIA: If this were true, then should I know this secret. I grant I am a woman; but withal a woman that Lord Brutus took to wife. I grant I am a woman; but withal a woman well-reputed, Cato's daughter. Think you I am no stronger than my sex, being so father'd and so husbanded? Tell me your counsels; I will not disclose 'em. I have made strong proof of my constancy, giving myself a voluntary wound here, in the thigh: can I bear that with patience, and not my husband's secrets?

BRUTUS: O ye gods, render me worthy of this noble wife!

[Rome, a hall in Caesar's palace]
[Thunder and lightning. Enter Julius Caesar, in his nightgown]

JULIUS CAESAR: Nor heaven nor earth have been at peace tonight. Thrice hath Calpurnia in her sleep cried out, "Help, ho! they murder Caesar!" Who's within? *[Enter Calpurnia]*

CALPURNIA: Caesar, I never stood on ceremonies, yet now they fright me. There is one within, besides the things that we have heard and seen, recounts most horrid sights seen by the watch. A lioness hath whelped in the streets; and graves have yawn'd, and yielded up their dead; fierce fiery warriors fight upon the clouds, in ranks and squadrons and right form of war, which drizzled blood upon the Capitol; the noise of battle hurtled in the air, horses did neigh, and dying men did groan; and ghosts did shriek and squeal about the streets. O Caesar, these things are beyond all use, and I do fear them! When beggars die, there are no comets seen;
The heavens themselves blaze forth the death of princes.

JULIUS CAESAR: Cowards die many time before their deaths; the valiant never taste of death but once. *[Enter servant]* What say the augurers?

SERVANT: They would not have you to stir forth to-day.

JULIUS CAESAR: The gods do this in shame of cowardice.

CALPURNIA: Do not go forth to-day: call it my fear that keeps you in the house, and not your own. We'll send Mark Antony to the senate-house; and he shall say you are not well to-day. Let me, upon my knee, prevail in this.

JULIUS CAESAR: Mark Antony shall say I am not well; and, for thy humour, I will stay at home. *[Enter Decius]* Here's Decius Brutus, he shall tell them so.

DECIUS BRUTUS: Caesar, all hail! good morrow, worthy Caesar. I come to fetch you to the senate-house.

JULIUS CAESAR: And you are come in very happy time, to bear my greeting to the senators, and tell them that I will not come to-day.

DECIUS BRUTUS: Most mighty Caesar, let me know some cause, lest I be laugh'd at when I tell them so.

JULIUS CAESAR: The cause is in my will, I will not come; that is enough to satisfy the senate. But, for your private satisfaction, because I love you, I will let you know, Calpurnia here, my wife, stays me at home. She dreamt to-night she saw my statua, which, like a fountain with an hundred spouts, did run pure blood; and many lusty Romans came smiling, and did bathe their hands in it.

DECIUS BRUTUS: This dream is all amiss interpreted; it was a vision fair and fortunate. Your statue spouting blood in many pipes, in which so many smiling Romans bathed, signifies that from you great Rome shall suck reviving blood; and that great men shall press for tinctures, stains, relics, and recognizance. This by Calpurnia's dream is signified.

JULIUS CAESAR: And this way have you well expounded it.

DECIUS BRUTUS: I have, when you have heard what I can say. And know it now, the senate have concluded to give, this day, a crown to mighty Caesar. If you shall send them word you will not come, their minds may change.

JULIUS CAESAR: How foolish do your fears seem now, Calpurnia! I am ashamed I did yield to them. Give me my robe, for I will go.

[Rome, a street near the Capitol]
[Enter Artemidorus]

ARTEMIDORUS: "Caesar, beware of Brutus; take heed of Cassius; come not near Casca; have an eye to Cinna; trust not Trebonius; mark well Metellus Cimber; Decius Brutus loves thee not: thou hast wrong'd Caius Ligarius. There is but one mind in all these men, and it is bent against Caesar. If thou beest not immortal, look about you: security gives way to conspiracy. The mighty gods defend thee! Thy lover, Artemidorus." Here will I stand till Caesar pass along, and as a suitor will I give him this. My heart laments that virtue cannot live out of the teeth of emulation. If thou read this, O Caesar, thou mayst live; if not, the Fates with traitors do contrive. *[Exit]*

[Rome, before the Capitol] [Enter Artemidorus and the soothsayer. Flourish. Enter Caesar, Brutus, Cassius, Casca, Decius, Metellus, Cinna, Antony, Publius, and others]
JULIUS CAESAR: The ides of March are come.
SOOTHSAYER: Ay, Caesar; but not gone.
ARTEMIDORUS: Hail, Caesar! Read this schedule.
DECIUS BRUTUS: Trebonius doth desire you to o'er-read, at your best leisure, this his humble suit.
ARTEMIDORUS: O Caesar, read mine first; for mine's a suit that touches Caesar nearer; read it, great Caesar.
JULIUS CAESAR: What touches us ourself, shall be last served.
ARTEMIDORUS: Delay not, Caesar; read it instantly.
CASSIUS: What, urge you your petitions in the street? Come to the Capitol. *[Caesar enters the Capitol,*

the rest following. All the Senators rise.]
JULIUS CAESAR: Are we all ready? What is now amiss that Caesar and his senate must redress?
METELLUS CIMBER: Most high, most mighty, and most puissant Caesar, Metellus Cimber throws before thy seat an humble heart. *[Kneeling]*
JULIUS CAESAR: I must prevent thee, Cimber. These couchings and these lowly courtesies might fire the blood of ordinary men, and turn pre-ordinance and first decree into the law of children. Thy brother by decree is banished. Know, Caesar doth not wrong; nor without cause will he be satisfied.
METELLUS CIMBER: Is there no voice more worthy than my own, for the repealing of my banish'd brother?
BRUTUS: I kiss thy hand, but not in flattery, Caesar; desiring thee that Publius Cimber may have an immediate freedom of repeal.
JULIUS CAESAR: What, Brutus!
CASSIUS: Pardon, Caesar; Caesar, pardon. As low as to thy foot doth Cassius fall, to beg enfranchisement for Publius Cimber.
JULIUS CAESAR: I could be well moved, if I were as you. But I am constant as the northern star. Let me a little show it, even in this, that I was constant Cimber should be banish'd, and constant do remain to keep him so.

CASCA: Speak, hands, for me!
[Stabbing Caesar]
JULIUS CAESAR: Et tu, Brute?
Then fall, Caesar!
CINNA: Liberty! Freedom! Tyranny
is dead! Run hence, proclaim, cry it
about the streets.
BRUTUS: People, and senators, be
not affrighted; fly not; stand still:
ambition's debt is paid, and let no
man abide this deed, but we the
doers. *[Enter Trebonius]*
CASSIUS: Where is Antony?
TREBONIUS: Fled to his house
amazed. Men, wives, and children
stare, cry out, and run as it were
doomsday.
BRUTUS: Stoop, Romans, stoop,
and let us bathe our hands in
Caesar's blood up to the elbows, and
besmear our swords. Then walk we
forth, even to the market-place, and,
waving our red weapons o'er our
heads, let's all cry, "Peace, freedom,
and liberty!" But here comes
Antony. *[Enter Antony]* Welcome,
Mark Antony.
ANTONY: O mighty Caesar! dost
thou lie so low? I know not,
gentlemen, what you intend, who
else must be let blood, who else is
rank. If I myself, there is no hour so
fit As Caesar's death's hour. I do
beseech ye, if you bear me hard,
now, whilst your purpled hands do
reek and smoke, fulfil your pleasure.
No place will please me so, no mean
of death as here by Caesar.

BRUTUS: O Antony, beg not your
death of us. To you our swords have
leaden points, Mark Antony, our
arms no strength of malice; and our
hearts, of brothers' temper, do
receive you in with all kind love,
good thoughts, and reverence.
CASSIUS: Your voice shall be as
strong as any man's in the disposing
of new dignities.
BRUTUS: Only be patient till we
have appeased the multitude, beside
themselves with fear, and then we
will deliver you the cause, why I,
that did love Caesar when I struck
him, have thus proceeded.
ANTONY: I doubt not of your
wisdom. Let each man render me his
bloody hand. That I did love thee,
Caesar, O, 'tis true. If, then, thy
spirit look upon us now, shall it not
grieve thee dearer than thy death, to
see thy Antony making his peace,
shaking the bloody fingers of thy
foes in the presence of thy corse?
CASSIUS: I blame you not for
praising Caesar so; but what compact
mean you to have with us?
ANTONY: Friends am I with you
all, and love you all; upon this hope,
that you shall give me reasons why
and wherein Caesar was dangerous.
And in the pulpit, as becomes a
friend, speak in the order of his
funeral.
BRUTUS: You shall, Mark Antony.
CASSIUS: Brutus, a word with you.
[aside] You know not what you do:
Do not consent that Antony speak in

his funeral. Know you how much the people may be moved by that which he will utter?

BRUTUS: By your pardon; I will myself into the pulpit first, and show the reason of our Caesar's death. What Antony shall speak, I will protest he speaks by leave and by permission.

CASSIUS: I know not what may fall; I like it not.

BRUTUS: Mark Antony, here, take you Caesar's body. You shall not in your funeral speech blame us, but speak all good you can devise of Caesar; and say you do't by our permission.

ANTONY: Be it so; I do desire no more.

BRUTUS: Prepare the body, then, and follow us. *[Exeunt all but Antony]*

ANTONY: O, pardon me, thou bleeding piece of earth, that I am meek and gentle with these butchers! Thou art the ruins of the noblest man That ever lived in the tide of times. *[Enter Octavius' servant]* You serve Octavius Caesar, do you not?

SERVANT: I do, Mark Antony.

ANTONY: Caesar did write for him to come to Rome.

SERVANT: He lies to-night within seven leagues of Rome.

ANTONY: Post back with speed, and tell him what hath chanced. Here is a mourning Rome, a dangerous Rome, no Rome of safety for Octavius yet; hie hence, and tell him so.

[The Forum, enter Brutus and Cassius]

CITIZENS: We will be satisfied; let us be satisfied.

FIRST CITIZEN: I will hear Brutus speak.

SECOND CITIZEN: I will hear Cassius; and compare their reasons. *[Brutus goes into the pulpit]*

THIRD CITIZEN: The noble Brutus is ascended: silence!

BRUTUS: Romans, countrymen, and lovers! hear me for my cause; believe me for mine honour; and have respect to mine honour, that you may believe why Brutus rose against Caesar. This is my answer, not that I loved Caesar less, but that I loved Rome more. Had you rather Caesar were living, and die all slaves, than that Caesar were dead, to live all free men? As Caesar loved me, I weep for him; as he was fortunate, I rejoice at it; as he was valiant, I honour him: but as he was ambitious, I slew him. Who is here so vile that will not love his country? If any, speak; for him have I offended. I pause for a reply.

CITIZENS: None, Brutus, none.

BRUTUS: *[Enter Antony with Caesar's body]* Here comes his body, mourn'd by Mark Antony who, though he had no hand in his death, shall receive the benefit of his dying, a place in the commonwealth;

as which of you shall not? With this I depart, that, as I slew my best lover for the good of Rome, I have the same dagger for myself, when it shall please my country to need my death.
CITIZENS: Live, Brutus! live, live!
BRUTUS: Good countrymen, let me depart alone, and, for my sake, stay here with Antony. Do grace to Caesar's corpse, and grace his speech tending to Caesar's glories; which Mark Antony, by our permission, is allow'd to make. I do entreat you, not a man depart, save I alone, till Antony have spoke.
[Exit]
ANTONY: Friends, Romans, countrymen, lend me your ears; I come to bury Caesar, not to praise him. The evil that men do lives after them; the good is oft interred with their bones; so let it be with Caesar. The noble Brutus hath told you Caesar was ambitious. If it were so, it was a grievous fault; and grievously hath Caesar answer'd it. For Brutus is an honourable man; so are they all, all honourable men, come I to speak in Caesar's funeral. He was my friend, faithful and just to me. But Brutus says he was ambitious; and Brutus is an honourable man. When that the poor have cried, Caesar hath wept. Ambition should be made of sterner stuff. Yet Brutus says he was ambitious; and Brutus is an honourable man. You all did see that on the Lupercal I thrice presented him a kingly crown, which he did thrice refuse: was this ambition? Yet Brutus says he was ambitious; and, sure, he is an honourable man. You all did love him once, not without cause. What cause withholds you, then, to mourn for him?
FIRST CITIZEN: Methinks there is much reason in his sayings.
SECOND CITIZEN: Poor soul! his eyes are red as fire with weeping.
ANTONY: If I were disposed to stir your hearts and minds to mutiny and rage, I should do Brutus wrong, and Cassius wrong, who, you all know, are honourable men. But here's a parchment with the seal of Caesar, I found it in his closet, 'tis his will. Let but the commons hear this testament.
FOURTH CITIZEN: We'll hear the will. Read it, Mark Antony.
ANTONY: It is not meet you know how Caesar loved you. You are not wood, you are not stones, but men. I fear I wrong the honourable men whose daggers have stabb'd Caesar; I do fear it.
FOURTH CITIZEN: They were traitors!
CITIZENS: The will! the testament!
ANTONY: You will compel me, then, to read the will? Then make a ring about the corpse of Caesar, and let me show you him that made the will. If you have tears, prepare to shed them now. I am no orator, as Brutus is; but, as you know me all, a plain blunt man, that love my friend; and that they know full well that

gave me public leave to speak of him. For I have neither wit, nor words, nor worth, action, nor utterance, nor the power of speech, to stir men's blood. You have forgot the will I told you of.

CITIZENS: Most true; the will. Let's stay and hear the will.

ANTONY: Here is the will, and under Caesar's seal. To every Roman citizen he gives to every several man, seventy-five drachmas. Moreover, he hath left you all his walks, his private arbours, and new-planted orchards, on this side Tiber; he hath left them you, and to your heirs for ever, common pleasures, to walk abroad, and recreate yourselves. *[Exeunt angry citizens for Brutus and others]*

SERVANT: Sir, Octavius is already come to Rome.

ANTONY: Where is he?

SERVANT: He and Lepidus are at Caesar's house.

ANTONY: And thither will I straight to visit him. He comes upon a wish. Fortune is merry, and in this mood will give us any thing. *[Exeunt]*

[Before Brutus' tent, in the camp near Sardis]

BRUTUS: No man bears sorrow better. Portia is dead. Impatient of my absence, and grief that young Octavius with Mark Antony have made themselves so strong; for with her death that tidings came; with this

she fell distract, and, her attendants absent, swallow'd fire.

CASSIUS: And died so?

BRUTUS: Even so. *[Enter Lucius]*

BRUTUS: Come in, Titinius! Welcome, good Messala. Now sit we close about this taper here, and call in question our necessities.

BRUTUS: Messala, I have here received letters, that young Octavius and Mark Antony come down upon us with a mighty power, bending their expedition toward Philippi.

MESSALA: Myself have letters of the selfsame tenour.

BRUTUS: With what addition?

MESSALA: That by proscription and bills of outlawry, Octavius, Antony, and Lepidus, have put to death an hundred senators.

BRUTUS: What do you think of marching to Philippi presently?

CASSIUS: I do not think it good.

BRUTUS: Your reason?

CASSIUS: This it is. 'Tis better that the enemy seek us: So shall he waste his means, weary his soldiers. Doing himself offence; whilst we, lying still, are full of rest, defence, and nimbleness.

BRUTUS: Good reasons must, of force, give place to better. The people 'twixt Philippi and this ground do stand but in a forced affection; for they have grudged us contribution. Our legions are brim-full, our cause is ripe. The enemy increaseth every day; we, at the height, are ready to decline. There is a tide in the affairs of men, which, taken at the flood, leads on to fortune; omitted, all the voyage of their life is bound in shallows and in miseries. On such a full sea are we now afloat; and we must take the current when it serves, or lose our ventures.

CASSIUS: Then, with your will, go on, we'll along ourselves, and meet them at Philippi.

BRUTUS: The deep of night is crept upon our talk, and nature must obey necessity; which we will niggard with a little rest. There is no more to say?

CASSIUS: No more. Good night.

[Enter the ghost of Caesar]

BRUTUS: How ill this taper burns! Ha! who comes here? I think it is the weakness of mine eyes that shapes this monstrous apparition. It comes upon me. Art thou any thing? Art thou some god, some angel, or some devil, that makest my blood cold, and my hair to stare? Speak to me what thou art.

GHOST OF CAESAR: Thy evil spirit, Brutus.

BRUTUS: Why comest thou?

GHOST OF CAESAR: To tell thee thou shalt see me at Philippi.

BRUTUS: Why, I will see thee at Philippi, then. *[Ghost vanishes]* Now I have taken heart thou vanishest. Ill spirit, I would hold more talk with thee.

[The plains of Philippi, enter Octavius, Antony]

OCTAVIUS CAESAR: Now, Antony, our hopes are answered. You said the enemy would not come down, but keep the hills and upper regions. It proves not so; their battles are at hand. Mark Antony, shall we give sign of battle?

ANTONY: No, Caesar. Make forth; the generals would have some words.

BRUTUS: Words before blows. Iis it so, countrymen?

OCTAVIUS CAESAR: Not that we love words better, as you do.

BRUTUS: Good words are better that bad strokes, Octavius.

ANTONY: In your bad strokes, Brutus, you give good words; witness the hole you made in Caesar's heart.

OCTAVIUS CAESAR: I draw a sword against conspirators; when think you that the sword goes up again? Never, till Caesar's three-and-thirty wounds be well avenged; or till another Caesar have added slaughter to the words of traitors.

BRUTUS: Caesar, thou canst not die by traitors' hands, unless thou bring'st them with thee.

OCTAVIUS CAESAR: So I hope; I was not born to die on Brutus' sword.

BRUTUS: O, if thou wert the noblest of thy strain, young man, thou couldst not die more honourable.

OCTAVIUS CAESAR: Come, Antony; away! Defiance, traitors, hurl we in your teeth. If you dare fight to-day, come to the field; if not, when you have stomachs. *[Exeunt]*

CASSIUS: Then, if we lose this battle, you are contented to be led in triumph thorough the streets of Rome?

BRUTUS: No, Cassius, no: think not, thou noble Roman, that ever Brutus will go bound to Rome. But this same day must end that work the ides of March begun. For ever, and for ever, farewell, Cassius! If we do meet again, why, we shall smile; if not, why, then, this parting was well made.

CASSIUS: For ever, and for ever, farewell, Brutus! If we do meet again, we'll smile indeed; if not, 'tis true this parting was well made.

[The plains of Philippi. The field of battle, Enter Brutus and Messala]

CASSIUS: O look, Titinius, look, the villains fly! Myself have to mine own turn'd enemy. This ensign here of mine was turning back; I slew the coward, and did take it from him.

TITINIUS: O Cassius, Brutus gave the word too early; who, having some advantage on Octavius, took it too eagerly. His soldiers fell to spoil, whilst we by Antony are all enclosed. *[Enter Pindarus]*

PINDARUS: Fly further off, my lord, fly further off; Mark Antony is in your tents, my lord. Fly, therefore, noble Cassius, fly far off.

CASSIUS: This hill is far enough. Look, look, Titinius; are those my tents where I perceive the fire?

TITINIUS: They are, my lord.

CASSIUS: Titinius, mount thou my horse, and hide thy spurs in him, till he have brought thee up to yonder troops, and here again; that I may rest assured whether yond troops are friend or enemy. *[Exit Titinius]* Go, Pindarus, get higher on that hill and tell me what thou notest about the field. Sirrah, what news?

PINDARUS: Titinius is enclosed round about with horsemen, that make to him on the spur; yet he spurs on. Now they are almost on him. He's ta'en; and hark! They shout for joy.

CASSIUS: Now be a freeman; and, with this good sword, that ran through Caesar's bowels, search this bosom. Stand not to answer. Here, take thou the hilts; and, when my face is cover'd, as 'tis now, guide thou the sword. Caesar, thou art revenged, even with the sword that kill'd thee. *[Dies]*

PINDARUS: So, I am free; yet would not so have been, durst I have done my will. O Cassius! Far from this country Pindarus shall run, where never Roman shall take note of him. *[Exit]* *[Enter Titinius with Messala]*

MESSALA: It is but change, Titinius; for Octavius is overthrown by noble Brutus' power, as Cassius' legions are by Antony.

TITINIUS: These tidings will well comfort Cassius.

MESSALA: Where did you leave him? Is not that he that lies upon the ground?

TITINIUS: He lies not like the living. O my heart!

MESSALA: Is not that he?

TITINIUS: No, this was he, Messala, but Cassius is no more.

MESSALA: Mistrust of good success hath done this deed. Why dost thou show to the apt thoughts of men the things that are not?

TITINIUS: What, Pindarus! where art thou, Pindarus?

MESSALA: Seek him, Titinius, whilst I go to meet the noble Brutus, thrusting this report into his ears. *[Exit Messala]*

TITINIUS: Why didst thou send me forth, brave Cassius? Did I not meet thy friends? and did not they put on my brows this wreath of victory, and bid me give it thee? Alas, thou hast misconstrued every thing! Come, Cassius' sword, and find Titinius' heart. *[Dies] [Alarums, Enter Messala, with Brutus, young Cato]*

BRUTUS: Where, where, Messala, doth his body lie?

MESSALA: Lo, yonder; and Titinius mourning it.

BRUTUS: Titinius' face is upward.

YOUNG CATO: He is slain.

BRUTUS: O Julius Caesar, thou art mighty yet! Thy spirit walks abroad, and turns our swords in our own proper entrails. Are yet two Romans living such as these? The last of all the Romans, fare thee well! It is impossible that ever Rome should breed thy fellow. *[Exeunt]*
[Enter Brutus, Dardanus, Clitus, Strato, and Voluminus to another part of the field]

BRUTUS: Come, poor remains of friends, rest on this rock. Sit thee down, Clitus. *[Whispers to him]*

CLITUS: What, I, my lord? No, not for all the world.

BRUTUS: Peace, then, no words.

CLITUS: I'll rather kill myself.

BRUTUS: Hark thee, Dardanius. *[Whispers to him]*

DARDANIUS: Shall I do such a deed?

CLITUS: What ill request did Brutus make to thee?

DARDANIUS: To kill him, Clitus.

BRUTUS: Come hither, good Volumnius; list a word. The ghost of Caesar hath appear'd to me two several times by night, at Sardis once, and, this last night, here in Philippi fields. I know my hour is come. Our enemies have beat us to the pit. It is more worthy to leap in ourselves, than tarry till they push us. I prithee, hold thou my sword-hilts, whilst I run on it.

VOLUMNIUS: That's not an office for a friend, my lord.

CLITUS: Fly, fly, my lord; there is no tarrying here.

BRUTUS: Farewell to you. I shall have glory by this losing day, more than Octavius and Mark Antony by this vile conquest shall attain unto. So, fare you well at once; for Brutus' tongue hath almost ended his life's history. Hence! I will follow. *[Exeunt]* I prithee, Strato, stay thou by thy lord. Hold, then, my sword, and turn away thy face, while I do run upon it. Wilt thou, Strato?

STRATO: Give me your hand first: fare you well, my lord.

BRUTUS: Farewell, good Strato. Caesar, now be still. I kill'd not thee with half so good a will.   *[Runs on sword and dies] [Enter Octavius, Antony, Messala]*

OCTAVIUS CAESAR: What man is that?

MESSALA: My master's man. Strato, where is thy master?

STRATO: Free from the bondage you are in, Messala. For Brutus only overcame himself, and no man else hath honour by his death.

MESSALA: How died my master, Strato?

STRATO: I held the sword, and he did run on it.

ANTONY: This was the noblest Roman of them all. All the conspirators, save only he, did that they did in envy of great Caesar; he only, in a general honest thought, and common good to all, made one of them. His life was gentle; and the elements so mix'd in him, that Nature might stand up and say to all the world, "This was a man!"

7. *A MIDSUMMER NIGHT'S DREAM*

The play

In *A Midsummer Night's Dream*, a play concerning the choice a woman faces between duty and her personal desires, Shakespeare introduces the theater audience to a young woman of strong beliefs surrounded by fairy mischief and confusion created by misdirected affections.

Theseus, Duke of Athens and betrothed of Hippolyta, is confronted by Egeus, father of the contrary Hermia, with a plea for help. Egeus is incapable of convincing Hermia of her responsibility to marry Demetrius who has been chosen by her father. Instead she proclaims her love for Lysander and refuses to submit to her father's will. Theseus decrees that she has four days in which to decide to honor her father. At the end of which time Hermia must chose between death or the convent for her disobedience. In defiance, Hermia and Lysander plot to meet in the forest and escape to a place far away from the "sharp law of Athens" where they will be safely married out of the reach of Hermia's father and the Duke's justice.

Hermia and Lysander are not the only characters in this play who are confounded by love. Helena, a dear friend of Hermia, is hopelessly in love with Demetrius who can no longer see her virtue due to his blinding love for Hermia. Helena has tried unsuccessfully to rekindle his affections but always fails since Demetrius appears to have permanently transferred his affections from Helena to Hermia.

It is not only the mortals who are being outwitted by love as the scene changes to the embattled Oberon and Titania, King and Queen of the fairies, who are at odds over a part-human-part-fairy page being raised and adored by Titania in violation of Oberon's order for her to release the child. When Titania refuses to relinquish the child, Oberon angrily puts a spell on her which will make her fall in love with the first living creature she sees. Having overheard Helena begging Demetrius to treat her as his lap dog rather than to ignore her, Oberon decides to send the fairy Puck to anoint the eyelids of Demetrius with the same love potion used on Titania in order to make Demetrius fall in love with Helena.

Unfortunately, Puck in his haste to please Oberon mistakes the sleeping Lysander for Demetrius who looks upon Helena and immediately falls in love with her forsaking Hermia. Helena, feeling herself mocked by her friend's betrothed, leaves the clearing only to be followed by the love-struck Lysander.

In this same clearing where Titania is sleeping, actors are practicing a play about Pyramus and Thisby which will be performed for Theseus' and Hippolyta's wedding festivities. They are not aware that Puck is watching and waiting for the chance to cause mischief, an opportunity which quickly presents itself as Puck turns the head of Bottom, one of the actors, into that of a mule. The rehearsal noises awaken Titania who sees the mule-headed Bottom and falls under the spell of the potion. She commands her fairies to serve him well, which pleases Bottom who immediately asks that his head and ears be scratched.

Oberon finds this situation amusing until Helena, pursued by Demetrius, enters the clearing. Now Oberon realizes that Puck's mistake is more far reaching than originally thought. Puck has changed the course of true love by causing Lysander to desire Helena and leaving Demetrius in love with Hermia. To set this right, Oberon casts a sleeping spell on Demetrius and applies the love potion to Demetrius' eyes himself in the hopes that the first person Demetrius sees will be Helena.

The noise of Helena being chased through the woods by Lysander wakens Demetrius who, as planned, falls in love with Helena as soon as he sees her. Helena now has two suitors, and, to further compound the confusion, Hermia immediately encounters this triangle of Lysander-Helena-Demetrius. She cannot believe that her beloved Lysander for whom she has disobeyed her father and fled from her home has abandoned her for another. Helena believes that the other triangle, Lysander-Hermia-Demetrius, has contrived to torture her by claiming that both men love her. Hermia feels betrayed by Helena who she believes is treating her as a "puppet" for the amusement of the men. The men prepare to fight a duel for Helena as the women square off for a cat fight caused by feelings of betrayal.

As Oberon watches the outcome of this confusion, he decides to dispatch Puck to undo the effects of the love potion by luring Lysander and Demetrius into a clearing where both will be lulled into a deep sleep. Helena and Hermia, following angrily after the men, are also quickly put to sleep. Puck is now free to apply the antidote to Lysander's eyes, thereby freeing him to again love Hermia and leaving Demetrius the sole suitor of Helena.

Now that the plight of the mortals is sorted out, Oberon sees Titania with the mule-headed Bottom and begins to feel sorry for the misdirected affection of his fairy queen and to desire reconciliation with her. Having obtained the young page from Titania in her drugged state, Oberon instructs Puck to undo the love spell on Titania and the mule-head spell on Bottom.

In the meantime, Theseus, Hippolyta, and Egeus enter the clearing where they find the sleeping Lysander, Hermia, Demetrius, and Helena. The Duke's troubadours awaken the couples who try to explain their presence in the woods by telling of the elopement plot and the subsequent pursuit of Helena after Demetrius, the restored love of Demetrius for Helena, and the true love of Lysander for Hermia. The contented Duke invites both couples to the temple where a double wedding ceremony awaits them.

During this happy exchange the newly restored Bottom awakens with an uneasy feeling that he has had a dream the re-telling of which would surely make him appear a mule to his friends. The very confused Bottom decides to remain silent saying, "The eye of man hath not heard, the ear of man hath not seen, man's hand is not able to taste, his tongue to conceive, nor his heart to report what my dream was."

After all return to the Duke's court, Theseus calls upon the thespians to perform the play *Pyramus and Thisby* over the objections of those who feel that the play is too long. However, despite critical comments made while watching the action, Theseus, Hippolyta, Lysander, Demetrius, and the others enjoy the play in which Pyramus and Thisby die for unrequited love, a play with remarkable similarity to their lives.

As the mortals retire before the bewitching hour in which the fairies emerge from the forest, Oberon, Titania, Puck, and the band of fairies silently appear. Oberon commands the fairies to make merry in celebration of the upcoming marriage of Theseus and Hippolyta and to bless the union of the newly married couples. As the fairies scatter to fulfill their tasks, Puck is left alone to explain that the play which the audience has just watched is only a dream and not to be taken to heart or allowed to offend.

Helena

Helena poses both a pathetic, comic figure, and a catalytic figure in this play of romantic triangles. She is the former love of Demetrius who abandons her affections for those of her friend Hermia causing Helena much suffering. Hermia, however, cannot abide Demetrius' attentions because of her love for Lysander. Helena, unfortunately, is incapable of abandoning her love of Demetrius who she feels will eventually return to his senses and her love. However, it is Helena's suffering which causes the actions of Oberon and the unfolding of the plot of the play as the affections of Demetrius are returned to her.

However, before the happy conclusion of this play can be reached, Helena is made the object of pity as she believes that not only Demetrius but Hermia and Lysander have betrayed her. Not realizing that Puck has confused Oberon's efforts at restoring Demetrius to her, Helena thinks that the three are mocking her for her love of Demetrius and his apathy toward her. Helena is deeply wounded when her friend, whom she considers as close as a sister, threatens to claw her eyes and calls her a "painted maypole." Poor Helena has lost Demetrius and her cherished friend. However, all is made right by Oberon when the triangle is undone and the proper relationships made to flourish.

Unlike *The Two Gentlemen of Verona* in which the relationship between the men is of primary importance, the relationship between the lovers is of concern in this play. Oberon, who sees Demetrius as a "disdainful youth" to Helena's "sweet Athenian lady," assumes the responsibility of righting the wrong done to Helena by Demetrius when he turns from her to pursue Hermia. As a result, Helena no longer feels inferior to Hermia due to Demetrius' neglect as she does in Act I, scene i in which she says,

> How happy some o'er other some can be!
> Through Athens I am thought as fair as she.
> But what of that? Demetrius thinks not so;
> He will not know what all but he do know.
> And as he errs, doting on Hermia's eyes,
> So I, admiring of his qualities.
> Things base and vile, holding no quantity,
> Love can transpose to form and dignity.
> Love looks not with the eyes, but with the mind,
> And therefore is winged Cupid painted blind.
> Nor hath Love's mind of any judgement taste;
> Wings, and not eyes, figure unheedy haste.
> And therefore is Love said to be a child,
> Because in choice he is so oft beguiled.
> As waggish boys in game themselves forswear,
> So the boy Love is perjured everywhere.
> For ere Demetrius looked on Hermia's eyne
> He hailed down oaths that he was only mine;
> And when this hail some heat from Hermia felt,
> So dissolved, and show'rs of oaths did melt.

I will go tell him of fair Hermia's flight.
Then to the wood will he to-morrow night
Pursue her; and for this intelligence
If I have thanks, it is a dear expense.
But herein mean I to enrich my pain,
To have his sight thither and back again.

Helena is the catalyst for the change which unfolds in the action of the play, rather than being a female character subservient to the male characters. It is through her constancy in love and determination to reclaim Demetrius that Oberon is capable of succeeding with the spell on him. It is Helena's plight and unrequited love which first speeds Oberon into action to redirect Demetrius' wandering eye.

Helena is a determined female persona who helps to guide the flow of the action and patiently waits for the wandering man to return. Although she occasionally feels some pity for herself when compared to the vivacious, dark-haired Hermia, the beautiful, blond Helena never abandons her efforts to regain the affection of her former betrothed. Unlike her friend Hermia who feels compelled to defy the teachings of society in order to marry the man of her choice, Helena is the epitome of the patient woman who continues to love despite rejection and believes that true love will conquer all.

Traitors' Gate, Tower of London, gate through which Anne Boleyn entered the Tower

8. MACBETH

<u>The play</u>

In *Macbeth* the theme of the unprofitably of murder is of utmost importance as the theater-goer watches the development of the characters as they are motivated by greed, ambition, and evil. However, the inner-workings of the personalities of the characters and the depth of the relationships between the characters as they struggle with the motivating factors is not shown. The theater-goer cannot describe the relationship between Macbeth and Lady Macbeth as anything other than that of co-conspirators, or determine whether they are capable of the emotions of love or remorse. Shakespeare portrays them as people whose main concern is obtaining power at all cost, even the cost of their sanity and immortal souls.

The play opens with the unknowing Macbeth, a thane or Scottish lord to King Duncan, being praised and rewarded for his valor in battle by being awarded the title of Thane of Cawdor in addition to his previous title of Thane of Glamis. Unfortunately, Macbeth encounters three witches who prophesied not only this good fortune but his continued rise in stature to king replacing Duncan. Macbeth is initially reluctant and afraid to accept the praises and predictions of the witches. However, the witches' accuracy about this new position as Thane of Cawdor leads Macbeth to believe that the other prophecies might be true. Macbeth begins to see the possibility that the witches might have truly foretold the future.

However, Lady Macbeth is not hesitant in believing the truth of the witches' prophecy. Upon hearing that Duncan is to accompany Macbeth to their home, Lady Macbeth begins to plot the king's murder and the fulfillment of the witches' prophecy that Macbeth will be king. Macbeth is reluctant to pursue the prophecy, not wishing to kill a kind, generous king who has only recently rewarded his bravery in combat. Relentlessly, Lady Macbeth continues to state her plan for the assassination of Duncan over Macbeth's objections. In her well formulated plan the king and his guards will be given sleeping potions in their wine at dinner. As soon as they are asleep, Macbeth will slip past the sleeping guards into the sedated king's chamber where he will kill Duncan. The bloody daggers will be placed in the hands of the guards who will be blamed for the death of Duncan as a crime of drunken insanity. Lady Macbeth chides her husband for his hesitancy so viciously that Macbeth finally, but reluctantly, agrees to the plan.

Macbeth continues to have misgivings even after the plan is set in motion. He thinks that he sees daggers floating before him in the air, but quickly realizes that he is only being tortured by his conscience. On the striking of the appointed bell, Macbeth enters Duncan's room and commits murder. Macbeth feels that he must also kill the sleeping guards in order to appear to avenge the murder of Duncan. After doing the foul deeds, Macbeth returns to Lady Macbeth with the blood-stained daggers only to be told that the daggers must remain with the bodies. Lady Macbeth returns the daggers to the bodies of the guards herself since Macbeth is unable to face the deed again. She returns with red stained hands, but a heart which she feels is still "white" or pure. She is confident that, since she did not commit the deed but only planned it, she is not as responsible as her husband.

In the morning when the king and his guards do not appear, the murders are discovered. Malcolm and Donalbain, the sons of the murdered king, flee to England and Ireland respectively to escape their own deaths. This quick departure only makes Macduff and Ross suspect them of having bribed the guards to commit the crime and then of having killed the guards to prevent them from talking, a suspicion pleasing to Macbeth. Their hasty departure also enables Macbeth to be crowned king, thereby fulfilling the witches' prophecy. Macbeth is afraid that there is still one person, Banquo, who knows of his involvement in the murder of the king. He commissions two murderers to kill Banquo and his son, Fleance. The murderers succeed in killing Banquo, but Fleance escapes. Macbeth, although free of Banquo, is not free of Banquo's ghost which haunts him at supper.

In order to gain more information and to bolster his confidence, Macbeth again visits the witches. He is warned of three things which can lead to his downfall. They are as follows: one, "Beware Macduff/Beware the thane of Fife;" two, "Laugh to scorn/The pow'r of man, for none of woman born/Shall harm Macbeth;" and three, "Macbeth shall never vanquished be until/Great Birnam Wood to high Dunsinane Hill/Shall come against him." (Act iv, sc ii) To rid himself of the potentially troublesome Macduff and his son, Macbeth sends murderers to Macduff's estate. Macduff is not in attendance but only his wife and child who are quickly slain in order to insure that no child of Macduff's will rise up against Macbeth. As the search continues for Macduff, Macbeth believes that these murders have removed one obstacle to his success.

While Macbeth is trying desperately to hold the throne taken by murder, Lady Macbeth is waging her own battle against insanity. She is often found by her gentlewomen walking alone at night in her sleep, rubbing in vain at the imaginary bloodstains on her hands. It would appear that her heart is not as pure as Lady Macbeth would think because long after the murder of Duncan and his guards, Lady Macbeth continues to see their blood on her hands until her death at her own hand.

All is lost to Macbeth in the final scenes as Macduff explains the three-fold prophecy in which he renders final judgement for Macbeth. It appears that Macduff was not born of a woman but was delivered by cesarean section, thereby rendering the murder of his son and wife unnecessary. It was the cesarean-delivered Macduff about whom the witches foretold, not his son. Also, Macduff has advanced his army under cover of branches cut from the trees of Great Birnam Wood thereby fulfilling the prophecy that Great Birnam Wood would contribute to the over throw of Macbeth; the trees have marched upon Macbeth's castle. Macduff is the embodiment of the prophecy, Macbeth is vanquished, and Macduff is the new king of Scotland.

<u>Lady Macbeth</u>

Lady Macbeth is a woman driven by ambition to seek a higher position for herself and for her husband. Upon hearing that Macbeth has been honored with a new title and more land, she quickly and coldly develops a plan whereby Macbeth can be more than a thane; he can be the king. The desire for power initially blots the traditional religious upbringing which teaches against murderous and covetous from her mind. It is only after the assassination of Duncan and his guards that Lady Macbeth is driven mad by the memory of the deeds and her conscience.

Shakespeare appreciated the spirit of the new Renaissance woman whom Lady Macbeth exemplifies as she relentlessly and ruthlessly obtains what she wants; she will not be stopped once her plan is in place. When Macbeth appears to be changing his mind about killing the king, Lady Macbeth accuses him of being less than a man and goads him into committing the act. As Macbeth refuses to place the dripping daggers beside the bodies of the murdered guards, it is Lady Macbeth who must perform the task. As Macbeth vacillates by saying that one new title and honor is enough, it is the ambitious Lady Macbeth who pushes him toward the throne without consideration of the cost.

Shakespeare wrote during a time which had in its recent memory the beheading of several of Henry VIII's wives as well as of Mary Queen of Scots and Lady Jane Grey who was the queen of England for nine days until beheading put an end to a conspiracy to keep Mary, Catholic daughter of Henry VIII, from ascending to the throne. It was not unheard of in either history or literature for a king to be assassinated for the throne by an ambitious cousin or uncle. There were several threats against the life of Elizabeth I, although she was very popular with the people. Considering the history of the times, Lady Macbeth's actions were not atypical, but rather predictable for a person desiring power and unable to acquire it in her own right. What was unusual was that the more ambitious of the co-conspirators was the woman since women were traditionally very much behind the scenes of life. Lady Macbeth was beginning to exercise that freedom and desire for power which had been exhibited by Anne Boleyn, Mary I, and Elizabeth I.

However, the influence of the church and the fear of the supernatural were still very strong in the lives of Renaissance men and women although the influence was declining as the secular world's impact on life was increasing. In this monologue in which Lady Macbeth is observed walking in her sleep and speaking of the blood stains in her hands, the effects of the church and her conscience on her soul are evident.

> Out, damned spot. Out I say! One-two-why then 'tis time to do't. Hell is murky. Fie, my lord, fie! a soldier and afeard? What need we fear who knows it, when none can call our power to accompt? Yet who would have thought the old man to have had so much blood in him? The Thane of Fife had a wife. Where is she now? What, will these hands ne'er be clean? No more o' that, my lord, no more o' that! You mar all with this starting. Hear's the smell of blood still. All the perfumes of Arabia will not sweeten this little hand. Oh, oh, oh! Wash your hands, put on your nightgown, look not so pale! I tell you yet again, Banquo's buried. He cannot come out on's grave. To bed, to bed! There's knocking at the gate. Come,   come,come, come, give me your hand! What's done cannot be undone. To bed, to bed, to bed!

No longer was the church the sole source of instruction, information, and culture for the citizenry. The theater and literature were alive and rapidly gaining popularity as the secular world and its delights replaced the somber teachings of hell and damnation by the church. However, Lady Macbeth was in many ways caught between the rigid world of the church and its teaching and the more relaxed secular world which allowed women to be strong figures in the image of Elizabeth I. In some ways Lady Macbeth's struggle for the throne was for herself as well as for Macbeth, for through him she could rule.

Cottage in Stratford-upon-Avon belonging to family of Anne Hathaway, wife of William Shakespeare

Round Tower of Windsor Castle which dates from 1070; location of St. George's Chapel burial site of Henry VIII

9. *MUCH ADO ABOUT NOTHING*

<u>The play</u>

In this comedy of love, Shakespeare portrays the human side of his characters as they struggle with the fear of loving and showing that love to someone who might not return the same feelings. It is through the wit and humanity of Beatrice and Benedick that the audience is delighted by the interactions of the characters in *Much Ado About Nothing*.

Much Ado About Nothing opens with Beatrice, niece to Leonato the governor of Messina, asking about the war record of Benedick as if doubting his valor when, in fact, she is secretly in love with him. Her uncle tells the messenger, who relays the story of Benedict's outstanding efforts in battle, to ignore her since "There is a kind of merry war betwixt Signior Benedick and her. They never meet but there's a skirmish of wit between them." Beatrice's efforts to disguise her affection for Benedick succeed as the messenger comments that it is obvious that Benedick is certainly not in her favor.

As Benedick enters with Don Pedro, Prince of Arragon, Claudio, Balthasar, attendant to Don Pedro, and Don John, the illegitimate brother of Don Pedro, the exchange between Beatrice and Benedick begins in earnest. Beatrice has already stated that at their last encounter she soundly thrashed Benedick in a battle of words leaving him with only one wit left. Now she earnestly tries to free him of that one wit by claiming teasingly "Courtesy itself must convert to/Disdain if you come in her presence." However she gets as good as she gives when Benedick retorts, "I would my horse had the speed of your tongue, and was so good a continuer."

All leave to seek entertainment in Leonato's house except Benedick and Claudio. Claudio confesses to the confirmed bachelor Benedick that he is in love with Hero, Leonato's daughter and Beatrice's cousin, but is unsure of the manner in which to woo the lady. Benedick tries to convince his friend that it is preferable to remain unmarried as he plans to do. However, Don Pedro who has returned to join the conversation says that he will one day live to see Benedick "pale with love." Benedick adamantly refuses to entertain the thought that he might fall to Cupid's arrow and says that if he ever should fall "hang me up in a bottle like a cat and shoot at me; and he that hits me, let him be clapped on the back and called Adam." Don Pedro advises Claudio that, not withstanding Benedick's views on marriage, he will speak to Leonato regarding Claudio's affection for Hero. They are not aware that Don John, who has only recently reconciled with his brother, plans to interfere with the course of the courting of Hero out of resentment for his place in life.

The similarities between Beatrice and Benedick, which cause their constant bickering, continue to increase in number as she tells Leonato that she would rather die and live in heaven among the bachelors than marry, for a man without a beard is too young and a man with a beard is too old for her consideration. Nevertheless, she is scolded by her uncle for having too sharp a tongue which might cause her desire for spinsterhood to come to fruition.

At the masked entertainment which follows, Don Pedro finds the opportunity to speak with Hero, leaving Beatrice to spend her evening with the masked Benedick. The masked Claudio is left alone only to be sought out by Don John who tells him that Don Pedro is actually wooing Hero for himself rather than for Claudio. Claudio begins to question the devotion of his friend Don Pedro and lament ever having asked him to be the go-between with Hero. Benedick further exacerbates Claudio's wound by telling him that he also has seen Don Pedro speaking with Hero. Claudio feeling twice betrayed, once by his own feelings and another by his friend, leaves in a great passion before Don Pedro has the opportunity to tell Claudio that he has succeeded in winning Hero's interest in him.

All is set right very shortly when Beatrice brings Claudio to Don Pedro who explains that Hero has expressed love for Claudio, and that Leonato has agreed to a marriage between the two. Claudio is restored to good humor and says that "Time goes on crutches till Love have all his rites." However, Hero and Claudio must wait a week before they marry in order to help Don Pedro win a match between Beatrice and Benedick.

Don John is more determined than ever to undo the pending marriage of Claudio and Hero as he listens to the scheme of Borachio, one of his men, who plans to tell Don Pedro that Hero is disloyal to Claudio and has been secretly entertaining another man from her window at night. To further dramatize the deception, Borachio plans to climb up to Hero's window and call to her maid Margaret who, pretending to be Hero, will appear at her mistress' window and will show her affection for him. This charade is to be witnessed by Claudio, Don Pedro, and Don John.

It is not long before Don Pedro, Claudio, and Leonato begin to place into action their plan to cajole Benedick into loving Beatrice. They come upon the sworn bachelor Benedick trying to hide himself from them. Knowing that he is within easy hearing, they begin to discuss the love which Beatrice has for Benedick and her fair appearance. As they leave, Benedick comes from his hiding place and finds to his surprise that a new feeling is awakening in him for Beatrice now that he understands that her sharp comments to him are actually a mask to hide her feelings for him. The confirmed bachelor finds himself recanting his words and looking on Beatrice in a different light saying, "When I said I should die a bachelor, I did not think I should live till I were married."

Meanwhile Hero, Ursula, and Margaret begin their efforts with Beatrice as they meet in an orchard and talk about the love-struck Benedick in words of highest praise. Knowing that Beatrice hides nearby, they discuss the love for her of which Benedick has often spoken to Don Pedro and Claudio but is reluctant to show because of Beatrice's sharp tongue. They are confident that Beatrice hears all and is now receptive to Benedick's attentions. Beatrice emerges from her hiding place to scold herself for being so sharp in her conversations with Benedick and, thereby causing him to hide his true affections.

> What fire is in mine eyes? Can this be true?
> Stand I condemned for pride and scorn so much?
> Contempt, farewell! and maiden pride, adieu!
> No glory lives behind the back of such,
> And, Benedick, love on; I will requite thee,
> Taming my wild heart to thy loving hand,
> If thou dost love, my kindness shall incite thee
> To bind our loves up in a holy band;
> For others say thou dost deserve, and I
> Believe it better than reportedly.

Soon Don Pedro, Claudio, and Leonato meet the freshly shaven, beardless, melancholy Benedick whom they accuse of having the expression of a man in love. Much to their satisfaction, Benedick asks Leonato to have words with him, presumably about the affection for his niece. As Benedick speaks with Leonato, Don John enters to tell Don Pedro and Claudio of his knowledge of Hero's disloyalty, which he feels he must do out of great affection for his brother. Don John invites Don Pedro and Claudio to accompany him to Leonato's house that night in order to witness Hero in her disloyal acts with another man, and reluctantly they agree. When they arrive at the selected spot, Don Pedro and Claudio think they see Hero speaking from her window to another man when in truth they see Margaret speaking with Borachio.

Both men are devastated and plan to disclose Hero's disloyalty the next morning, the morning of the wedding. That same night Borachio is apprehended by the watchmen of Leonato's house who have overheard him bragging to another man about the deed he has recently committed against Don Pedro and Claudio at the direction of Don John. He must now explain to the constable his part in the undoing of a loyal, virtuous woman.

Next morning at the church Claudio refuses to marry Hero calling her a "rotten orange" which he quickly returns to her father. Further, Don Pedro says that he feels dishonored that he has engaged his friend to a "common stale" or prostitute. As Don Pedro recounts the discovery of the previous night, Hero faints at hearing her honor and reputation so sullied as Leonato in disgrace asks, "Hath no man's dagger here a point for me?" When Don Pedro, Claudio, and Don John leave, the friar tries to uncover any possible explanation for these stories. It is Benedick who offers the one plausible explanation of the wickedness of Don John who might have concocted the plot against the happiness of Claudio in order to do evil against those whom he feels are against him.

Quickly the friar suggests that Hero be allowed to pretend death in the hopes of causing either the falseness of the accusation to be disclosed or for the love of Claudio to be restored to her. All agree to assume the disposition of mourners for the wronged Hero as they plan a fitting revenge on Don Pedro, Claudio, and Don John. If all fails, the friar suggests that Hero be spirited away to live in secrecy the remainder of her life.

Before Benedick leaves to spread the word that Hero has died at losing both honor and the love of Claudio, Benedick confesses to Beatrice that he loves her. However, Beatrice is so distraught over the tragic downfall of her beloved cousin that she can take no joy in Benedick's confession of love for her. Beatrice's only thought is that if Benedick loves her, he should kill Claudio for dishonoring Hero. In order to prove himself, Benedick accepts the loathsome task and leaves to challenge his dear friend Claudio in a duel.

In the hearing room in Messina, Dogberry the constable is drawing a confession from Borachio as to his role and that of Don John in the conspiracy to dishonor Hero. At the same time, Antonio is trying to comfort his brother Leonato who will not be comforted saying, "My griefs cry louder than advertisement." Antonio counsels Leonato not to suffer alone but to make those who dishonored Hero suffer along with him. As Don Pedro and Claudio enter,

Leonato immediately accuses Claudio of wronging Hero. Claudio and Don Pedro try to explain that the disloyalty of Hero has been justly witnessed and not planned as idle gossip or as a trick to avoid marriage. Leonato and Antonio will not be comforted but leave to further their plans of revenge.

Immediately following the exit of the elderly gentlemen, Benedick enters and promptly challenges Claudio to a duel for his role in the death of Hero. Both Don Pedro and Claudio are surprised at the change in Benedick from a man of wit and humor who laughs at everything and takes nothing seriously to a man of great sadness and determination who is set on accomplishing his task. The challenge of the duel is, nevertheless, accepted by Claudio who believes that Benedick is under the influence of his love for Beatrice.

Before Don Pedro and Claudio can retire to prepare for the duel, the constable enters with the prisoner Borachio who has confessed not only his role in the dishonoring of Hero but the extent of Don John's involvement. Both Don Pedro and Claudio are sick at heart for having fallen prey to the vengeful Don John and offer Leonato the right to impose any punishment on them that he chooses for their part in Hero's death. Leonato proposes that they pray at Hero's tomb and tell everyone of the town that Hero is indeed a virtuous woman, that they disclose their unwitting part in Don John's deception, and that Claudio marry the "twin" to Hero. Don Pedro and Claudio readily agree to Leonato's terms. Leonato continues to enjoy his revenge on Claudio for dishonoring Hero as he tells Hero and the other ladies to withdraw until summoned and then to appear with their faces masked in order to continue the punishment of Claudio and preside at his marriage.

Benedick seizes the opportunity to ask the waiting friar to perform a marriage ceremony in which he and Beatrice will wed. However, the wary Beatrice who has witnessed the inconstant nature of man's love will not consent to marry Benedick thinking that his love is not true. When asked if she loves him, she responds "Why no; no more than reason." She continues to use her wit to send Benedick's heart on a merry chase not acknowledging if she loves him or does not. Finally, Beatrice consents to marry her beloved Benedick "partly to save your life." Before she can utter another word, Benedick seals her lips with a lover's kiss. The once confirmed bachelor cannot too highly recommend love and marriage as he tells Don Pedro "Get thee a wife, get thee a wife! There is no staff more reverent than one tipped with horn."

Beatrice

Beatrice, a witty woman whose wit works both for and against her is, unlike Kate of *The Taming of the Shrew*, careful not to allow her sharp tongue to push her into shrewishness. She challenges men word-for-word and does not relent in her self-confidence. She does not hide behind the conventions of the times which demand that a woman be sweet and fluffy, rather than outspoken and determined. However, this wit and free speech almost cost her the man she loves.

Beatrice, although witty and quick to speak her mind, is shy when confronted by Benedick and hides her true feelings for him behind her sharp retorts. Beatrice and Benedick have been snapping at each other without either realizing that the other has strong feelings which are being hidden. It is not until Don Pedro, Leonato, and Claudio open Benedick's eyes to the woman with whom he has been arguing without seeing her virtue that Benedick realizes his long hidden love for Beatrice. Likewise, it takes the interaction of Hero to awaken in Beatrice the confidence to speak somewhat guardedly to Benedick about her long concealed love for him. Each has been looking for the qualities of the other without seeing the qualities possessed in the person at whom the bickering is directed. Benedick says in justifying his desire to remain unmarried that it is not until all of the graces of his ideal woman are contained in one woman that he will marry. As soon as he hears that Beatrice loves him, Benedick quickly realizes that the graces he has long desired are in one woman and that the one woman is Beatrice. For Beatrice, it is hearing her pride spoken of as an impediment to her happiness that awakens her to take action to overcoming both her pride and her sharp tongue. Once these obstacles are removed, Beatrice and Benedick quickly find each other.

However, in the end, some of the old Beatrice remains. After watching her cousin Hero be insulted and abused by love and her betrothed, Beatrice once again becomes cautious of involvement with Benedick and hides behind her wit. She is again reluctant to disclose her love for him and even more reluctant to agree to marry him. Finally, in the guise of an act of charitable kindness rather than as an act of love, Beatrice agrees to marry him. Fortunately, Benedick is now aware of Beatrice's love, fears, and the method she uses to hide her true feelings and meets her half way.

Unlike Kate, Beatrice does not rage in her wit and is never unkind to others. Also unlike Kate, Beatrice is loved by her uncle and cousin who are like father and sister to her. She is not treated like a second class citizen by a beautiful sister. Beatrice is actually a much more prominent figure in the play and the lives of the other characters than Hero. In this play, Hero is the lesser character and the pawn in a terribly unfair game in which a woman's character is slandered with little effort and with little more proof that the word of several men. Beatrice never allows herself to be put in the position of being scandalized and is actually the catalyst in sending Benedick forward to duel with Claudio to avenge the undoing of Hero.

Also unlike *The Taming of the Shrew*, the theater-goer is certain at the end of the play that Beatrice will continue to match wits with Benedick in a very happy and equal marriage since the two possess the same spirit and joy of living. The theater-goer can only wonder who will in the long run gain the upper hand in the marriage of Kate to Petruchio. Perhaps the stronger force in the marriage will be Kate who is capable at the end of the play of leading Petruchio away from the entertainment of the night in pursuit of her. In *Much Ado About Nothing* the theater-goer knows that two equals are equally matched.

Round Tower of Windsor Castle which dates from 1070; location of St. George's Chapel burial site of Henry VIII

10. *OTHELLO THE MOOR OF VENICE*

<u>The play</u>

Othello the Moor of Venice is a play in which the weakness of over-confidence allows the protagonist to be influenced by the words and actions of lesser, mean-spirited men into doubting himself and the faithfulness of the woman he loves. This over-confidence finally results in not only the decline of Othello's political and military powers but his personal happiness and brings about his death.

The play opens with Iago, Othello's trusted, war-toughened ensign complaining to Roderigo that Othello has passed him over for promotion in order to promote Michael Cassio who has never seen battle. Iago's dissatisfaction and feeling of jealously have progressed to a state of hatred for Othello. When asked by his confidant Roderigo why he continues to follow Othello, Iago states "I am not what I am" and discloses his plan to discredit Othello and Cassio in order to assume their positions of power.

Iago's first attempt at discrediting Othello occurs when he and Roderigo, the rejected suitor of Desdemona, waken Brabantio, Desdemona's father, claiming that his daughter against his wishes has married Othello who, although well decorated for victorious conduct in battle, is still black and an inappropriate husband for the daughter of a wealthy Venetian. Brabantio immediately pursues the lovers to try to stop their union. However, Iago does not stay to help look for Othello and Desdemona saying that he must "show out a flag and sign of love, /Which is indeed but a sign" for Othello in order to remain in Othello's confidence in order to accomplish his final plan of discrediting him.

Iago dutifully warns Othello of Brabantio's anger at hearing of the marriage. Othello does not suspect the duplicity of his ensign and confides in Iago that he does not fear any words which Brabantio might say to prevent his marriage to Desdemona because he has shown himself in battle to be worthy of anyone he should select. Even when faced by the angry father Othello, trusting in his abilities to handle and conquer the adversary, remains calm telling his men and those of Brabantio to "Keep up your bright swords, for the dew will rust them."

Brabantio decides to ask the Duke to solve the problem of the relationship between Othello and Desdemona. He finds the Duke and the Senate at work considering the need to fortify Cyprus against invasion and the likelihood of sending Othello to fight against the enemy. Standing in a shadow cast by Othello, Brabantio begs the Duke to rescue his daughter from the bewitching effects of Othello. Initially the Duke agrees that the law protects against casting spells which would lure daughters away from their duty to their fathers. However, when he hears that Othello has not bewitched Desdemona but simply shared her love and married her, the Duke counsels Brabantio to accept his new son-in-law. Brabantio reluctantly welcomes Othello with the warning "Look to her, Moor, if thou hast eyes to see:/She has deceived her father, and may thee."

Iago's initial step to discredit Othello has not progressed as planned. However, he is confident that the relationship between Othello and Desdemona will not last as soon as the suspicion of infidelity between Desdemona and Cassio is made known. Iago plans to continue his vengeful efforts on Cyprus.

Upon their arrival in Cyprus, Iago, Desdemona, and Emilia, Iago's wife, engage Desdemona in conversation in order to calm her nerves while waiting for Othello to return from the battle front. Cassio is drawn into the conversation and Iago's plot when Cassio touches Desdemona's hand after greeting her with the customary kiss of welcome. This kiss and touch will later be used by Iago to position Cassio as Desdemona's secret lover. Iago tells Roderigo the details of the plan in which Cassio is to be engaged in a sword fight which will show his rougher side. Roderigo is not convinced that this plan will succeed, but he complies with Iago hoping to one day win the hand of Desdemona.

Iago engages Cassio and several sailors of Cyprus in drinking and riotous singing until Cassio who seldom drinks is quite drunk. As Cassio staggers away to assume his guard post with the vengeful Roderigo following behind, Iago represents Cassio as a drunkard to Montano, the governor of Cyprus, saying that Cassio drinks to drunkenness each night before going to bed. While they are speaking, Cassio enters chasing Roderigo with drawn sword. Montano attempts to stop Cassio from doing harm only to enter into a sword fight with the drunken Cassio himself. When Othello arrives Cassio is too intoxicated to explain his actions, and Montano is too severely wounded to explain his involvement. This leaves the telling of the incidents to Iago who has instigated the entire episode. Othello, being ignorant of Iago's part in orchestrating the incident, removes Cassio from his position as lieutenant. Left alone on stage with him, Iago comforts Cassio who can little remember the squabble with Roderigo and does not know what happened in the duel. Iago counsels Cassio to plead his case with Desdemona who will speak on his behalf to Othello. All is falling nicely into Iago's plan of establishing Cassio as Desdemona's lover.

Iago plants the seeds of jealousy in Othello when Cassio is witnessed departing from Desdemona's room after he asks her to plead for his reinstatement as Othello's lieutenant. Knowing that Cassio often has served as the go-between in Othello's wooing of Desdemona, Iago suggests that an inappropriate closeness has been developing between Cassio and Desdemona for some time. Othello contends that he trusts his wife totally and that the only relationship between Cassio and Desdemona is friendship based on their love of him. Iago can easily read Othello's mood and knows that sparks of jealousy have been kindled by his inferences.

As the suspicions of misconduct between Desdemona and Cassio fester, Desdemona tries to comfort her husband without knowing the cause of his misery. He rejects her and in so doing causes Desdemona to drop a handkerchief given to her by him. The forgotten handkerchief is retrieved by Emilia who takes it to Iago not knowing that he plans to use it as further proof of the relationship between Cassio and Desdemona.

The seeds of mistrust sown by Iago have begun to drive Othello to distraction as he doubts Desdemona's virtue and Cassio's loyalty. Iago seizes the opportunity to place the handkerchief in the hands of the town courtesan presumably as a gift from Cassio who himself supposedly received the handkerchief from Desdemona. Othello is driven mad by the perceived infidelity of his wife, strikes her, calls her a devil, and accuses her of infidelity.

The loving, honorable Desdemona suffers greatly from the abuse heaped upon her by Othello. She begs Iago to instruct her in the manner in which to soothe Othello and to convince him of her constancy; Iago advises that she allow Othello's temper to cool naturally. Unfortunately, Desdemona follows Iago's advice, feeling that Othello's friend knows him better than a wife of so short a time.

Although Othello is slowly falling prey to Iago's hateful plans, Roderigo is beginning to doubt the sincerity of Iago's intentions to help him win the love of Desdemona. Iago senses the disquiet of Roderigo and kills him before the plans can be disclosed.

Othello, torn by love, doubt, regret, and jealousy, demands that Desdemona confess her infidelity with Cassio; an act which she cannot do since she is free of guilt. The injured Othello smothers her moments before Emilia can tell him about Iago's "pernicious soul" and the foul deeds and trickeries orchestrated by Iago. Othello, faced with the truth about Iago, his murder of

Desdemona, and his disbelief of Cassio, rushes forward to kill Iago who is quickly taken into custody for his crimes. Othello asks those in attendance not to think too harshly of him and to remember him as "one who loved not wisely, but too well" as he stabs himself and dies.

Desdemona

Desdemona is a woman of wealth and respected family who betrays the customs of society and her father's wishes in order to marry Othello the Moor, a black general about whom she knows very little. She knows of his valiant effort on the battlefield but little of his inner-self. She loves the glory of his victories, pities the slain warriors who opposed his mighty strength, and wants to make a life in the shadow of his adventures, just as her father once stood in the shadow of Othello's physical size. From the first act of the play, the theater-goer knows that this young woman who betrays her father's wishes will be the cause of Othello's downfall. It is only Othello and Desdemona who do not know that she is leading them into the pitfalls established by a society, in the person of Iago, which cannot completely accept their relationship and a black man's fortune and fame.

Desdemona is a woman who has been taught to honor and respect her father and to satisfy her duty to him by marrying the man of his choosing. However, in keeping with the new liberties being assumed by women during the reign of Elizabeth I, Desdemona takes control of her own fate by selecting her own spouse. She also flies in the face of a society which honors the black soldier with titles but does not accept him as an equal and discourage intermarriage. Her actions not only cause misery to herself and Othello but shorten her father's life, for he is incapable of justifying to himself either her new freedom, her marriage, or her parental disobedience.

Desdemona at the last appears to know that her fate is sealed as she instructs Emilia "If I should die before thee prithee shroud me/In one of those same sheets," the sheets on which she plans to sleep that night. She continues to foreshadow her death as she tells Emilia of the maid once employed by her mother who died singing a tale of her lover's madness.

My mother had a maid called Barbary.
She was in love, and he she loved proved mad
And did foresake her. She had a song of 'Willow';
And old thing 'twas; but it expressed her fortune,
And she died singing it. That song to-night
Will not go from my mind; I have much to do
But to go hang my head all at one side
And sing it like poor Barbary. Prithee dispatch.

Singing

'The poor soul sat sighing by a sycamore tree,
    Sing all a green willow;
Her hand on her bosom, her head on her knee,
    Sing willow, willow, willow;
The fresh streams ran by her and murmured her moans;
    Sing willow, willow, willow;
Her salt tears fell from her, and soft'ned the stones-
    Sing willow, willow, willow;
Sing all a green willow must be my garland.
Let nobody blame him; his scorn I approve'-

In this tragedy of unwise love, duplicity of man, schemes, and lies, Desdemona and Othello are victims of a time which is not prepared to tolerate the success and equality of people of color and interracial marriages. Othello is the source of much envy and jealousy for his valor on the battlefield and his rise to power. His selection of a white woman from a noble family to be his wife further aggravates those who are against him. Othello has placed himself in their society by gaining favor with the Duke and in marrying one of their rank, but he is never accepted. In marrying him, Desdemona places herself in a position of scorn as a woman whose determination to assert herself is placed above the morés of the times. Both Desdemona and Othello suffer for their disregard of the expectations of society. Desdemona suffers the most since she lives in the shadow of her famous husband and is the unwitting tool of his destruction.

The theater-goer cannot help but wonder how two people could have been so blinded by their efforts for freedom of choice and equality as to not see the evil of prejudice threatening to undo them. The over-confidence in their ability to surmount the heavily weighted odds eventually led to their downfall. Desdemona never faced the result of her actions, being spared the realization by murder. Othello faced reality at his death.

Othello the Moor: One Act Play

Approximate running time twenty-five minutes

DRAMATIS PERSONAE
OTHELLO
    The Moor
CASSIO
    Lieutenant of Othello
IAGO
RODERIGO
    A Venetian gentleman
MONTANO
    Governor of Cyprus
BRABANTIO
    A senator; father of Desdemona

DESDEMONA
    Wife of Othello
THE DUKE OF VENICE
EMILIA
    Wife of Iago
GRATIANO
            Brother of Brabantio
BIANCA
    Mistress of Cassio
LODOVICO
    Kinsman of Desdemona

SENATORS, MESSENGER, SAILOR, HERALD, OFFICERS, GENTLEMEN, ATTENDANTS.

[Venice]

[Enter Roderigo and Iago]
RODERIGO: Thou told'st me thou didst hold him in thy hate.
IAGO: Despise me, if I do not.
RODERIGO: I would not follow him, then.
IAGO: O, sir, content you; I follow him to serve my turn upon him. In following him, I follow but myself; Heaven is my judge, not I for love and duty, but seeming so, for my peculiar end.
IAGO: Call up her father, rouse him: make after him, poison his delight.
RODERIGO: Here is her father's house; I'll call aloud.

RODERIGO: What, ho, Brabantio! Signior Brabantio, ho!
IAGO: Awake! what, ho, Brabantio! thieves! thieves! thieves! Look to your house, your daughter, and your bags! Thieves! thieves! *[Brabantio appears above]*
BRABANTIO: What is the reason of this terrible summons? What is the matter there?
IAGO: Zounds, sir, y'are robb'd; for shame, put on your gown; Your heart is burst, you have lost half your soul; Even now, now, very now, an old black ram is tupping your white ewe. Arise, arise; Awake the snorting citizens with the bell, or else the devil will make a grandsire of you. Arise, I say.

BRABANTIO: What, have you lost your wits?

BRABANTIO: What profane wretch art thou?

IAGO: I am one, sir, that comes to tell you your daughter and the Moor are now making the beast with two backs.

BRABANTIO: Thou art a villain.

IAGO: You are--a senator.

BRABANTIO: This thou shalt answer: I know thee, Roderigo.

RODERIGO: Sir, I will answer any thing. But, I beseech you, if't be your pleasure and most wise consent, as partly I find it is, that your fair daughter, at this odd-even and dull watch o' the night, transported, with no worse nor better guard but with a knave of common hire, a gondolier, to the gross clasps of a lascivious Moor.

BRABANTIO: Strike on the tinder, ho! Give me a taper!- call up all my people! This accident is not unlike my dream. *[Exit]*

IAGO: Farewell; for I must leave you. It seems not meet, nor wholesome to my place, to be produced against the Moor. Though I do hate him as I do hell-pains, yet, for necessity of present life, I must show out a flag and sign of love, which is indeed but sign. That you shall surely find him, lead to the Sagittary the raised search; and there will I be with him. So, farewell.

[Exit. Enter Brabantio]

BRABANTIO: It is too true and evil: gone she is; and what's to come of my despised time is naught but bitterness. Now, Roderigo, where didst thou see her? O unhappy girl! with the Moor, say'st thou? Are they married, think you?

RODERIGO: Truly, I think they are.

BRABANTIO: O heaven! How got she out? O treason of the blood! Fathers, from hence trust not your daughters' minds by what you see them act. Call up my brother. O, would you had had her! Do you know where we may apprehend her and the Moor?

RODERIGO: I think I can discover him,if you please to get good guard, and go along with me.

BRABANTIO: Pray you, lead on. At every house I'll call.

[Another street]
[Enter Othello, Iago]

IAGO: Though in the trade of war I have slain men, yet do I hold it very stuff o' the conscience to do no contrived murder: I lack iniquity sometimes to do me service: nine or ten times I had thought t'have yerk'd him here under the ribs.

OTHELLO: 'Tis better as it is.

IAGO: Nay, but he prated, and spoke such scurvy and provoking terms against your honour. But, I pray you, sir, are you fast married? Be assured of this, that the magnifico is much beloved; and hath, in his effect, a voice potential as double as the duke's: he will divorce you; or put upon you what restraint and grievance
The law--with all his might t'enforce it on--will give him cable.

OTHELLO: Let him do his spite. My services which I have done the signiory shall out-tongue his complaints. Which, when I know that boasting is an honour, I shall promulgate, I fetch my life and being from men of royal siege; and my demerits may speak, unbonneted, to as proud a fortune as this that I have reach'd: for know, Iago, but that I love the gentle Desdemona, I would not my unhoused free condition put into circumscription and confine for the sea's worth. But, look! what lights come yond?

IAGO: Those are the raised father and his friends. You were best go in.

OTHELLO: Not I; I must be found. My parts, my title, and my perfect soul shall manifest me rightly. Is it they?

IAGO: By Janus, I think no. *[Enter Cassio and certain Officers with torches]*

OTHELLO: The servants of the duke, and my lieutenant. The goodness of the night upon you, friends! What is the news?

CASSIO: The duke does greet you, general, and he requires your haste-post-haste appearance even on the instant.

OTHELLO: What is the matter, think you?

CASSIO: Something from Cyprus, as I may divine. You have been hotly call'd for; when, being not at your lodging to be found, the senate hath sent about three several quests to search you out.

OTHELLO: 'Tis well I am found by you. I will but spend a word here in the house, and go with you. *[Exit]*

CASSIO: Ancient, what makes he here?

IAGO: He's married.

CASSIO: To who? *[Enter Othello]*

CASSIO: Here comes another troop to seek for you.

IAGO: It is Brabantio. *[Enter Brabantio, Roderigo, and Officers]*

OTHELLO: Holla! stand there!

RODERIGO: Signior, it is the Moor.

BRABANTIOL Down with him, thief!

IAGO: You, Roderigo! come, sir, I am for you.

OTHELLO: Keep up your bright swords, for the dew will rust them. Good signior, you shall more command with years than with your weapons.

BRABANTIO: O thou foul thief, where hast thou stow'd my daughter? Damn'd as thou art, thou hast enchanted her; for I'll refer me to all things of sense, if she in chains of magic were not bound, whether a maid so tender, fair, and happy, so opposite to marriage that she shunn'd the wealthy curled darlings of our nation, would ever have, t'incur a general mock, run from her guardage to the sooty bosom of such a thing as thou, to fear, not to delight. Lay hold upon him. If he do resist, subdue him at his peril.

OTHELLO: Hold your hands, both you of my inclining, and the rest. Were it my cue to fight, I should have known it without a prompter. Where will you that I go to answer this your charge?

BRABANTIO: To prison; till fit time of law, and course of direct session, call thee to answer.

OTHELLO: What if I do obey? How may the duke be therewith satisfied, whose messengers are here about my side, upon some present business of the state to bring me to him?

FIRST OFFICER: 'Tis true, most worthy signior; he duke's in council, and your noble self, I am sure, is sent for.

BRABANTIO: How! the duke in council! In this time of the night! Bring him away; mine's not an idle cause: the duke himself, or any of my brothers of the state, cannot but feel this wrong as 'twere their own; for if such actions may have passage free, bond-slaves and pagans shall our statesmen be. *[Exeunt]*

[A council chamber]
[The Duke and Senators sitting at a table]

FIRST OFFICER: A messenger from the galleys. *[Enter a Sailor]*

DUKE: Now, what's the business?
SAILOR: The Turkish preparation makes for Rhodes; so was I bid report here to the state by Signior Angelo.
DUKE: How say you by this change?
FIRST SENATOR: This cannot be, by no assay of reason: tis a pageant, To keep us in false gaze. When we consider th'importancy of Cyprus to the Turk. *[Enter a messenger]*
MESSENGER: The Ottomites, reverend and gracious, steering with due course toward the isle of Rhodes, have there injointed them with an after fleet.
FIRST SENATOR: Ay, so I thought. How many, as you guess?
MESSENGER: Of thirty sail.
DUKE: 'Tis certain, then, for Cyprus. Marcus Luccicos, is not he in town?
FIRST SENATOR: He's now in Florence.
DUKE: Write from us to him; post-post-haste dispatch.
FIRST SENATOR: Here comes Brabantio and the valiant Moor.*[Enter Brabantio Othello, Iago, Roderigo, and Officers]*
DUKE: Valiant Othello, we must straight employ you against the general enemy Ottoman. *[to Brabantio]* I did not see you; welcome, gentle signior. We lack'd your counsel and your help to-night.
BRABANTIO: So did I yours. Good your Grace, pardon me. Neither my place, nor aught I heard of business, hath raised me from my bed; for my particular grief is of so flood-gate and o'erbearing nature that it engluts and swallows other sorrows, and it is still itself.
DUKE: Why, what's the matter?
BRABANTIO: My daughter! O, my daughter!
DUKE and SENATOR: Dead?

BRABANTIO: Ay, to me; he is abused, stol'n from me, and corrupted by spells and medicines bought of mountebanks; for nature so preposterously to err, being not deficient, blind, or lame of sense, sans witchcraft could not.
DUKE: Whoe'er he be that, in this foul proceeding, hath thus beguiled your daughter of herself, and you of her.
BRABANTIO: Here is the man, this Moor; whom now, it seems, your special mandate, for the state-affairs, hath hither brought.
DUKE and SENATOR: We are very sorry for't.
DUKE: *[to Othello]* What, in your own part, can you say to this?
OTHELLO: Most potent, grave, and reverend signiors, my very noble and approved good masters, that I have ta'en away this old man's daughter, it is most true; true, I have married her. Yet, by your gracious patience, I will a round unvarnish'd tale deliver of my whole course of love; what drugs, what charms, what conjuration, and what mighty magic, for such proceeding I am charged withal, I won his daughter.
BRABANTIO: A maiden never bold; Of spirit so still and quiet, that her motion blush'd at herself; and she in spite of nature, of years, of country, credit, every thing to fall in love with what she fear'd to look on! It is a judgement maim'd and most imperfect, that will confess perfection so could err against all rules of nature; and must be driven to find out practices of cunning hell, why this should be.
FIRST SENATOR: But, Othello, speak. Did you by indirect and forced courses subdue and poison this young maid's affections? Or came it by request, and such fair question as soul to soul affordeth?

OTHELLO: I do beseech you, send for the lady to the Sagittary, and let her speak of me before her father. If you do find me foul in her report, the trust, the office, I do hold of you, not only take away, but let your sentence even fall upon my life.

DUKE: Fetch Desdemona hither.

OTHELLO: *[Exeunt Iago]* And, till she come, as truly as to heaven I do confess the vices of my blood, so justly to your grave ears I'll present how I did thrive in this fair lady's love, and she in mine.

DUKE: Say it, Othello.

OTHELLO: Her father loved me; oft invited me; still question'd me the story of my life, from year to year, the battles, sieges, fortunes, that I have pass'd. I ran it through, even from my boyish days to the very moment that he bade me tell it. I did consent; and often did beguile her of her tears, when I did speak of some distressful stroke that my youth suffer'd. My story being done, she gave me for my pains a world of sighs. She swore, in faith, 'twas strange, 'twas passing strange; 'twas pitiful, 'twas wondrous pitiful. She wish'd she had not heard it: yet she wish'd that heaven had made her such a man. She thank'd me; and bade me, if I had a friend that loved her, I should but teach him how to tell my story, and that would woo her. Upon this hint I spake. She loved me for the dangers I had pass'd; and I loved her that she did pity them. This only is the witchcraft I have used. Here comes the lady; let her witness it. *[Enter Desdemona with Iago]*

DUKE: I think this tale would win my daughter too. Good Brabantio, take up this mangled matter at the best. Men do their broken weapons rather use than their bare hands.

BRABANTIO: I pray you, hear her speak. If she confess that she was half the wooer, destruction on my head, if my bad blame light on the man! Come hither, gentle mistress.Do you perceive in all this noble company where most you owe obedience?

DESDEMONA: My noble father, I do perceive here a divided duty. To you I am bound for life and education. How to respect you; you are the lord of duty, I am hitherto your daughter: but here's my husband; and so much duty as my mother show'd to you, preferring you before her father, so much I challenge that I may profess due to the Moor my lord.

BRABANTIO: God be wi' you! I have done. Please it your Grace, on to the state-affairs. I had rather to adopt a child than get it. Come hither, Moor. I here do give thee that with all my heart which, but thou hast already, with all my heart I would keep from thee. For your sake, jewel, I am glad at soul I have no other child; for thy escape would teach me tyranny, to hang clogs on them. I have done, my lord.

DUKE: Othello, the fortitude of the place is best known to you; and though we have there a substitute of most allow'd sufficiency, yet opinion, a sovereign mistress of effects, throws a more safer voice on you: you must therefore be content to slubber the gloss of your new fortunes with this more stubborn and boisterous expedition.

OTHELLO: The tyrant custom, most grave senators, hath made the flinty and steel couch of war my thrice-driven bed of down. Most humbly, therefore, bending to your state, I crave fit disposition for my wife; due reference of place and exhibition;with such accommodation and besort as levels with her breeding.

DUKE: If you please, be't at her father's.

BRABANTIO: I'll not have it so.

OTHELLO: Nor I.

DESDEMONA: Nor I; I would not there reside, to put my father in impatient thoughts by being in his eye. Most gracious duke, to my unfolding lend your prosperous ear; and let me find a charter in your voice, t'assist my simpleness.

DUKE: What would you, Desdemona?

DESDEMONA: That I did love the Moor to live with him, let me go with him.

DUKE: Be it as you shall privately determine, either for her stay or going: th'affair cries haste, and speed must answer it.

FIRST SENATOR: You must away to-night.

DUKE: At nine i'the morning here we'll meet again. Othello, leave some officer behind, and he shall our commission bring to you.

OTHELLO: So please your Grace, my ancient; a man he is of honesty and trust. To his conveyance I assign my wife, with what else needful your good Grace shall think to be sent after me.

DUKE: Let it be so. Good night to every one. *[to Brabantio]* And, noble signior, if virtue no delighted beauty lack, your son-in-law is far more fair than black.

BRABANTIO: Look to her, Moor, if thou hast eyes to see. She has deceived her father, and may thee. *[Exeunt Duke and others]*

OTHELLO: Honest Iago, my Desdemona must I leave to thee. I prithee, let thy wife attend on her; and bring them after in the best advantage. Come, Desdemona; I have but an hour of love, of worldly matters and direction, to spend with thee: we must obey the time. *[Exeunt Othello and Desdemona]*

IAGO: He holds me well; the better shall my purpose work on him. Cassio's a proper man: let me see now; to get his place, and to plume up my will in double knavery. How, how? Let's see. After some time, to abuse Othello's ear that he is too familiar with his wife. He hath a person, and a smooth dispose, to be suspected; framed to make women false. The Moor is of a free and open nature, that thinks men honest that but seem to be so; and will as tenderly be led by th'nose as asses are. I have't; it is engender'd: hell and night must bring this monstrous birth to the world's light. *[Exit]*

[A seaport town in Cyprus, Enter Cassio, Desdemona, Iago, Emilia, and Roderigo]

CASSIO: The riches of the ship is come on shore! Ye men of Cyprus, let her have your knees. Hail to thee, lady! and the grace of heaven before, behind thee, and on every hand, enwheel thee round!

DESDEMONA: I thank you, valiant Cassio. What tidings can you tell me of my lord?

CASSIO: He is not yet arrived: nor know I aught but that he's well, and will be shortly here.

IAGO: *[aside]* He takes her by the palm: ay, well said, whisper: with as little a web as this will I ensnare as great a fly as Cassio. Ay, smile upon her, do; I will gyve thee in thine own courtship. *[Trumpet]* The Moor! I know his trumpet.

DESDEMONA: Let's meet him, and receive him. *[Enter Othello]*

OTHELLO: O my fair warrior!

DESDEMONA: My dear Othello!

OTHELLO: It gives me wonder great as my content to see you here before me. O my soul's joy!

DESDEMONA: The heavens forbid But that our loves and comforts should increase, even as our days do grow!

OTHELLO: Amen to that, sweet powers! Come, let us to the castle. News, friends; our wars are done, the Turks are drown'd. I prithee, good Iago, go to the bay and disembark my coffers. Bring thou the master to the citadel; he is a good one, and his worthiness does challenge much respect. Come, Desdemona, once more well met at Cyprus. *[Exeunt all but Iago and Roderigo]*

IAGO: List me. The lieutenant to-night watches on the court-of-guard first, I must tell thee this; Desdemona is directly in love with him.

RODERIGO: With him! why, 'tis not possible.

IAGO: Her eye must be fed; and what delight shall she have to ;look on the devil? When the blood is made dull with the act of sport, there should be- again to inflame it, and to give satiety a fresh appetite- loveliness in favour, sympathy in years, manners, and beauties; all which the Moor is defective in.

RODERIGO: I cannot believe that in her; she's full of most bless'd condition.

IAGO: The wine she drinks is made of grapes: if she had been bless'd, she would never have loved the Moor: bless'd pudding! Didst thou not see her paddle with the palm of his hand? didst not mark that?

RODERIGO: Yes, that I did; but that was but courtesy.

IAGO: Lechery, by this hand; an index and obscure prologue to the history of lust and foul thoughts. They met so near with their lips, that their breaths embraced together.

Watch you to-night; for the command, I'll lay't upon you: Cassio knows you not. I'll not be far from you: do you find some occasion to anger Cassio, either by speaking too loud, or tainting his discipline. Sir, he is rash, and very sudden in choler, and haply may strike at you. Provoke him, that he may. So shall you have a shorter journey to your desires, by the means I shall then have to prefer them; and the impediment most profitably removed, without the which there were no expectation of our prosperity.

RODERIGO: I will do this, if I can bring it to any opportunity. *[Exit]*

IAGO: That Cassio loves her, I do well believe it; that she loves him, 'tis apt, and of great credit. The Moor- howbeit that I endure him not- Is of a constant, loving, noble nature; and I dare think he'll prove to Desdemona a most dear husband. I'll have our Michael Cassio on the hip; abuse him to the Moor in the rank garb, make the Moor thank me, love me, and reward me, for making him egregiously an ass, and practising upon his peace and quiet even to madness. 'Tis here, but yet confused. Knavery's plain face is never seen till used. *[Exit]*

[A hall in the castle.Enter Othello, Desdemona, and Cassio]

OTHELLO: Good Michael, look you to the guard to-night. Let's teach ourselves that honourable stop, not to outsport discretion.

CASSIO: Iago hath direction what to do; gut, notwithstanding, with my personal eye will I look to't. *[Exit Othello, enter Iago]*

CASSIO: Welcome, Iago; we must to the watch.

IAGO: Not this hour, lieutenant; 'tis not yet ten o' the clock. Our general cast us thus early for the love of his Desdemona; who let us not therefore blame; he hath not yet made wanton the night with her; and she is sport for Jove.

CASSIO: She's a most exquisite lady.

IAGO: Come, lieutenant, I have a stoop of wine; and here without are a brace of Cyprus gallants that would fain have a measure to the health of black Othello.

CASSIO: Not to-night, good Iago: I have very poor and unhappy brains for drinking. I could well wish courtesy would invent some other custom of entertainment.

IAGO: O, they are our friends; but one cup: I'll drink for you.

CASSIO: I have drunk but one cup to-night, and that was craftily qualified too, and, behold, what innovation it makes here: I am unfortunate in the infirmity, and dare not task my weakness with any more. *[Exit]*

IAGO: If I can fasten but one cup upon him, with that which he hath drunk to to-night already, he'll be as full of quarrel and offence as my young mistress' dog. Now, my sick fool Roderigo, whom love hath turn'd almost the wrong side out, have I to-night fluster'd with flowing cups, and they watch too. Now, 'mongst this flock of drunkards am I to put our Cassio in some action that may offend the isle: but here they come. *[Enter Cassio, Montano, and Gentlemen]*

CASSIO: 'Fore God, they have given me a rouse already.

MONTANO: Good faith, a little one; not past a pint, as I am a soldier.

CASSIO: To the health of our general!

MONTANO: I am for it, lieutenant; and I'll do you justice.

CASSIO: Do not think, gentlemen, I am drunk. This is my ancient; this is my right hand, and this is my left. I am not drunk now; I can stand well enough, and speak well enough.

ALL: Excellent well. *[Exit Cassio]*

IAGO: *[to Montano]* You see this fellow that is gone before; he is a soldier fit to stand by Caesar and give direction: and do but see his vice; 'tis to his virtue a just equinox, the one as long as th'other: 'tis pity of him. I fear the trust Othello puts him in, on some odd time of his infirmity, will shake this island.

MONTANO: But is he often thus?

IAGO: 'Tis evermore the prologue to his sleep.

MONTANO: It were well the general were put in mind of it. Perhaps he sees it not; or his good nature prizes the virtue that appears in Cassio, and looks not on his evils: is not this true? *[Enter Roderigo]*

IAGO: *[aside to Roderigo]* How now, Roderigo! I pray you, after the lieutenant; go. *[Exit Roderigo]*

MONTANO: And 'tis great pity that the noble Moor should hazard such a place as his own second with one of an ingraft infirmity. It were an honest action to say so to the Moor. *[Enter Cassio, driving in Roderigo]*

CASSIO: Zounds, you rogue! you rascal!

MONTANO: What's the matter, lieutenant?

CASSIO: A knave teach me my duty! but I'll beat the knave into a twiggen bottle.

RODERIGO: Beat me!

CASSIO: Dost thou prate, rogue? *[Striking Roderigo]*

MONTANO: Nay, good lieutenant; I pray you, sir, hold your hand.

CASSIO: Let me go, sir, or I'll knock you o'er the mazard.

MONTANO.
Come, come, you're drunk.

CASSIO: Drunk!   *[They fight]*
IAGO: *[aside to Roderigo]* Away, I say, go out; and cry a mutiny! *[Exit Roderigo]* Nay, good lieutenant, God's will, gentlemen; Help, ho! Lieutenant, sir, Montano, sir; Help, masters! Here's a goodly watch indeed! *[Enter Othello and Attendants]*
OTHELLO: What is the matter here?
MONTANO: Zounds, I bleed still; I am hurt to the death.   *[Faints]*
OTHELLO: Hold, for your lives!
IAGO: Hold, ho! Lieutenant, sir, Montano, gentlemen, have you forgot all sense of place and duty? Hold! the general speaks to you; hold, hold, for shame!
OTHELLO: Why, how now, ho! from whence ariseth this?
IAGO: I cannot speak any beginning to this peevish odds; and would in action glorious I had lost those legs that brought me to a part of it!
OTHELLO: How comes it, Michael, you are thus forgot?
CASSIO: I pray you, pardon me; I cannot speak.
OTHELLO: Worthy Montano, you were wont be civil.
MONTANO: Worthy Othello, I am hurt to danger. Your officer, Iago, can inform you.
OTHELLO: Now, by heaven, my blood begins my safer guides to rule. Give me to know how this foul rout began, who set it on.
IAGO: I had rather have this tongue cut from my mouth than it should do offence to Michael Cassio; yet, I persuade myself, to speak the truth shall nothing wrong him. Thus it is, general. Montano and myself being in speech, there comes a fellow crying out for help; and Cassio following him with determined sword to execute upon him. Sir, this gentleman steps in to Cassio, and

entreats his pause: myself the crying fellow did pursue, he, swift of foot, outran my purpose; and I return'd the rather for that I heard the clink and fall of swords. When I came back, for this was brief, I found them close together, at blow and thrust; even as again they were when you yourself did part them. More of this matter cannot I report.
OTHELLO: Cassio, I love thee; but never more be officer of mine. *[Exeunt all but Iago and Cassio]*
CASSIO: Reputation, reputation, reputation! O, I have lost my reputation! I have lost the immortal part of myself, and what remains is bestial. My reputation, Iago, my reputation!
IAGO: As I am an honest man, I thought you had received some bodily wound.
CASSIO: I will rather sue to be despised than to deceive so good a commander with so slight, so drunken, and so indiscreet an officer.
IAGO: What was he that you follow'd with your sword? What had he done to you?
CASSIO: I remember a mass of things, but nothing distinctly; a quarrel, but nothing wherefore.
IAGO: Our general's wife is now the
general. Importune her help to put you in your place again. This broken joint between you and her husband entreat her to splinter; and, my fortunes against any lay worth naming, this crack of your love shall grow stronger than it was before.
CASSIO: You advise me well. In the morning I will beseech the virtuous Desdemona to undertake for me. *[Exit]*
IAGO: Good night, lieutenant; I must to the watch. For whiles this honest fool plies Desdemona to repair his fortunes, and she for him

pleads strongly to the Moor, I'll pour this pestilence into his ear, that she repeals him for her body's lust; and by how much she strives to do him good, she shall undo her credit with the Moor. So will I turn her virtue into pitch; and out of her own goodness make the net that shall enmesh them all. *[Exit]* *[Enter Emilia, Cassio, Iago]*
EMILIA: Good morrow, good lieutenant: I am sorry for your displeasure; but all will sure be well. The general and his wife are talking of it; and she speaks for you stoutly: the Moor replies, that he you hurt is of great fame in Cyprus and great affinity, and that in wholesome wisdom he might not but refuse you; but he protests he loves you, and needs no other suitor but his likings to take the safest occasion by the front to bring you in again.
CASSIO: Yet, I beseech you, if you think fit, or that it may be done, give me advantage of some brief discourse with Desdemona alone.
EMILIA: Pray you, come in. I will bestow you where you shall have time to speak your bosom freely.
CASSIO: I am much bound to you. *[Exeunt]*

[The garden of the castle] *[Enter Othello and Iago]*
OTHELLO: Was not that Cassio parted from my wife?
IAGO: Cassio, my lord! No, sure, I cannot think it, that he would steal away so guilty-like, seeing you coming.
OTHELLO: I do believe 'twas he. *[Enter Desdemona]*
DESDEMONA: How now, my lord! I have been talking with a suitor here, a man that languishes in your displeasure.
OTHELLO: Who is't you mean?

DESDEMONA: Why, your lieutenant, Cassio. Good my lord, if I have any grace or power to move you, his present reconciliation take.
OTHELLO: Went he hence now?
DESDEMONA: Ay, sooth; so humbled, that he hath left part of his grief with me, to suffer with him. Good love, call him back.
OTHELLO: Not now, sweet Desdemona; some other time.
DESDEMONA: But shall't be shortly? I prithee, name the time; but let it not exceed three days: in faith, he's penitent.
OTHELLO: I will deny thee nothing. Whereon, I do beseech thee, grant me this, to leave me but a little to myself.
DESDEMONA: Farewell, my lord.
OTHELLO: Excellent wretch! perdition catch my soul, but I do love thee! and when I love thee not, chaos is come again.
IAGO: My noble lord,-
OTHELLO: What dost thou say, Iago?
IAGO: Did Michael Cassio, when you woo'd my lady, know of your love?
OTHELLO: He did, from first to last: why dost thou ask?
IAGO: I did not think he had been acquainted with her.
OTHELLO: O, yes; and went between us very oft. Is he not honest?
IAGO: I think Cassio's an honest man.
OTHELLO: Nay, yet there's more in this. I prithee, speak to me as to thy thinkings.
IAGO: Good name in man and woman, dear my lord, is the immediate jewel of their souls. Who steals my purse steals trash; 'tis something, nothing; 'twas mine, 'tis his, and has been slave to thousands; but he that filches from me my good

name robs me of that which not enriches him, and makes me poor indeed.

OTHELLO: By heaven, I'll know thy thoughts!

IAGO: O, beware, my lord, of jealousy; it is the green-eyed monster, which doth mock the meat it feeds on: that cuckold lives in bliss who, certain of his fate, loves not his wronger; but, O, what damned minutes tells he o'er who dotes, yet doubts, suspects, yet strongly loves!

OTHELLO: Why, why is this? Think'st thou I'ld make a life of jealousy, to follow still the changes of the moon with fresh suspicions? 'Tis not to make me jealous to say my wife is fair, feeds well, loves company, is free of speech, sings, plays, and dances well; where virtue is, these are more virtuous. For she had eyes, and chose me. No, Iago; I'll see before I doubt.

IAGO: I am glad of it; for now I shall have reason to show the love and duty that I bear you with franker spirit. Look to your wife; observe her well with Cassio; wear you eye thus, not jealous nor secure. She did deceive her father, marrying you; and when she seem'd to shake and fear your looks, she loved them most.

OTHELLO: And so she did.

IAGO: Why, go to, then; she that, so young, could give out such a seeming, to seal her father's eyes up close as oak.

OTHELLO: I do not think but Desdemona's honest. And yet, how nature erring from itself.

IAGO: Long live she so! and long live you to think so! Ay, there's the point. Not to affect many proposed matches of her own clime, complexion, and degree, whereto we see in all things nature tends. I do not in position distinctly speak of her; though I may fear her will, recoiling to her better judgement, may fall to match you with her country forms, and happily repent.

OTHELLO: Farewell, farewell. If more thou dost perceive, let me know more; set on thy wife to observe: leave me, Iago.

IAGO: My lord, I take my leave. *[Exit]*

OTHELLO: Why did I marry? This honest creature doubtless sees and knows more, much more, than he unfolds. Desdemona comes. If she be false, O, then heaven mocks itself! I'll not believe't. *[Enter Desdemona and Emilia]*

DESDEMONA: How now, my dear Othello! Your dinner, and the generous islanders by you invited, do attend your presence.

OTHELLO: I have a pain upon my forehead here.

DESDEMONA: Faith, that's with watching; 'twill away again. Let me but bind it hard, within this hour it will be well.

OTHELLO: Your napkin is too little.*[Drops handkerchief]* I'll go in with you.

EMILIA: I am glad I have found this napkin. This was her first remembrance from the Moor. My wayward husband hath a hundred times woo'd me to steal it; but she so loves the token, for he conjured her she should ever keep it, that she reserves it evermore about her to kiss and talk to. I'll have the work ta'en out, and give't Iago. What he will do with it heaven knows.*[Enter Iago]*

IAGO: How now! what do you here alone?

EMILIA: Do not you chide; I have a thing for you.

IAGO: A good wench; give it me.

EMILIA: What will you do with't, that you have been so earnest to have me filch it?

IAGO: Why, what's that to you?

EMILIA: If't be not for some purpose of import, give't me again: poor lady, she'll run mad when she shall lack it.

IAGO: Be not acknown on't; I have use for it. Go, leave me. *[Exit Emilia]* I will in Cassio's lodging lose this napkin, and let him find it. Trifles light as air are to the jealous confirmations strong as proofs of holy writ: this may do something. The Moor already changes with my poison. *[Enter Othello]*

OTHELLO: Villain, be sure thou prove my love a whore, be sure of it; give me the ocular proof; or, by the worth of man's eternal soul, thou hadst been better have been born a dog than answer my waked wrath! Make me to see't; or, at the least, so prove it, that the probation bear no hinge nor loop to hang a doubt on; or woe upon thy life!

IAGO: Take note, take note, O world, to be direct and honest is not safe.

OTHELLO: By the world, I think my wife be honest, and think she is not; I think that thou art just, and think thou art not. I'll have some proof. Her name, that was as fresh as Dian's visage, is now begrimed and black as mine own face.

IAGO: I see, sir, you are eaten up with passion.

OTHELLO: Give me a living reason she's disloyal.

IAGO: Tell me but this, have you not sometimes seen a handkerchief spotted with strawberries in your wife's hand?

OTHELLO: I gave her such a one; 'twas my first gift.

IAGO: Such a handkerchief--I am sure it was your wife's--did I to-day see Cassio wipe his beard with. If it be that, or any that was hers, it speaks against her with the other proofs.

OTHELLO: Within these three days let me hear thee say that Cassio's not alive.

IAGO: My friend is dead; 'tis done at your request. But let her live.

OTHELLO: Damn her, lewd minx! O, damn her! *[Exeunt]*

[Before the castle, enter Desdemona and Emilia]

DESDEMONA: Where should I lose that handkerchief, Emilia?

EMILIA: I know not, madam.

DESDEMONA: Believe me, I had rather have lost my purse.

EMILIA: Is he not jealous?

DESDEMONA: Who, he? I think the sun where he was born drew all such humours from him. I will not leave him now till Cassio be call'd to him.*[Enter Othello]* How is't with you, my lord?

OTHELLO: How do you, Desdemona? Give me your hand: this hand is moist, my lady.

DESDEMONA: It yet hath felt no age nor known no sorrow.

OTHELLO: This argues fruitfulness and liberal heart. Hot, hot, and moist: this hand of yours requires a sequester from liberty, fasting and prayer, much castigation, exercise devout; for here's a young and sweating devil here, that commonly rebels.'Tis a good hand.

DESDEMONA: You may, indeed, say so; for 'twas that hand that gave away my heart. Come now, your promise.

OTHELLO: What promise, chuck?

DESDEMONA: I have sent to bid Cassio come speak with you.

OTHELLO: Lend my thy handkerchief, that which I gave you.

DESDEMONA: I have it not about me.

OTHELLO: That is a fault. That handkerchief did an Egyptian to my mother give; she was a charmer, and could almost read the thoughts of people: she told her, while she kept it,'twould make her amiable, and subdue my father entirely to her love; but if she lost it, or made a gift of it, my father's eye should hold her loathed, and his spirits should hunt after new fancies. She, dying, gave it me; and bid me, when my fate would have me wive, to give it her.'Tis true: there's magic in the web of it.

DESDEMONA: It is not lost; but what an if it were?

OTHELLO: Fetch't, let me see't.

DESDEMONA: Why, so I can, sir, but I will not now. This is a trick to put me from my suit. Pray you, let Cassio be received again.

OTHELLO: Fetch me the handkerchief: my mind misgives.

DESDEMONA: Come, come. You'll never meet a more sufficient man. I pray, talk me of Cassio.

OTHELLO: The handkerchief! Away! *[Exit]*

EMILIA: Is not this man jealous?

DESDEMONA: I ne'er saw this before. Sure, there's some wonder in this handkerchief. I am most unhappy in the loss of it. *[Enter Cassio and Iago]*

IAGO: There is no other way; 'tis she must do't.

DESDEMONA: How now, good Cassio! what's the news with you?

CASSIO: Madam, my former suit: I do beseech you that by your virtuous means I may again exist, and be a member of his love whom I with all the office of my heart entirely honour.

DESDEMONA: Alas, thrice-gentle Cassio! My advocation is not now in tune; my lord is not my lord; nor should I know him.

IAGO: Is my lord angry?

EMILIA: He went hence but now, and certainly in strange unquietness. Pray heaven it be state-matters, as you think, and no conception nor no jealous toy concerning you.

DESDEMONA: I will go seek him. Cassio, walk hereabout. If I do find him fit, I'll move your suit, and seek to effect it to my uttermost.

CASSIO: I humbly thank your ladyship. *[Exeunt Desdemona, Emilia, and Iago. Enter Bianca]*

BIANCA: Save you, friend Cassio!

CASSIO: How is it with you, my most fair Bianca? I' faith, sweet love, I was coming to your house.

BIANCA: And I was going to your lodging, Cassio. What, keep a week away? seven days and nights?

CASSIO: Pardon me, Bianca. I have this while with leaden thoughts been press'd. *[Giving her Desdemona's handkerchief]* Take me this work out.

BIANCA: O Cassio, whence came this? This is some token from a newer friend.

CASSIO: Go to, woman! Throw your vile guesses in the devil's teeth,

BIANCA: Why, whose is it?

CASSIO: I know not neither: I found it in my chamber. I like the work well. I'ld have it copied. Take it, and do't; and leave me for this time.*[Exit Bianca]*

[Before the castle. Enter Othello and Iago]

IAGO: Stand you awhile apart; confine yourself but in a patient list. Whilst you were here o'erwhelmed with your grief, passion most unfitting such a man, Cassio came hither: I shifted him away, and laid good 'scuse upon your ecstasy; bade him anon return, and here speak with me; the which he promised. Do but encave yourself, and mark the fleers, the gibes, and notable scorns, that dwell in every region of his face; for I will make him tell the tale anew, where, how, how oft, how long ago, and when he hath, and is again to cope your wife. I say, but mark his gesture. Marry, patience; or I shall say y'are all in all in spleen, and nothing of a man. Will you withdraw? *[Othello exits]* Now will I question Cassio of Bianca, a housewife that, by selling her desires, buys herself bread and clothes: it is a creature that dotes on Cassio, as 'tis the strumpet's plague to beguile many and be beguiled by one. He, when he hears of her, cannot refrain from the excess of laughter: here he comes. As he shall smile, Othello shall go mad; and his unbookish jealousy must construe poor Cassio's smiles, gestures, and light behaviour, quite in the wrong. *[Enter Cassio]* How do you now, lieutenant?

CASSIO: The worser that you give me the addition whose want even kills me.

IAGO: Ply Desdemona well, and you are sure on't. *[Lowers voice]* Now, if this suit lay in Bianca's power, how quickly should you speed!

OTHELLO: *[in hiding]* Look, how he laughs already!

IAGO: I never knew a woman love man so.

OTHELLO: Now he denies it faintly, and laughs it out. To tell it o'er: go to; well said, well said.

IAGO: She gives it out that you shall marry her. Do you intend it?

CASSIO: Ha, ha, ha! I marry her! what, a customer! Prithee, bear some charity to my wit; do not think it so unwholesome:- ha, ha, ha!

OTHELLO: So, so, so, so: they laugh that win.

CASSIO: This is the monkey's own giving out: she is persuaded I will

marry her, out of her own love and flattery, not out of my promise.

OTHELLO: Iago beckons me; now he begins the story.

CASSIO: She was here even now; she haunts me in every place. I was, the other day, talking on the sea-bank with certain Venetians; and thither comes the bauble, and by this hand she falls me thus about my neck.

OTHELLO: *[aside]* Crying "O dear Cassio!" as it were: his gesture imports it. Now he tells how she pluck'd him to my chamber.

IAGO: Before me! look, where she comes.

CASSIO: *[Enter Bianca]* What do you mean by this haunting of me?

BIANCA: Let the devil and his dam haunt you! What did you mean by that same handkerchief you gave me even now? I was a fine fool to take it. I must take out the work?- A likely piece of work, that you should find it in your chamber, and not know who left it there! This is some minx's token, and I must take out the work? *[Exit]*

OTHELLO: By heaven, that should be my handkerchief!

IAGO: After her, after her.

CASSIO: Faith, I must; she'll rail i' the street else. *[Exit Cassio]*

OTHELLO: *[coming out of hiding]* How shall I murder him, Iago?

IAGO: Did you perceive how he laugh'd at his vice? And did you see the handkerchief?

OTHELLO: Was that mine?

IAGO: Yours, by this hand: and to see how he prizes the foolish woman your wife! she gave it him, and he hath given it his whore.

OTHELLO: I would have him nine years a-killing. A fine woman! a fair woman! a sweet woman!

IAGO: Nay, you must forget that.

OTHELLO: Ay, let her rot, and perish, and be damn'd to-night; for

she shall not live: no, my heart is
turned to stone; I strike it, and it
hurts my hand.
IAGO: Nay, that's not your way.
She's the worse for all this.
OTHELLO: Nay, that's certain: but
yet the pity of it, Iago! O Iago, the
pity of it, Iago!
IAGO: If you are so fond over her
iniquity, give her patent to offend;
for, if it touch not you, it comes near
nobody.
OTHELLO: I will chop her into
messes. Cuckold me!
IAGO: O, 'tis foul in her.
OTHELLO: With mine officer!
IAGO: That's fouler.
OTHELLO: Get me some poison,
Iago; this night. I'll not expostulate
with her, lest her body and beauty
unprovide my mind again--this night,
Iago.
IAGO: Do it not with poison,
strangle her in her bed, even the bed
she hath contaminated.
OTHELLO: Good, good: the justice
of it pleases: very good.
IAGO: And for Cassio, let me be his
undertaker. You shall hear more by
midnight.
OTHELLO:Excellent good.*[Exeunt]*

*[A room in the castle. Enter Othello
and Emilia]*
OTHELLO: You have seen nothing,
then?
EMILIA: Nor ever heard, nor ever
did suspect.
OTHELLO: Yes, you have seen
Cassio and she together.
EMILIA: But then I saw no harm,
and then I heard each syllable that
breath made up between them.
OTHELLO: What, did they never
whisper? Nor send you out o'
th'way? To fetch her fan, her gloves,
her mask, nor nothing?
EMILIA: Never, my lord. I durst,
my lord, to wager she is honest, 'ay

down my soul at stake: if you think
other, remove your thought, it doth
abuse your bosom.
OTHELLO: Bid her come hither:
go.*[Exit Emilia]* She says enough;
yet she's a simple bawd that cannot
say as much. This is a subtle whore,
a closet-lock-and-key of villainous
secrets. And yet she'll kneel and
pray; I have seen her do't. *[Enter
Desdemona with Emilia]*
DESDEMONA: My lord, what is
your will?
OTHELLO: Let me see your eyes;
look in my face.
OTHELLO: *[to Emilia]* Some of
your function, mistress; leave
procreants alone, and shut the door;
cough, or cry "hem" if any body
come. *[Exit Emilia]*
OTHELLO: Why, what art thou?
DESDEMONA: Your wife, my
lord; your true and loyal wife.
OTHELLO: Come, swear it, damn
thyself. Swear thou are honest.
DESDEMONA: Heaven doth truly
know it.
OTHELLO: Heaven truly knows
that thou art false as hell.
DESDEMONA: To whom, my lord?
with whom? how am I false? Alas
the heavy day! Why do you weep?
Am I the motive of these tears, my
lord? I hope my noble lord esteems
me honest.
OTHELLO: O, ay; as summer flies
are in the shambles, that quicken
even with blowing. O thou weed,
who art so lovely fair, and smell'st
so sweet, that the sense aches at thee,
would thou hadst ne'er been born!
DESDEMONA: Alas, what ignorant
sin have I committed?
OTHELLO: Was this fair paper, this
most goodly book, made to write
"whore" upon? What committed! O
thou public commoner! What
committed! Impudent strumpet!

DESDEMONA: By heaven, you do me wrong. No, as I am a Christian. If to preserve this vessel for my lord from any other foul unlawful touch, be not to be a strumpet, I am none. O, heaven forgive us!
OTHELLO: I cry you mercy, then. I took you for that cunning whore of Venice that married with Othello. *[Enter Emilia]* You, you, ay, you! We have done our course; there's money for your pains. I pray you, turn the key, and keep our counsel. *[Exit]*
EMILIA: Good madam, what's the matter with my lord? He that is yours, sweet lady.
DESDEMONA: I have none: do not talk to me, Emilia; I cannot weep; nor answer have I none, but what should go by water. Prithee, to-night lay on my bed my wedding-sheets, remember; and call thy husband hither. *[Exit Emilia]*
DESDEMONA: 'Tis meet I should be used so, very meet. How have I been behaved, that he might stick the small'st opinion on my least misuse? *[Enter Emilia with Iago]*
IAGO: What is your pleasure, madam? How is't with you?
DESDEMONA: I cannot tell.
IAGO: What's the matter, lady?
EMILIA: Alas, Iago, my lord hath so bewhored her. Hath she forsook so many noble matches, her father, and her country, and her friends, to be call'd whore? would it not make one weep?
DESDEMONA: It is my wretched fortune.
EMILIA: I will be hang'd, if some eternal villain, some busy and insinuating rogue, some cogging, cozening slave, to get some office, have not devised this slander; I'll be hang'd else.
DESDEMONA: If any such there be, heaven pardon him!

DESDEMONA: O good Iago, what shall I do to win my lord again?
IAGO: I pray you, be content; 'tis but his humour. The business of the state does him offence, and he does chide with you.
DESDEMONA: If 'twere no other,-
IAGO: Hark, how these instruments summon to supper! *[Exeunt]*

[A room in the castle] [Enter Othello, Desdemona, and Lodovico]
OTHELLO to Lovodico: 'Twill do me good to walk. Desdemona, get you to bed on th'instant; I will be return'd forthwith: dismiss your attendant there: look't be done.
DESDEMONA: I will, my lord. *[Exit all but Desdemona and Emilia]*
DESDEMONA:He hath commanded me to go to bed, and bade me to dismiss you.
EMILIA: Dismiss me!
DESDEMONA: It was his bidding; therefore, good Emilia, give me my nightly wearing.
EMILIA: I have laid those sheets you bade me on the bed.
DESDEMONA: If I do die before thee, prithee, shroud me in one of those same sheets.My mother had a maid call'd Barbara. She was in love; and he she loved proved mad, and did forsake her: she had a song of "willow;" an old thing 'twas, but it express'd her fortune, and she died singing it: that song to-night will not go from my mind; I have much to do, but to go hang my head all at one side, and sing it like poor Barbara. Prithee, dispatch.
EMILIA: Shall I go fetch your night-gown?
DESDEMONA: No, unpin me here. *[Exit Emilia][Song]*"The poor soul sat sighing by a sycamore tree,
    Sing all a green willow;
Her hand on her bosom, her head on her knee,

Sing willow, willow, willow:
The fresh streams ran by her, and
murmur'd her moans;
    Sing willow, willow, willow;
Her salt tears fell from her, and
soften'd the stones;-
Lay by these:-
    Sing willow, willow, willow;
Sing all a green willow must be my
garland.
Let nobody blame him; his scorn I
approve.

[A street. Enter Iago and Roderigo]
IAGO: Here, stand behind this bulk;
straight will he come.
RODERIGO: Be near at hand; I may
miscarry in't.
IAGO: Here, at thy hand: be bold,
and take thy stand.*[Retires to a little
distance] [Enter Cassio]*
RODERIGO: I know his gait, 'tis
he. Villain, thou diest!
CASSIO: That thrust had been mine
enemy indeed. *[Draws and wounds
Roderigo]*
RODERIGO: O, I am slain! *[Iago
cuts Cassio behind in the leg, and
exit]*
CASSIO: I am maim'd for ever.
Help, ho! murder! murder!*[Enter
Othello]*
OTHELLO: The voice of Cassio.
Iago keeps his word.
CASSIO: O, help, ho! light! a
surgeon!
RODERIGO: Nobody come? then
shall I bleed to death. *[Enter Iago
and others, with a light]*
IAGO: Who's there? whose noise is
this that cries on murder?
LODOVICO: We do not know.
CASSIO: Here, here! for heaven's
sake, help me!
IAGO: What are you here that cry
so grievously?
CASSIO: Iago? O, I am spoil'd,
undone by villains! Give me some
help.

RODERIGO: O, help me here!
CASSIO: That's one of them.
IAGO: O murderous slave! O
villain! *[Stabs Roderigo]*
RODERIGO: O damn'd Iago! O
inhuman dog!
IAGO: I cry you mercy. Here's
Cassio hurt by villains.*[Enter
Bianca]*
BIANCA: What is the matter, ho?
who is't that cried? O my dear
Cassio! my sweet Cassio! *[Enter
Emilia]*
EMILIA: 'Las, what's the matter?
what's the matter, husband?
IAGO: Cassio hath here been set on
in the dark by Roderigo, and fellows
that are scaped. He's almost slain,
and Roderigo dead. Kind gentlemen,
let's go see poor Cassio dress'd.
[Exeunt]

*[A bedchamber in the castle,
Desdemona in bed asleep] [Enter
Othello]*
OTHELLO: It is the cause, it is the
cause, my soul. Yet I'll not shed her
blood; nor scar that whiter skin of
hers than snow, and smooth as
monumental alabaster. Yet she must
die, else she'll betray more men.
[Kissing her] O balmy breath, that
dost almost persuade justice to break
her sword! She wakes.
DESDEMONA: Who's there?
Othello? Will you come to bed, my
lord?
OTHELLO: Have you pray'd to-
night, Desdemona? I would not kill
thy soul.
DESDEMONA: Talk you of killing?
Then heaven have mercy on me!
OTHELLO: Amen, with all my
heart!
DESDEMONA: If you say so, I
hope you will not kill me. And yet I
fear you; for you are fatal then when
your eyes roll so. Why I should fear

I know not, since guiltiness I know not; but yet I feel I fear.

OTHELLO: Think on thy sins. That handkerchief which I so loved and gave thee thou gavest to Cassio.

DESDEMONA: No, by my life and soul! Send for the man, and ask him. Lord have mercy on me! And have you mercy too! I never did offend you in my life; never loved Cassio but with such general warranty of heaven as I might love; I never gave him token.

OTHELLO: By heaven, I saw my handkerchief in's hand. I saw the handkerchief.

DESDEMONA: He found it. I never gave it him: send for him hither. Let him confess a truth.

OTHELLO: He hath confess'd that he hath used thee.

DESDEMONA: He will not say so.

OTHELLO: No, his mouth is stopp'd; honest Iago hath ta'en order for't.

DESDEMONA: Alas, he is betray'd, and I undone!

OTHELLO: Out, strumpet! weep'st thou for him to my face?

DESDEMONA: O, banish me, my lord, but kill me not! But while I say one prayer!

OTHELLO: It is too late. [Smothers her]

EMILIA: [within] What, ho! my lord, my lord!

OTHELLO: Who's there?

EMILIA: [within] O, good my lord, I would speak a word with you!

OTHELLO: Yes: 'tis Emilia. Shall she come in? What's best to do? If she come in, she'll sure speak to my wife. My wife! my wife! what wife! I have no wife.

OTHELLO: I had forgot thee: O, come in, Emilia. Let me the curtains draw.   [Enter Emilia]

EMILIA: O, my good lord, yonder's foul murders done! Cassio, my lord,

hath kill'd a young Venetian call'd Roderigo.

OTHELLO: Roderigo kill'd! And Cassio kill'd!

EMILIA: No, Cassio is not kill'd.

OTHELLO: Not Cassio kill'd! then murder's out of tune, and sweet revenge grows harsh.

DESDEMONA: O falsely, falsely murder'd!

EMILIA: Alas, what cry is that? that was my lady's voice. Help! help, ho! help! O lady, speak again! Sweet Desdemona! O sweet mistress, speak!
O, who hath done this deed?

DESDEMONA: Nobody, I myself. Farewell. Commend me to my kind lord: O, farewell!

OTHELLO: Why, how should she be murder'd? You heard her say herself, it was not I. She's, like a liar, gone to burning hell. 'Twas I that kill'd her.

EMILIA: O, the more angel she, and you the blacker devil!

OTHELLO: She turn'd to folly, and she was a whore. She was false as water.

EMILIA: Thou art rash as fire, to say
That she was false: O, she was heavenly true!

OTHELLO: Cassio did top her; ask thy husband else

EMILIA: My husband!

OTHELLO: Thy husband. Ay, 'twas he that told me first. An honest man he is, and hates the slime that sticks on filthy deeds.

EMILIA: If he say so, may his pernicious soul rot half a grain a day! he lies to th'heart. She was too fond of her most filthy bargain. This deed of thine is no more worthy heaven than thou wast worthy her.

OTHELLO: Peace, you were best.

EMILIA: Thou hast not half that power to do me harm as I have to be

hurt. I care not for thy sword; I'll
make thee known. The Moor hath
kill'd my mistress! Murder! murder!
[Enter Montano, Grantio, and Iago]
MONTANO: What is the matter?-
How now, general!
EMILIA: O, are you come, Iago?
you have done well, that men must
lay their murders on your neck.
Disprove this villain, if thou be'st a
man. He says thou told'st him that
his wife was false.
IAGO: I told him what I thought;
and told no more than what he found
himself was apt and true.
EMILIA: But did you ever tell him
she was false?
IAGO: I did.
EMILIA: You told a lie; an odious,
damned lie. My mistress here lies
murder'd in her bed and your reports
have set the murder on.
OTHELLO: Nay, stare not, masters:
it is true, indeed.
IAGO: What, are you mad? I charge
you, get you home.
EMILIA: Good gentlemen, let me
have leave to speak. 'Tis proper I
obey him, but not now. Perchance,
Iago, I will ne'er go home.
OTHELLO: O! O! O! *[Falling on
the bed]*
EMILIA: Nay, lay thee down and
roar; for thou hast kill'd the sweetest
innocent that e'er did lift up eye.
OTHELLO: O, she was foul!
GRATIANO: Poor Desdemona! I
am glad thy father's dead. Thy
match was mortal to him, and pure
grief shore his old thread in twain:
did he live now, this sight would
make him do a desperate turn.
OTHELLO: 'Tis pitiful; but yet Iago
knows that she with Cassio hath the
act of shame a thousand times
committed; Cassio confess'd it. And
she did gratify his amorous works
with that recognizance and pledge of
love which I first gave her; I saw it in

his hand. It was a handkerchief, an
antique token my father gave my
mother.
EMILIA: O heaven! O heavenly
powers!
IAGO: Come, hold your peace.
EMILIA: No, I will speak as liberal
as the north. O thou dull Moor! that
handkerchief thou speak'st of I found
by fortune, and did give my husband;
for often, with a solemn earnestness.
More than, indeed, belong'd to such
a trifle. He begg'd of me to steal it.
IAGO: Villainous whore!
EMILIA: She give it Cassio! no,
alas, I found it, and I did give't my
husband.
OTHELLO: Are there no stones in
heaven but what serve for the
thunder? Precious villain! *[Runs at
Iago who stabs Emilia, and exits]*
GRATIANO: The woman falls;
sure, he hath kill'd his wife.
EMILIA: Ay, ay: O, lay me by my
mistress' side.
MONTANO: 'Tis a notorious
villain. Take you this weapon, which
I have here recover'd from the Moor.
Come, guard the door without; let
him not pass, but kill him rather. I'll
after that same villain, for 'tis a
damned slave. *[Exeunt Montano and
Gratiano]*
OTHELLO: I have another weapon
in this chamber; it is a sword of
Spain, the ice-brook's temper. O,
here it is. Behold, I have a weapon; a
better never did itself sustain upon a
soldier's thigh. Be not afraid, though
you do see me weapon'd. Here is
my journey's end, here is my butt. O
cursed, cursed slave! Whip me, ye
devils, from the possession of this
heavenly sight! Blow me about in
winds! roast me in sulphur! Wash me
in steep-down gulfs of liquid fire! O
Desdemona! Desdemona! *[Enter
others with Iago]*

LODOVICO: Where is this rash and most unfortunate man?

OTHELLO: That's he that was Othello; here I am.

LODOVICO: Where is that viper? bring the villain forth.

OTHELLO: I look down towards his feet, but that's a fable. If that thou be'st a devil, I cannot kill thee. *[Wounds Iago]*

IAGO: I bleed, sir; but not kill'd.

OTHELLO: I am not sorry neither: I'ld have thee live, for, in my sense, 'tis happiness to die.

LODOVICO: O thou Othello, that wert once so good, fall'n in the practice of a damned slave, what shall be said to thee? This wretch hath part confess'd his villainy. Did you and he consent in Cassio's death?

OTHELLO: Ay.

CASSIO: Dear general, I never gave you cause.

OTHELLO: I do believe it, and I ask your pardon.

LODOVICO: Sir, you shall understand what hath befall'n, which, as I think, you know not. Here is a letter found in the pocket of the slain Roderigo; and here another: the one of them imports the death of Cassio to be undertook by Roderigo.

OTHELLO: O villain!

LODOVICO: Now here's another discontented paper, found in his pocket too; and this, it seems, Roderigo meant t' have sent this damned villain; but that, belike, Iago in the interim came in and satisfied him.

OTHELLO: O the pernicious caitiff! How came you, Cassio, by that handkerchief that was my wife's?

CASSIO: I found it in my chamber. And he himself confess'd but even now that there he dropp'd it for a special purpose which wrought to his desire.

LODOVICO: You must forsake this room, and go with us. Your power and your command is taken off, and Cassio rules in Cyprus. For this slave, if there be any cunning cruelty than can torment him much and hold him long, it shall be his. You shall close prisoner rest, till that the nature of your fault be known to the Venetian state. Come, bring away.

OTHELLO: Soft you; a word or two before you go. I have done the state some service, and they know; No more of that. I pray you, in your letters, when you shall these unlucky deeds relate, speak of me as I am; nothing extenuate, nor set down aught in malice: then must you speak of one that loved not wisely, but too well; of one not easily jealous, but, being wrought, perplex'd in the extreme; of one whose hand, like the base Indian, threw a pearl away richer than all his tribe; of one whose subdued eyes, albeit unused to the melting mood, drop tears as fast as the Arabian trees their medicinable gum. Set you down this; and say besides, that in Aleppo once, where a malignant and a turban'd Turk beat a Venetian and traduced the state, I took by th'throat the circumcised dog, and smote him--thus. *[Stabs himself]* I kiss'd thee ere I kill'd thee. *[Falling upon Desdemona]* Killing myself, to die upon a kiss. *[Dies]*

CASSIO: This did I fear, but thought he had no weapon; For he was great of heart.

LODOVICO: *[to Iago]* O Spartan dog, more fell than anguish, hunger, or the sea! Look on the tragic loading of this bed; this is thy work. Myself will straight aboard, and to the state this heavy act with heavy heart relate. *[Exeunt]*

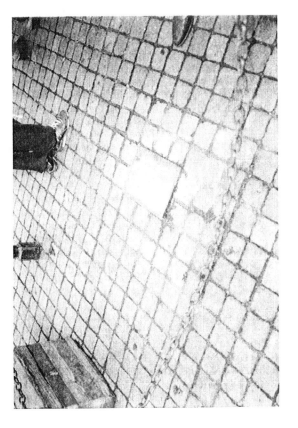

Site of scaffold used for the execution of Anne Boleyn, second wife of Henry VIII; Katherine Howard, fifth wife of Henry VIII;Lady Jane Grey, uncrowned queen of nine days

11. *THE TAMING OF THE SHREW*

The play

The Taming of the Shrew is a comedy in which Kate, the older daughter, is wooed by a somewhat impoverished gentleman in spite of her reputation as a shrew. Much to the surprise of her family and friends, the marriage to Petruchio changes Kate from a head strong young woman into a well mannered wife.

One day a disheveled, drunken "gentleman" by the name of Petruchio arrives in Padua from Verona in search of a wife and her dowry. His friend, Hortensio, a suitor to the fair younger sister Bianca, arranges for him to meet and woo Kate. Although amused and somewhat off-put by Kate's spirited behavior, the equally high spirited and financially depressed Petruchio begins the wooing process which rapidly leads to a betrothal.

While Kate is being wooed by Petruchio, Bianca is being wooed by Lucentio, Hortensio, and Gremio, three suitors. Of the three suitors, only Lucentio is young and handsome, as well as wealthy; the others are peers of Baptista and far older than Bianca. Since Bianca is not marriageable until after the marriage of her sister, Lucentio chooses to pose as a tutor in order to see the fair Bianca, while Hortensio poses as a music teacher for the same purpose. Gremio, being the preferred suitor and close friend of Baptista, woos Bianca under the guise of visiting Baptista. Bianca is quickly won by the face and charm of Lucentio and agrees without the blessing of her father to marry. Lucentio knowing of the upcoming marriage of Kate to Petruchio feels that he has outsmarted the other suitors and has won a wonderful, much sought-after prize from them. Their secret is discovered and a formal, church wedding is planned for the lucky couple as soon as Kate is married.

In the meantime, Petruchio marries Kate after making her endure a long wait at the church for his arrival. Not only does Petruchio arrive late to his own wedding, but he arrives attired in rags, riding upon a mule, and smelling even more foul than the poor animal. This is certainly not the proper behavior for a bride-groom of a wealthy young woman who would be expected to arrive punctually, dressed in his finest attire, riding in a carriage, and bearing gifts and flowers for all. Further, Petruchio tricks a furious Kate into saying the wedding vows as she is about to rage in anger and denounce him for a fool. Her fate is cast, she is now Petruchio's wife. The theater-goer is aware that Petruchio is beginning the process of taming his head-strong, stubborn, and vain bride by behaving more boorishly than usual. Petruchio's asides in previous scenes have set the stage for his pretendings. Kate, however, is not aware of the purpose behind Petruchio's behavior, and feels that she is to marry a madman. Not only is Petruchio's arrival at the wedding late and scandalous, but he will not allow her to attend the wedding feast in her honor. Instead, Petruchio whisks Kate away, under the guise of protecting her from others who would steal 'my household stuff," dressed in her wedding finery into a terrible rain storm to begin the journey home to Verona on a mule.

Arrival at Petruchio's house does not provide Kate with better treatment or more pleasant companions and surroundings. The house is in total disarray, the servants are dirty and undisciplined, and there is no food prepared to warm them after a very uncomfortable journey during which Kate is thrown from the mule into a muddy pool of water. When food is prepared for them, Petruchio refuses to allow Kate to eat any of it claiming that the meat is improperly cooked. Kate is forced to retire for the night on an empty stomach to a room which has not been properly aired, dusted, or warmed. The next morning finds Kate taking control of the domestic situation in her new home as the servants scrub, polish, and wax the house into perfect order. Petruchio wonders if this could possibly be the beginning of the new, tamed Kate.

Time passes and Kate and Petruchio are invited to the wedding of Bianca and Lucentio. Petruchio, without the knowledge of his wife, selects a wardrobe of exquisitely designed clothes for her to wear to the wedding. Unfortunately, Kate exhibits some of her old vanity in her reaction to the clothes. Everything she likes and praises as wonderfully flattering to her figure and face, Petruchio says is offensive and ill-made. Petruchio destroys the wonderful wardrobe as another lesson in obedience for Kate. Kate does not know that there is a second, equally as beautiful wardrobe waiting for the departure the next day, assuming she modifies her behavior.

The journey to Padua is, alas, not an uneventful one as Kate and Petruchio have a discussion as to whether it is the sun or the moon which shines on their daytime travel. Before Kate will agree that the celestial orb is whatever Petruchio might chose to name it, Petruchio must threaten to return home rather than continue the journey to the wedding. Kate, having experienced the full force of

Petruchio's anger on other occasions, agrees that it is indeed the sun, moon, or whatever else pleases Petruchio.

Kate must undergo one more test on the journey home. She and Petruchio meet an elderly gentlemen along the road whom Petruchio addresses as if he were a fair maiden. Kate, remembering the threat of an immediate return to Verona, agrees that the aged man is indeed a fair maiden. When Petruchio reverses his opinion and instructs Kate that the stranger is a wrinkled, elderly man, she accepts the change willingly. Petruchio is convinced that his stubborn, ill-tempered wife is tamed and is a prize worthy of all the trouble of conquering as they continue the journey to Padua in all of their finery.

At the wedding feast, Petruchio responds to the chiding of Kate by the other wives and offers a wager to Lucentio, the bride-groom of Bianca, and Hortensio, the recent husband of the local widow, that Kate will respond more rapidly when summoned from another room than will their wives. He knows that Kate must prove herself to be better than these other wives in order to forever prove to the people of Padua that the name of "Kate the curst" is no longer justified. One-by-one the wives are summoned, and one-by-one the wives refuse to respond saying that they are too busy to come at their husband's call. Petruchio begins to feel a sense of doubt as even the formerly fair, obedient Bianca refuses to appear; however, it is too late to turn back. Petruchio summons Kate hoping that he has not been mislead by the new obedience and tranquility she has shown. To the surprise of all in attendance not only does Kate appear, but she drags behind her the unwilling widow and Bianca. Kate chides these unruly wives and reminds them that the role of the wife is to be the helpmate of her husband. The play ends with Petruchio claiming victory over the other husbands and following Kate from the wedding festivities.

Kate

Shakespeare has painted an intricate picture of the changing expectations of the times in this play which treats the roles of the marriage partners in a light-hearted manner. Women of the time of Shakespeare were expected to manage the home and obey their husband's will; they were owned by their husbands. However, the question arises as to whether Shakespeare intends the audience to merely witness this on-going tradition as the subservience demanded of the Middle Ages, or if he wants the theater-goer to see the modification of the relationship between Petruchio and Kate as a mirror of the changing role of Renaissance couples which considers the weaknesses and strengths of both part-ners.

The audience can quickly see that Kate learns to obey the will of Petruchio and becomes the ideal wife. That which is more difficult to see is that Petruchio is tamed of his unruly, drunken ways by Kate's kindness and conformity to the expectations of society and gentile people and her willingness to place his desires before her own. Petruchio begins to see the value in treating other people with kindness and respect, something which he has not done in the past. He also begins to learn the difference self-respect can make in successful relationships. Petruchio is no longer the slovenly, drunken person who arrived on Hortensio's doorstep in search of a wife and her dowry. He conforms to society's expectations of orderly dress and appearance.

A further change for the audience to ponder is that through the transformation of the personalities of Kate and Petruchio from willful and selfish to considerate and respectful, the true "shrews" of the play are identified. Bianca and the widow, who have been playing the role of proper, considerate women in order to appear socially correct and marriageable, are exposed as the selfish, self-centered women they become as soon as they are married and settled in their own homes. Underneath the masks of convention are women with quick tempers, sharp tongues, and strong wills. Under Kate's mask, however, is a young woman who uses a sharp tongue to cover up the pain of being ignored and neglected by a father who shows preferential treatment to the fair-haired, fashionable younger daughter. During the Middle Ages and the Renaissance, women with milk-white skin, blonde hair, and blue eyes were considered more beautiful than women with darker hair and complexions. This appearance was so desirable that women used many elaborate and potentially lethal compounds on their hair and skin in order to acquire the fashionable look. Under Kate's mask is a kind woman, willing to please and love as soon as someone accepts her for what and who she is without the traditional bias toward fair beauty.

As illustrated in this speech from the final scene of the play given by Kate upon being summoned by Petruchio, she has accepted her role as wife quite seriously and chides the other women for their disrespect and disobedience toward their husbands. In essence Kate is exhibiting the new gentler side, the side which has also tamed Petruchio's wild, dirty, drunken ways.

> Fie, fie, unknit that threat'ning unkind brow
> And dart not scornful glances from those eyes
> To wound thy lord, thy king, thy governor.
> It blots thy beauty as frosts do bite the meads,
> Confounds thy fame as whirlwinds shake fair buds,
> And in no sense is meet or amiable.
> Thy husband is thy lord, thy life, thy keeper,
> Thy head, thy sovereign; one that cares for thee

And for thy maintenance; commits his body
To painful labor both by sea and land,
To watch the night in storms, the day in cold,
Whilst thou li'st warm at home, secure and safe;
And craves no other tribute at thy hands
But love, fair looks, and true obedience-
Too little payment for so great a debt.
I am ashamed that women are so simple
To offer war where they should kneel for peace,
Or seek for rule, supremacy, and sway,
When they are bound to serve, love, and obey.
Come, come, you froward and unable worms,
My mind hath been as big as one of yours,
To bandy word for word and frown for frown.
But now I see our lances are but straws,
Our strength as weak, our weakness past compare,
That seeming to be most which we indeed least are.
Then vail your stomachs, for it is not boot,
And place your hands below your husband's foot,
In token of which duty, if he please,
My hand is ready, may it do him ease.

Just as the women are exposed as selfish, shrewish females, the refined, cultured husbands, who agree to the wager, are exposed as uncaring men who would wager on the feelings and self-esteem of their wives as quickly as they would wager on a horse or any other possession. All of the courtship words of love have been exposed as mere gibberish as the women are reduced to chattel by the men who once placed them on pedestals; they are not perceived as partners but pawns in a game. Whereas, under Petruchio's rough exterior is a man who believes in his wife's newly surfaced gentleness. Although reluctant to test his wife for fear of embarrassment, he knows that Kate must prove herself to be a changed person to the people of Padua. Petruchio is pleased and complimentary when she succeeds and is willingly lead from the room by Kate as the prize for her obedience as he says to the other husbands, "We three are married, but you two are sped (done for)./ 'Twas I won the wager, though you hit the white (bull's eye, play on Bianca's name),/And being a winner, God give you good night." (Act V, scene ii)

The Taming of the Shrew: One Act Play

Approximate running time twenty minutes

DRAMATIS PERSONAE
TRAVELER   WIDOW
JUGGLER   BAPTISTA
LUCENTIO   PETRUCHIO
KATE   GREMIO
BIANCA   TRANIO
HORTENSIO

[Set in Padua, Italy]
TRAVELER: Ladies and Gentlemen, Follow me to Padua whence the rich and noble Baptista seeks a husband for his daughter, Kate, the curst. Meet you there Bianca, the fair and beautiful who waits for love until her older sister, Kate, is wed. Watch as Lucentio plots to woo Bianca. Watch as Petruchio tames Kate. Or is Petruchio tamed?? Marry, to Padua!!*[Exit Traveler as cast enters]* *Enter Baptista with his two daughters Kate and Bianca, Gremio, an old gentleman, and Hortensio, suitor to Bianca. Lucentio and Tranio stand apart.*

BAPTISTA: *[Standing with men except Lucentio and Tranio and Bianca]* Gentlemen, importune me no further, for how I firmly am resolved you know. That is, not to bestow my youngest daughter before I have a husband for the elder. If either of you both love Katherina, because I know you well and love you well, leave shall you have to court her at your pleasure.
GREMIO: To cart her rather, she's too rough for me. There, there, Hortensio, will you any wife?
KATE: *[Standing alone with anger]*

I pray you, sir, is it your will? To make a stale of me amongst these mates?

HORTENSIO: 'Mates,'maid, how mean you that? No mates for you. Unless you were of gentler, milder mold.

KATE: I'faith, sir, you shall never need to fear: Iwis it is not halfway to her heart. But if it were, doubt not her care should be to comb your noodle with a three-legged stool and paint your face and use you like a fool.

HORTENSIO: From all such devils, good Lord deliver us.

GREMIO: And me too, good Lord.

TRANIO: [Standing aside from others] Hush, master, here's some good pastime toward. That wench is stark mad or wonderful froward.

LUCENTIO: But in the other's silence do I see maid's mild behavior and sobriety. Peace, Tranio!

TRANIO: Well said, master; mum, and gaze your fill.

BAPTISTA: Gentlemen, that I may soon make good what I have said-- Bianca, get you in, and let it not displease thee, good Bianca, for I will love thee ne'er the less, my girl.

KATE: A pretty peat! it is best put finger in the eye, an she knew why.

BIANCA: [with humility and fear] Sister, content you in my discontent. Sir, to your pleasure humbly I subscribe. My books and instruments shall be my company, on them to look and practice by myself.

LUCENTIO: [aside] Hark, Tranio, thou mayst hear Minerva speak.

HORTENSIO: Signior Baptista, will you be so strange. Sorry am I that our good will effects Bianca's grief.

GREMIO: Why, will you mew her up, Signior Baptista, for this fiend of hell and make her bear the penance of her tongue?

BAPTISTA: Gentlemen, content ye, I am resolved. Go in, Bianca. [Exit Bianca, followed sullenly by Kate] [Conversation continues silently while Tranio speaks]

TRANIO: O pray, sir, tell me, is it possible that love should of a sudden take such hold?

LUCENTIO: O Tranio, till I found it to be true I never thought it possible or likely. But see, while idly I stood looking on, I found the effect of love-in-idleness and now in plainness do confess to thee, that art to me as secret and as dear as Anna to the Queen of Carthage was, Tranio, I burn, I pine, I perish, Tranio, if I achieve not this young modest girl. Counsel me, Tranio, for I know thou canst. Assist me, Tranio, for I know thou wilt.

TRANIO: Master, it is no time to chide you now. Affection is not rated from the heart, if love have touched you, nought remains but so, 'Redime te captum, quam queas minimo.'

LUCENTIO: Granmercies, lad. Go forward, this contents; The rest will comfort, for thy counsel's sound.

TRANIO: Master, you looked so longly on the maid, perhaps you marked not what's pith of all.

LUCENTIO: O yes, I saw sweet beauty in her face, such as the daughter of Agenor had, that made great Jove to humble him to her hand when with his knees he kissed the Cretans strand.

TRANIO: Saw you no more? Marked you not how her sister began to scold and raise up such a storm that mortal ears might hardly endure the din?

LUCENTIO: Tranio, I saw her coral lips to move, and with her breath she did perfume the air. Sacred and sweet was all I saw in her.   *[Exit Lucentio and Tranio]*

BIANCA: *[Enter Bianca dragged by Kate to center stage]* Good sister, wrong me not, nor wrong yourself, To make a bondmaid and a slave of me--That I disdain. But for these other gawds, unbind my hands, I'll pull them off myself, yea, all my raiment, to my petticoat, or what you will command me will I do, so well I know my duty to my elders.

BAPTISTA: Why, how now, dame, whence grows this insolence? Bianca, stand aside. Poor girl, she weeps. Go ply thy needle, meddle not with her. For shame, thou hilding of a devilish spirit, why dost thou wrong her that did ne'er wrong thee? When did she cross thee with a bitter word? What, in my sight? Bianca, get thee in.   *[Exit Bianca]*

KATE: Will you not suffer me? Nay, now I see she is your treasure, she must have a husband; I must dance barefoot on her wedding-day, and for your love to her lead apes in hell. Talk not to me, I will go sit and weep till I can find occasion of revenge. *[Exit with great displeasure]*

BAPTISTA: Was ever gentleman thus grieved as I? But who comes here? *[Enter Gremio, Lucentio as schoolmaster, Petruchio with Hortensio as music-master, Tranio as Lucentio with Biondello bearing lute and books]*

GREMIO: Good morrow, neighbor Baptista.

BAPTISTA: Good morrow, neighbor Gremio. God save you, gentlemen.

PETRUCHIO: *[bows with great flourish]* And you, good sir. Pray, have you not a daughter called Katherina, fair and virtuous?

BAPTISTA: I have a daughter, sir, called Katherina.

PETRUCHIO: I am a gentleman of Verona, sir, that hearing of her beauty and her wit, her affability and bashful modesty, her wondrous qualities and mild behavior.   Am bold to show myself a forward guest within your house, to make mine eye the witness

Of that report which I so oft have heard. And for an entrance to my entertainment I do present you with a man of mine, *[Presents Hortensio]* cunning in music and the mathematics, to instruct her fully in those sciences, whereof I know she is not ignorant. Accept of him or else you do me wrong. His name is Litio, born in Mantua.

BAPTISTA: Y'are welcome, sir, and he for your good sake. But for my daughter Katherine, this I know, she is not for your turn, the more my grief.

PETRUCHIO: I see you do not mean to part with her, or else you like not of my company.

BAPTISTA: Mistake me not, I speak but as I find. Whence are you, sir? What may I call your name?

PETRUCHIO: Petruchio is my name, Antonio's son, a man well known throughout all Italy.

BATISTA: *[to Hortensio]* Proceed in practice with my younger daughter. She's apt to learn and thankful for good turns. Signior Petruchio, will you go with us or shall I send my daughter Kate to you?

PETRUCHIO: I pray you do. I will attend her here. *[Exit Baptista, Gremio, Hortensio]* And woo her with some spirit when she comes. Say that she rail, why then I'll tell her plain she sings as sweetly as a nightingale. Say that she frown, I'll say she looks as clear as morning roses newly washed with dew. Say she be mute and will not speak a word, then I'll commend her volubility and say she uttereth piercing eloquence. If she do bid me pack I'll give her thanks as though

she bid me stay by her a week. If she deny to wed I'll crave the day when I shall ask the banns, and we be married. *[Enter Kate with haughty airs]* But her she comes, and now, Petruchio, speak. Good morrow, Kate, for that's your name, I hear.

KATE: *[with disdain, paces stage, pauses to listen and deliver lines]* Well have you heard, but something hard of hearing. They call me Katherine that do talk of me.

PETRUCHIO: You lie, in faith, for you are called plain Kate, and bonny Kate, and sometimes Kate the curst. But Kate, the prettiest Kate in Christendom, Kate of Kate-Hall, my super-dainty Kate, for dainties are all cates, and therefore, Kate, take this of me, Kate of my consolation: Hearing thy mildness praised in every town, thy virtues spoke of, and thy beauty sounded, yet not so deeply as to thee belongs, myself am moved to woo thee for my wife.

KATE: Moved? In good time: let him that moved you hither remove you hence. I knew you at the first, you were a movable.

PETRUCHIO: Come, come, you wasp, i'faith you are too angry.

KATE: If I be waspish best beware my sting.

PETRUCHIO: My remedy is then to pluck it out.

KATE: Ay, if the fool could find it where it lies.

PETRUCHIO: Who knows not where a wasp does wear his sting? In his tail.

KATE: In his tongue.

PETRUCHIO: Whose tongue?

KATE: Yours, if you talk of tales, and so farewell.

PETRUCHIO: 'Twas told me you were rough and coy and sullen, and now I find report a very liar, for thou art pleasant, gamesome, passing courteous, but slow in speech, yet sweet as springtime flowers. Thou canst not frown, thou canst not look askance, nor bite the lip as angry wenches will, nor hast thou pleasure to be cross in talk. But thou with mildness entertain'st thy wooers, with gentle conference, soft and affable. Why does the world report that Kate doth limp? O sland'rous world! Kate like a hazel-twig is straight and slender, and as brown in hue as hazelnuts and sweeter than the kernels. O let me see thee walk. Thou dost not halt.

KATE: Whence did you study all this goodly speech?

PETRUCHIO: It is extempore, from my mother-wit.

KATE: A witty mother, witless else her son.

PETRUCHIO: Am I not wise?

KATE: Yes, keep you warm.

PETRUCHIO: Marry, so I mean, sweet Katherine, in thy bed. And therefore, setting all this chat aside, thus in plain terms. Your father hath consented that you shall be my wife, your dowry 'greed upon, and will you, nill you, I will marry you. Now, Kate, I am a husband for your turn, for by this light, whereby I see thy beauty-Thy beauty that doth make me like thee well-Thou must be married to no man but me. [Enter Baptista, Gremio, Tranio] For I am he am born to tame you, Kate, and bring you from a wild Kate to a Kate conformable as other household Kates. Here comes your father. Never make denial, I must and will have Katherine to my wife. [Grabs Kate's arm behind her back. Kate struggles]

BAPTISTA: Now, Signior Petruchio, how speed you with my daughter?

PETRUCHIO: [Holding Kate's arm behind her back forcefully] How but well, sir? How but well? It were impossible that I should speed amiss.

BAPTISTA: Why, how now, daughter Katherine? In your dumps?

KATE: Call you me daughter? Now, I promise you-you have showed a tender fatherly regard to wish me wed to one half lunatic, a madcap ruffian and a swearing Jack, that thinks with oaths to face the matter out.

PETRUCHIO: Father, 'tis thus. Yourself and all the world that talked of her have talked amiss of her. If she be curst it is for policy, for she's not froward but modest as the dove. She is not hot but temperate as the morn. And, so conclude, we have 'greed so well together that upon Sunday is the wedding-day.

KATE: I'll see thee hanged on Sunday first.

PETRUCHIO:Be patient, gentlemen, I choose her for myself. If she and I be pleased, what's that to you? 'Tis bargained 'twixt us twain, being alone, that she shall still be curst in company. I tell you, 'tis incredible to believe how much she loves me. O the kindest Kate! She hung about my neck, and kiss on kiss she vied so fast, protesting oath on oath, that in a wink she won me to her love. O you are novices. 'Tis a world to see how tame, when men and women are alone, a meacock wretch can make the curstest shrew. Give me thy hand, Kate, I will unto Venice to buy apparel 'gainst the wedding-day. Provide the feast, father, and bid the guests. I well be sure my Katherine shall be fine.

BAPTISTA: I know not what to say-but give me your hands. God send you joy! Petruchio, 'tis a match.

GREMIO, TRANIO: Amen, say we, we will be witnesses.

PETRUCHIO: Father, and wife, and gentlemen, adieu, I will to Venice. Sunday comes apace. We will have rings and things and fine array, and kiss me, Kate 'We will be married a Sunday.' *[Exit Kate (struggling) and Petruchio]*

NARRATOR TWO, the JUGGLER: *[Enters juggling]* Marry, Petruchio and Kate are wed a week and now return to Baptista's home for the marriage of the fair Bianca. Watch what happens when a traveller is met on the road. Watch how Petruchio tame Kate. Ay, see how the sun shines...or is it the moon?*[Exit juggling--reenter Juggler with moon and sun figures-stands in background]*

PETRUCHIO: Come on, a God's name, once more toward our father's. Good Lord, how bright and goodly shines the moon! *[Juggler turns moon/sun figures to match words of Kate and Petruchio]*

KATE: The moon? The sun. It is not moonlight now.

PETRUCHIO: I say it is the moon that shines so bright.

KATE: I know it is the sun that shines so bright.

PETRUCHIO: Now by my mother's son, and that's myself, it shall be moon or star or what I list, or e'er I journey to you father house.

KATE: Forward, I pray, since we have come so far, and be it moon or sun or what you please. And if you please to call it a rush-candle, henceforth I vow it shall be so for me.

PETRUCHIO: I say it is the moon.

KATE: I know it is the moon.

PETRUCHIO: Nay, then you lie. It is the blessed sun.

KATE: Then God be blessed, it is the blessed sun, but sun it is not when you say it is not, and the moon changes even as your mind. What you will have it named, even that it is, and so it shall be still for Katherine. *[Juggler leaves in outward disgust, dragging the moon/sun]*

PETRUCHIO:*[to elderly gentleman]* Good morrow, gentle mistress, where away? Tell me, sweet Kate, and tell me truly too, hast thou beheld a fresher gentlewoman? Such war of white and red within her cheeks! What stars do spangle heaven with such beauty? As those two eyes become that heavenly face? Fair lovely maid once more good day to thee. Sweet Kate, embrace her for her beauty's sake.

K A T E : *[sweetly to elderly gentleman]* Fair budding virgin, fair and fresh and sweet, whither away, or where is thy abode? Happy the parents of so fair a child, happier the man whom favorable stars allots thee for his lovely bedfellow.

PETRUCHIO: Why, how now, Kate, I hope thou are not mad. This is a man, old, wrinkled, faded, withered, and not a maiden, as thou sayst he is.

KATE: *[humbly, demurely]* Pardon, old father, my mistaking eyes that have been so bedazzled with the sun that everything I look on seemeth green. Now I perceive thou art a reverend father. Pardon, I pray thee, for my mad mistaking. *[Exit Petruchio, Kate, and Lucentio]*

NARRATOR THREE: *[Member of the Wedding Party, enters as Kate and Petruchio exit]* Baptista is a happy,fortunate man today. His fair Bianca is wed to her loving Lucentio. Guests are dressed and ready for the happy celebration. Lucentio thinks he has a better wife than Petruchio. Friend Hortensio thinks his wife the better. Petruchio hopes he has the better wife. Join me at the wedding feast and watch!

WIDOW: *[wife of Hortensio to Kate tartly]* Your husband, being troubled with a shrow, measures my husband's sorrow by his woe-and now you know my meaning.

KATE: *[sorrowfully]* A very mean meaning.

WIDOW: Right, I mean you.

KATE: *[with slightly increased anger]* And I am mean indeed, respecting you.

PETRUCHIO: To her, Kate!

HORTENSIO: To her, widow!

PETRUCHIO: *[boastfully, sarcastically]* A thousand marks my Kate does put her down.

BAPTISTA: *[sorrowfully, shaking head]* Now, in good sadness, son Petruchio, I think thou hast the veriest shrew of all.

PEETRUCHIO: Well, I say no. And therefore, for assurance, let's each one send unto his wife, and he whose wife is most obedient, to come at first when he doth send for her, shall win the wager which we will propose.

HORTENSIO: Content. What's the wager?

LUCENTIO: Twenty crowns.

PETRUCHIO: Twenty crowns? I'll venture so much of my hawk or hound, but twenty times so much upon my wife.

LUCENTIO: A hundred then.

HORTENSIO: Content

PETRUCHIO: A match, 'tis done.

HORTENSIO: Who shall begin?

LUCENTIO: That will I. Go, Biondello, bid your mistress come to me.

BIONDELLO: I go. *[Exit, skipping]*

BAPTISTA: Son, I'll be your half, Bianca comes.

LUCENTIO: I'll have no halves; I'll bear it all myself. *[Enter Biondello, bewildered]* How now, what news?

BIONDELLO: Sir, my mistress sends you word that she is busy and she cannot come.

PETRUCHIO: How? 'She is busy and she cannot come'? Is that an answer?

GREMIO: Ay, and a kind one too. Pray God, sir, your wife send you not a worse.

PETRUCHIO: I hope better.

HORTENSIO: Sirrah Biondello, go and entreat my wife to come to me forth with. *[Exit Biondello, hesitantly]*

PETRUCHIO: O ho, 'entreat her'! Nay, then she must needs come.

HORTENSIO: I am afraid, sir, do what you can, yours will not be entreated. *[Enter Biondello, woefully]*

Now where's my wife?

BIONDELLO: She says you have some goodly jest in hand. She will not come. She bids you come to her.

PETUCHIO: Worse and worse,'she will not come'! O vile, intolerable, not to be endured! Sirrah Grumio, go to your mistress, say I command her come to me.*[Exit Grumio, SLOWLY]*

HORTENSIO: I know her answer. She will not.

PETRUCHIO: See where she comes and brings you froward wives as prisoners to her womanly persuasion.

KATE: *[Enters pushing other wives who sit poutingly]* Fie, fie, unknit that threat'ning unkind brow and dart not scornful glances from those eyes to wound thy lord, thy king, thy governor. It blots thy beauty as frosts do bite the meads, confounds thy fame as whirlwinds shake fair buds, and in no sense is meet or amiable. Thy husband is thy lord, thy life, thy keeper, thy head, thy sovereign; one that cares for thee and for thy maintenance; commits his body to painful labour to watch the night in storms, the day in cold, whilst thou li'st warm at home, secure and safe; And craves no other tribute at thy hands but love, fair looks, and true obedience--Too little payment for so great a debt. I am ashamed that women are so simple to offer war where they should kneel for peace, or seek for rule, supremacy, and sway, when they are bound to serve, love, and obey. Come, come, you froward

and unable worms, my mind hath
been as big as one of yours, to bandy
word for word and frown for frown.
But now I see our lances are but
straws, our strength as weak, our
weakness past compare, that seeming
to be most which we indeed least are.
Then vail your stomachs, for it is not
boot, and place your hands below
your husband's foot, in token of
which duty, if he please, my hand is
ready, may it do him ease. *[Holds
hand up to Petruchio, gazes up at
him lovingly]*
PETRUCHIO: Why, there's a
wench! Come on and kiss me, Kate!
*[Reaches down to take Kate's
outstretched hand, freezes in position
as play ends]*

12. ANTONY AND CLEOPATRA

The play

The action in *Antony and Cleopatra* centers on the all encompassing love between the Roman general Mark Antony and the Egyptian queen Cleopatra. Both are strong figures who face love, life, and duty to each other and their countries with great determination. It is Cleopatra's force of will and love which inspires Mark Antony to greatness and to despair.

The play opens with Mark Antony refusing to receive messengers who might be from either his estranged wife or Caesar by saying "Let Rome in Tiber meet and the wide arch/Of the ranged empire fall/Here is my space." Followers of Mark Antony feel that he is disgracing and lowering himself by his almost submissive love of Cleopatra; the man who was "the triple pillar of the world transformed/Into a strumpet's fool."

It is not long before Mark Antony receives word that his wife is dead. As he laments the relationship with Cleopatra which has caused him to be a less than perfect husband and has added to his wife's rebellious nature, Mark Antony is reminded by his friend Enobarbus that he may have lost a wife, but he still has another love to console him, Cleopatra.

Antony is convinced that he must end his relationship with Cleopatra not only because of his role in his wife's death, but because of his need to more closely observe the increasing power of Sextus Pompeius, son of Pompey the Great, who is quickly positioning himself to outmaneuver Mark Antony with Caesar. As Mark Antony tries to tell Cleopatra of the two pressing reasons for his departure, she pretends illness and betrayal, and mocks his despair at leaving. She will not graciously accept his promise of love for her which will survive "an honorable trial." Their parting is in anger rather than in love as Mark Antony had hoped. Meanwhile, Caesar anxiously awaits Antony's return to squash the young Pompey. As Cleopatra laments the lack of Antony's company and receives a pearl as token of his eternal love, she is reminded of her own changeable heart which in her "salad days" allowed her to love Julius Caesar and Pompey and to sing their praises.

Upon returning to Rome, Mark Antony is challenged by Caesar to explain why he has not offered the promised assistance against the enemies of Caesar with more speed. To each question Mark Antony has a quick and reasonable explanation for his slow responds. Seeing that this conversation is not advancing the cause of either man with the other, Agrippa, a friend of Caesar, suggests that Caesar give his sister Octavia in marriage to the newly widowed Mark Antony in order to bind them together as brothers and replace the rebellious deceased wife.

As soon as Mark Antony marries Octavia he is advised by a soothsayer, who appeals to his vanity as a general, not to stay with Caesar for fear of becoming subservient to him and forfeiting his powers. Mark Antony, realizing that these words are true and feeling himself to be equal to Caesar, quickly decides to leave Rome again for Egypt where he wears the title of Emperor. While Mark Antony is en route to Egypt, Cleopatra receives word of Antony's marriage to Octavia and flies into a rage against the messenger and falls into a melancholy state, thinking that Mark Antony is lost to her forever.

Meanwhile Caesar, Mark Antony, and Pompey meet to discuss the reason for their apparent disharmony. Pompey explains that he only wants to vindicate the noble name of his father who was slain by Julius Caesar, not to fight against two brave men such as Caesar and Mark Antony. Agreeing on at least a momentary friendship, Pompey, Mark Antony, Caesar, and their close advisors drink and enjoy each other's company.

Soon it is time for Mark Antony and Octavia, whose beauty is openly and disparagingly discussed by Cleopatra, to part company. Octavia hopes that the relationship between Caesar and Mark Antony sealed by her marriage to Mark Antony will be a constant bond between loyal brothers. The relationship, however, is doomed from the beginning. Octavia thinks that Mark Antony has left for Athens, but he is actually in Egypt entertaining assorted kings in thoughts of war against Caesar following the advice of the soothsayer. Once again Mark Antony has shaken the power of Caesar and asserted his own strength; thereby, breaking treasonously with him.

It is not long before Caesar and his followers undertake war against Mark Antony, Cleopatra, and their followers. Against the advise of his men, Mark Antony allows himself to be lured into an ill-conceived sea battle when his strength is on land. Just at a time when the sea battle appears to be progressing in favor of Mark Antony, Cleopatra leaves the fight with Mark Antony following behind her like a love-struck boy leaving the soldiers to fight without leadership and thinking Mark Antony a coward in battle. For this apparent cowardice, Mark

Antony loses the respect and support of his generals and friends as they give their support to Caesar.

Immediately Mark Antony regrets having followed Cleopatra's ship out of the battle. She claims not to have desired his company, thinking him too engaged in fighting to realize she was leaving. The love-struck Mark Antony replies that "My heart was to they rudder tied by th'strings/And those shouldst tow me after." All that is left to Mark Antony, a man who has forsaken everything for a woman, is to disband what is left of his navy in Egypt, divide his treasures among his officers as apology, and obtain safe passage through Octavius Caesar's men for them. For himself, Mark Antony asks to spend his years in Egypt or, if this is not possible, Athens. He requests that the victorious Caesar allow Cleopatra to pay homage to him and keep some property for herself and her heirs. Caesar denies Antony's request saying that anything Cleopatra desires is hers, if she will either drive Mark Antony from Egypt or kill him there.

However, out of respect for Cleopatra's title and position, Caesar sends a messenger to Cleopatra asking that she name the many treasures which he can bestow in exchange for her loyalty to him. As Cleopatra pretends to entertain thoughts of loyalty to Caesar, Mark Antony enters and orders the messenger whipped for delivering such a request to Cleopatra. After receiving a scolding for what Mark Antony perceives as lack of faith in his strength and reputation, Cleopatra again pledges devotion to him.

Mark Antony, being convinced that he can still outmaneuver Caesar, sets off to wage a land battle against him with Cleopatra's support. Enobarbus, one of Mark Antony's last loyal friends, reads all of these personality changes in Mark Antony as weaknesses and seeks the opportunity to leave his company rather than to be part of Mark Antony's folly over a woman. Not only is Enobarbus observing Mark Antony but Caesar's advisors counsel him to proceed slowly and allow Mark Antony's own misguided judgement to be his downfall. Mark Antony tries without success to rally his supporters with words of courage which actually speak of his own demise rather than of success and triumph.

However, the next morning Mark Antony is again the warrior commanding his men in battle. Unfortunately, Mark Antony finds that Enobarbus has defected in favor of Caesar and will no longer have his men join Mark Antony in battle. Mark Antony sends a soldier with Enobarbus' accumulated treasures plus words of gratitude for his past valiant service. These expressions greatly touch the heart of Enobarbus who declines to fight against Mark Antony choosing instead "Some ditch wherein to die: the foul'st best fits/My latter part of life." As the fates appear to be on the side of Mark Antony, Enobarbus kills himself for his act of treason and disloyalty against his dear friend Mark Antony.

Again Mark Antony abandons his land advantage in pursuit of Caesar's troupes on the sea, and again he faces defeat as the Egyptian troupes quickly surrender to Caesar's men. In his moment of defeat and humiliation, Mark Antony berates Cleopatra for her lack of loyalty, having given her affections to Pompey, Julius Caesar, and now himself while never truly being faithful to any of them.

Much disturbed by Mark Antony's words, Cleopatra sends a message that she has died as the result of the loss of his love. This message proves fatal because the defeated Mark Antony, having lost valor, honor, loyalty, and now love, falls on his sword in a suicide attempt in order to join Cleopatra in the after-life rather than continue living without her. The wound is not immediately fatal, affording Mark Antony the time to be moved to Cleopatra's monument in which she is hiding from Caesar. Mark Antony dies in her arms, warning Cleopatra not to thrust those around Caesar and asking that she not sorrow for his death but think of his "former fortunes,/Wherein I lived the greatest prince o' th' world."

In due course, Caesar sends a messenger to discover Cleopatra's demands for surrender. She replies with queenly confidence that what he will give is rightfully already hers. Further, she will never allow herself to be Caesar's slave.

Sir, I will eat no meat, I'll not drink, sir-
If idle talk will once be necessary-
I'll not sleep neither. This mortal house I'll ruin,
Do Caesar what he can. Know, sir, that I
Will not wait pinioned at your master's court
Nor once be chastised with the sober eye
Of dull Octavia. Shall they hoist me up
And show me to the shouting varletry
Of censuring Rome? Rather a ditch in Egypt
Be gentle grave unto me! Rather on Nilus' mud
Lay me stark-nak'd and let the waterflies
Blow me into abhorring! Rather make
My country's high pyramids my gibbet
And hang me up in chains!

Knowing that Cleopatra will doubt the words of a messenger, Caesar visits her himself in an effort to convince her that both her safety and dignity are secure with him. Cleopatra does not believe Caesar and is warned by a friend of Caesar not to trust his words since the plan exists to parade Cleopatra along the route to Rome as a prized trophy. Rather than be Caesar's prize, Cleopatra accepts the bite of a poisonous asp and dies. Caesar enters to find all dead and orders Cleopatra buried with Mark Antony saying, "No grave upon the earth shall clip in it/A pair so famous."

Cleopatra

Cleopatra is a queen who has loved and been loved by three powerful men: Pompey, Julius Caesar, and Mark Anthony. Her presence is so forceful that Mark Antony leaves his men in battle when she sails away, and finds that Cleopatra's kisses repay all that may have been won or lost in the battle he has abandoned in pursuit of her. However, Cleopatra suffers from the usual insecurities of one in love when she hears that Mark Antony has married Octavia and sharply questions a messenger regarding the appearance of her rival for Antony's affections.

As a woman in love not as a queen, Cleopatra tests Antony's devotion to her rather than to battle by allowing the rumor to reach him that she is dead. Mark Antony, unable to live without her, promptly inflicts himself with a mortal wound. The heart broken Cleopatra feels that all is lost when Mark Antony dies in her arms and says, "The crown o' the earth doth melt." She chastises herself for having thought too highly of herself and for losing Mark Antony as payment for such conceit, for she realizes that she has been "commanded/By such poor passions as the maid that milks/And does the meanest chares" for daring to compare her position and power to that of the gods.

In an unqueenly fashion, Cleopatra has placed the attributes of Mark Antony above all others in ability, fairness, and power. To her Mark Antony is not only the emperor of Egypt with her as his queen, he has been raised to the heights of ruler of the world by her love. Her adoration of Mark Antony has given him qualities which, in her dreams and heart, enable him to possess a face which is "as the heav'ns, and therein struck/A sun and moon, which kept their course and lighted/The little O, th'earth." In Cleopatra's eyes Mark Antony rules supreme and "His legs bestride the ocean:his reared arm/Crested the world." Cleopatra's love of an already powerful, valiant man raises him to heights which Mark Antony not only desired and fought to maintain, but heights which were recognized as loftier than those of other men that were his opponents; even Caesar recognized the all encompassing presence of the couple.

However, for all of her womanly love of Mark Antony and despair at his death, Cleopatra is a proud sovereign who refuses in defeat to allow herself to be disgraced and paraded as a spoil of war. Even as the surrender to Caesar nears, Cleopatra demands her robe and crown so that in death she might rule the other inhabitants of the heavens and be recognized as the queen. She sees herself as the loftier immortal elements of fire and air rather than as the more base elements of water and earth which belong to lesser mortals. As Cleopatra dies from the asp's bite, she appears sorrowful only that the asp cannot speak "That I might hear thee call great Caesar ass/Unpolicied (outwitted)."

As her reign over Egypt and three great Roman men comes to an end, Cleopatra places herself above Caesar by taking her own life rather than allowing him to rob her of dignity, for in death Cleopatra looks "As she would catch another Mark Antony/In her strong toil (net) of grace." Cleopatra, who has ruled Egypt and the men she has loved on her terms, dies with her power and influence intact as she exits dressed in regal finery to conquer new territory.

13. *TWELFTH NIGHT: OR WHAT YOU WILL*

<u>The play</u>

In *Twelfth Night: or What You Will*, a play set in Illria on the coast of the Adriatic which centers on love, long lost siblings, mistaken identity, and the importance of the relationships between the male lead characters, the women act as the catalyst which sparks the subterfuge and confusion of the play.

Viola and her brother, Sebastian, have been separated by a shipwreck and are now orphaned. Viola realizes that she must marry in order to secure a sound future and position in society. She hears of an unmarried and wealthy duke on whom she sets her sights. She also believes that her brother frequents the duke's court. Viola decides to dress as a page in order to be close to Duke Orsino, learn his ways, gain his confidences, and eventually disclose her true gender and marry him. She is not aware, however, that the Duke is unsuccessfully trying to woo the countess Lady Olivia.

Olivia has tried to convince Duke Orsino that she is not interested in his advances since she is in mourning for her father and brother, but he continues to woo her. After Viola presents herself as a page in the Duke's service, the Duke sends her under the assumed name of Cesario to deliver his messages of love to Olivia. When Olivia sees Viola in her disguise as Cesario, she immediately falls in love and sends her man-servant with a ring for "him" claiming that it was left behind by Cesario.

Upon her return to Duke Orsino's court, Viola is asked about her success in wooing Olivia for the Duke. When she reports failure, Duke Orsino asks his trusty page what type man he would love, if he were a woman. Viola as Cesario describes the Duke much to his pleasure. When asked to describe the woman Cesario would love, Viola describes herself. Duke Orsino remains unaware that Viola is a woman.

The Duke again sends Viola to press his suit with Olivia who this time willingly welcomes the "man" with whom she has fallen in love. Viola hardly has any opportunity to tell Olivia of Duke Orsino's love for her before Olivia tells Viola as Cesario that she is in love with him and never wants to hear of the Duke again. Viola quickly departs claiming that she has no intentions of ever loving a woman. The passage from Act II, scene ii not only illustrates Viola's frustration at having to place herself in the guise of a man but her sympathy for the deceived Olivia who is trying to win the love of Cesario. Her sympathy for Olivia is also a form of self pity as Viola empathizes with Olivia's plight as that of all women in a hopeless love relationship.

> I left no ring with her. What means this lady?
> Fortune forbid my outside have not charmed her.
> She made good view of me; indeed, so much
> That methought, her eyes had lost their tongue,
> For she did speak in starts distractedly.
> She loves me sure; the cunning of her passion
> Invites me in this churlish messenger.
> None of my lord's ring? Why, he sent her none.
> I am the man. If it be so, as 'tis,
> Poor lady, she were better love a dream.
> Disguise, I see thou art a wickedness
> Wherein the pregnant enemy does much.
> How easy is it for the proper false
> In women's waxen hearts to set their forms!
> Alas, our frailty is the cause not we,
> For such as we are made of, such we be.

Upon returning to the Duke's court, Viola is immediately challenged to a duel by a rejected suitor of Olivia's who is insulted that his suit would not be accepted by the her, whereas, the attentions of a mere messenger would be encouraged. Just as Viola is planning to confess that she is a woman, she is rescued by an unknown sea captain who takes up the duel in her place claiming that it is his job to defend her life. A relieved but confused Viola watches as the sea captain is taken away for a past crime by the police while shouting out the name of Sebastian, her long, separated brother. Viola now knows that her hunch is correct, and that her brother is alive and in Illyria. Her future is not as bleak as it would have seemed only days before now that the protection of a male family member is in the foreseeable future.

To further complicate the plot, Sebastian, under the name of Roderigo and in search of his sister, arrives in Illyria at the very spot on which Viola has been saved from a duel by the sea captain and is immediately set upon by the same offended suitor who makes another challenge of a duel. Sebastian is saved from the duel by Olivia who thinks that she has rescued Cesario not realizing that she has rescued the twin brother. Sebastian allows the eager Olivia to take care of him and agrees to her proposal of marriage, not for love but for money and property.

Not long after the marriage of Olivia and Sebastian, the sea captain is brought before Duke Orsino for his past dueling crimes. The sea captain sees Viola who he thinks is Sebastian and tells the Duke of saving Sebastian's life and caring for him for the last three months. At the same time, Olivia enters the courtyard, sees Viola who she thinks is Sebastian, and begins saying all manner of sweet, flattering things. The Duke immediately feels betrayed by his messenger, thinking that Cesario has pressed his own suit instead of his employer's interest. The Duke and Viola do not understand that Olivia and the sea captain know the real Sebastian.

Just as Duke Orsino is warning his unfaithful messenger Viola to never set foot in his court again, the real Sebastian appears and addresses Olivia as his rightful wife. Duke Orsino and Olivia cannot believe that before them stand two men with the same face. As the confusion unravels, Viola takes this opportunity to admit that she is in fact a woman in search of a long, lost brother. Olivia realizes that she has fallen in love with a woman and, thankfully, has married a man. Sebastian discovers his long, lost sister and understands that his new wife's initial and sudden show of affection was mistakenly but conveniently directed at him. Duke Orsino marries Viola who he favors as a page for her deportment and carriage and finds even more pleasant as a woman. Most importantly, the twins, Viola and Sebastian are reunited to live happily ever after in Illryia.

Viola

Viola learns the harsh reality of the need for male protection when, as an orphan, she feels it necessary to set out in search of her twin brother in order to secure some degree of financial security. Viola learns that without the protective umbrella of a man's home, a woman in the late Middle Ages is often unable to support herself or to live comfortably. Even in the search for her brother, Viola is faced with the reality that a woman cannot travel alone without the worry of harassment by undisciplined ruffians. She must travel in the disguise of a man in order to seek her protector.

However, Viola is not without some defense mechanisms of her own. She is capable of convincing Duke Orsino and Lady Olivia that she is a young man worthy of the most intimate confidences from one and the love of another. Viola befriends the Duke and counsels him on affairs of the heart, and she wins the heart of the sorrowful Olivia with her kindness and refined manners. Both are convinced that Viola is a caring person who is above reproach.

It is only after the marriage of Sebastian to Olivia that the Duke begins to believe that Viola is not as faithful as he originally thought. He questions the treason which has led Viola as Cesario to betray him and his confidences by wooing and winning Olivia. When the confusion and mistaken identity are corrected, a very relieved Duke Orsino immediately forgets his misdirected and unreturned love for Olivia and sees Viola as a caring, concerned woman. The Duke proposes to the woman who as his page has managed to share his thoughts and has shown an understanding of his nature. The true Viola has exerted an impact on the lives of those with whom she has come in contact.

Although not a complicated plot and certainly not a cast of complicated characters, Shakespeare in this play has portrayed in one person many much desired personality traits. Viola is diligent in the search for her brother when she could have abandoned the effort and thrown herself as a hopeless female on the pity of Duke Orsino, a fairly benevolent duke. She also could have forsaken her efforts on behalf of Duke Orsino to woo the Lady Olivia as soon as the lady began to make advances toward her as the page, Cesario. However, Viola does not abandon her independent search for her brother or the mission of winning Olivia for Duke Orsino. She remains ever-constant and dedicated. It is only when her identity is unmasked by the appearance of Sebastian that Viola is forced to relinquish her pursuits and dedication to the tasks at hand.

In this simplistic play and with this uncomplicated woman, Shakespeare has captured the mind of the theater-goer with the ideals of devotion and dedication of purpose much like the morality plays before Shakespeare would have attempted to do. However, unlike the morality plays with their somber tones, Shakespeare has used comedy as the vehicle for enlightening, instructing, and depicting strong, desirable virtues.

14. *ROMEO AND JULIET*

<u>The play</u>

Romeo and Juliet is a tragedy about young love, hopes, dreams, and the circumstances which make them impossible to be realized. The plot is set in Verona and revolves around an old family quarrel which continues to separate the two most prominent families of the city, the Capulets and the Montagues in spite of efforts by the prince to establish peace and tranquility.

The handsome, impetuous Romeo, a Montague, arrives uninvited and masked at a party given by the Capulets. He has come to see Rosaline, a Capulet cousin, with whom he is infatuated from a distance and to compare her beauty to that of the other young women who will be attending the party. When he sees Juliet dancing with unspeakable grace, Romeo forgets Rosaline and falls madly in love with Juliet, not knowing that she is the daughter of the head of the Capulet family, saying "O, she doth teach the torches to burn bright!". Juliet, assuming that all of the men attending the party are Capulets or friends of the Capulets, falls in passionate love with Romeo, declaring "My only love, sprung from my only hate! Too early seen unknown, and known too late!". Too late each is informed that their love cannot be since the object of affection is the enemy.

Later that night when all is quiet, Romeo climbs the wall of the garden below Juliet's balcony where he overhears her talking to herself proclaiming her love for him and her desire to abandon even her family to be with him. Romeo tries to swear the lasting nature of his love for Juliet on the moon only to be reminded by her of the inconstancy of the moon "that monthly changes in her circled orb." Romeo responds that he, too, is overcome with love which will cause him also to abandon his family. They agree to meet the next day and marry, if all can be arranged.

Romeo and Juliet meet and marry, assisted by Friar Laurence who initially scolds Romeo for his changeable heart which flits from one woman to another. The Friar warns Romeo that this love may not be any more permanent that the others saying, "they stumble that run fast." However, the earnestness of their young love convinces the Friar that Romeo and Juliet should not "stay alone/Till Holy Church incorporate two in one."

Upon returning to their homes, Romeo is forced into a duel with Tybalt, Juliet's cousin, in order to avenge the murder of Mercutio, Romeo's cousin. Initially, Romeo tries to dissuade Tybalt from fighting the duel saying that not only has the prince forbidden fighting, but he loves Tybalt "better than thou canst divine." However, as Romeo is trying to separate Tybalt and Mercutio, Mercutio is killed, causing Romeo to take up the duel. Romeo kills Tybalt and escapes to Friar Laurence's monastery from where he dispatches a message to Juliet prior to banishment from Verona. Romeo is convinced by the Friar to leave Verona for Mantua where he will stay until the Friar can tell everyone that Romeo and Juliet are married, and, hopefully, smooth the hard feelings between the families.

Initially upon hearing of the murder of her cousin, Juliet hates Romeo for killing Tybalt, but eventually her love for her new husband Romeo overshadows the loss of a cousin. Meanwhile, Romeo in distress at his exile from Juliet, threatens suicide which causes the Friar to chastise him for having womanish tears and rash actions which would not only kill him but Juliet who "in thy life lives." As the Friar reveals the plan for Romeo's escape to Mantua, he points out to Romeo that "a pack of blessings light upon thy back," noting that the penalty of death has been commuted to banishment which still provides the opportunity for Romeo and Juliet to meet. Romeo visits Juliet that night and explains the Friar's plan, parting at daybreak trusting that the Friar Laurence will succeed, and that they will be reunited to live as husband and wife "with twenty thousand times more joy than thou wentst forth in lamentation."

However, this security does not last. Juliet's father arranges a marriage for her with Paris, a young count and relative of the prince of Verona. Juliet refuses to marry Paris which causes her father to state that she will be turned out of the house and out of his life if she continues to refuse to marry Paris. Her mother's dissatisfaction is shown in the prophetic statement, "I wish the fool were married to her grave!" Juliet turns to her nurse for comfort but only hears that since Romeo can never return for her, she should marry Paris. Pretending to give thought to the nurse's words, Juliet stays alone to plan her visit to the Friar saying "I'll to the friar to know his remedy. If all else fail, myself have power to die."

In great distress, Juliet goes to the Friar to beg his assistance. The Friar, being somewhat knowledgeable in the practice of apothecary, mixes a potion which will temporarily simulate death. The plan is for Juliet to "undertake a thing like death to chide away this shame" long enough for Romeo to be summoned from Mantua, return, and as Juliet revives, take her away forever.

Asking her mother to leave her, Juliet drinks the potion which simulates death. The next morning, Juliet's body is found by the nurse who comes to dress Juliet for the day calling her a "slug-abed." Great lamentation ensures as the household learns of Juliet's death with Capulet crying, "Death is my son-in-law. Death is my heir;/My daughter he hath wedded. My child is dead,/And with my child my joys are buried!"

Unfortunately, Romeo receives news from Mantua that Juliet is dead before learning of the details of the Friar's plan. Believing Juliet to be dead, Romeo visits an apothecary who provides him with a deadly poison and returns to the crypt in order to be forever united with Juliet. After a brief scuffle with the grieving Paris, which results in his death, Romeo enters the crypt and drinks the potion. He dies as Friar Laurence arrives to be with Juliet as she awakens. However, Friar Laurence is too late to save Romeo. Juliet awakens expecting to hear that Romeo is on his way to complete the plan and take her away, but to her horror she finds her beloved Romeo dead. Not wishing to live without him, Juliet stabs herself with Romeo's dagger and dies never more to be parted from her beloved by a foolish age-old family quarrel.

The play ends with both families realizing the terrible result of needless feuding as they bury their children. The lovers, Romeo and Juliet, are eternally united, as the prince says "never was a story of more woe/Than this of Juliet and her Romeo."

Juliet

Juliet is a young woman of barely fourteen years who is enjoying her first and only encounter with love. She falls in love with Romeo without knowing that he is a Montague and an enemy of the Capulets. Once Romeo's identity is made known, Juliet refuses to abandon this new love. She is capable of seeing Romeo, not as the son of her family's enemy, but as an attractive, personable, daring young man with whom she would like to spend the rest of her life. To the modern theater-goer, fourteen seems too young for us to consider a boy-girl relationship as anything more than a flirtation. However to Juliet, whose mother is twenty-eight and a mother herself at fourteen, fourteen is the perfect age for marriage.

Despite her innocence, lack of experience, and great affection for Romeo, Juliet realizes that the heart of a young man is often fickle and offers Romeo the opportunity to think rationally about the love he professes and the marriage which is the required course of that love in this speech from Act II, scene ii.

Dost thou love me? I know thou wilt say 'Ay';
And I will take thy word. Yet, if thou swear'st,
Thou mayst prove false. At lovers' perjuries,

They say Jove laughs. O gentle Romeo,
If thou dost love, pronounce it faithfully.
Or if thou thinkest I am too quickly won,
I'll frown and be perverse and say thee nay,
So thou wilt woo; but else, not for the world.
In truth fair Montague, I am too fond,
And therefore thou mayst think my havior light;
But trust me, gentleman, I'll prove more true
Than those that have more cunning to be strange.
I should have been more strange, I must confess,
But that thou overheard'st, ere I was ware,
My true-love passion. Therefore pardon me,
And not impute this yielding to light love,
Which the dark night hath so discovered.

By suggesting a brief interval for reflection, Juliet is showing a maturity and an understanding of the seriousness of the state of matrimony. She states that their attraction has occurred too quickly but might prove to be substantive the next day after the glow of love-at-first-sight wears off, if it is meant to be.

Although young and innocent, Juliet possesses a mature understanding of not only love but duty. When first informed that Romeo has killed her cousin Tybalt, Juliet feels betrayed and grieves for Tybalt while despising Romeo. However, it is not long before her love for Romeo and her sense of wifely duty cause her to worry about the safely of Romeo, her husband of barely three hours. She realizes that it is her duty to defend Romeo whose banishment causes more pain than even the death of a family member.

Later, Juliet shows her dedication to this new marriage by seeking Friar Laurence's help in avoiding the marriage to Paris proposed by her parents and stubbornly refused by her to the displeasure of her father. Juliet, remains constant to her vows of marriage to Romeo in the face of one more obstacle while wishing to be reunited with him at all cost. She agrees to drink a sleeping potion which will simulate death knowing that when she awakens, she will flee with Romeo to Mantua where they can live as a married couple until their parents accept them.

Even after the plan fails and Romeo kills himself believing Juliet to be dead, Juliet does not abandon her love for him. She looks for and finds a means of being with Romeo rather than spending a lifetime without him in a convent as suggested by Friar Laurence. She uses Romeo's dagger as a means of uniting them in death proving the constancy of her love.

Juliet is more than just a young, love-struck girl. She is the embodiment of the requirements of the Middle Ages for a good wife, namely loyalty, devotion, and domesticity, which she combines with the new freedom of choice to select a spouse desired by the woman of the Renaissance. Juliet is strong and determined to follow the path she has chosen for herself. She is not at all similar to Bianca who pretends to follow the manners of the times in order to be well considered by the townspeople while hiding a willful side from view. Juliet knows that following her heart will mean disappointing her parents and might mean banishment or death. However, she has chosen Romeo and would rather face life away from the security of Mantua than live life without him.

Romeo and Juliet: One Act Play

Approximate running time twenty minutes

DRAMATIS PERSONAE
ROMEO
JULIET
MONTAGUE
LADY MONTAGUE
CAPULET
LADY CAPULET
MERCUTIO
    Kinsman of Prince Escalus
TYBALT
    Nephew of Lady Capulet
ESCALUS
    Prince of Verona

NURSE.
FRIAR JOHN
AN APOTHECARY
THREE MUSICIANS
FRIAR LAURENCE
BENVOLIO
    Nephew of Montague
PARIS
    A young nobleman
SERVING-MEN
    Servants of Capulet
BALTHASAR

PAGE to Paris; another PAGE; an OFFICER
CITIZENS of Verona; KINSFOLK of both houses; MASKERS,
GUARDS, WATCHMEN, AND ATTENDANTS.
CHORUS.
PROLOGUE.
[Enter chorus]
CHORUS.
Two households, both alike in
dignity,
In fair Verona, where we lay our
scene,
From ancient grudge break to new
mutiny,
Where civil blood makes civil hands
unclean.
From forth the fatal loins of these
two foes
A pair of star-cross'd lovers take
their life;
Whose misadventured piteous
overthrows

Doth with their death bury their
parents' strife.   *[Exit] [Verona,
Enter Benvolio]*
BENVOLIO: Part, fools! Put up your
swords; you know not what you do.
[Enter Tybalt]
TYBALT: What, art thou drawn
among these heartless hinds? Turn
thee, Benvolio, look upon thy death.
BENVOLIO: I do but keep the
peace: put up thy sword, or manage
it to part these men with me.
TYBALT: What, drawn, and talk of
peace! I hate the word, as I hate hell,
all Montagues, and thee: Have at
thee, coward! *[Enter citizens]*
CITIZENS: Clubs, bills, and
partisans! strike! beat them down!
Down with the Capulets! down with

the Montagues! *[Enter old Capulet in his gown and Lady Capulet]*
CAPULET: My sword, I say! Old Montague is come, and flourishes his blade in spite of me. *[Enter old Montague and Lady Montague]*
MONTAGUE: Thou villain Capulet! Hold me not, let me go.
LADY MONTAGUE: Thou shalt not stir one foot to seek a foe.*[Enter Prince Escalus]*
PRINCE ESCALUS: Rebellious subjects, enemies to peace, profaners of this neighbour-stained steel. Will they not hear? You men, you beasts, that quench the fire of your pernicious rage with purple fountains issuing from your veins, on pain of torture, from those bloody hands throw your mistemper'd weapons to the ground, and hear the sentence of your moved prince. Three civil brawls, bred of an airy word, by thee, old Capulet, and Montague, have thrice disturb'd the quiet of our streets. If ever you disturb our streets again, your lives shall pay the forfeit of the peace. You, Capulet, shall go along with me; and, Montague, come you this afternoon, to know our further pleasure in this case. *[Exeunt all but Montague, Lady Montague and Benvolio]*
MONTAGUE: Who set this ancient quarrel new abroach? Speak, nephew, were you by when it began?
BENVOLIO: Here were the servants of your adversary, and yours, close fighting, ere I did approach. I drew to part them: in the instant came the fiery Tybalt, with his sword prepared. Till the prince came, who parted either part.
LADY MONTAGUE: O, where is Romeo? Saw you him to-day?
BENVOLIO: Madam, an hour before the worshipp'd sun peer'd forth the golden window of the east, a troubled mind drove me to walk abroad; so early walking did I see your son. Towards him I made; but he was ware of me, and stole into the covert of the wood.
MONTAGUE: Many a morning hath he there been seen, with tears augmenting the fresh morning's dew, Adding to clouds more clouds with his deep sighs.
BENVOLIO: My noble uncle, do you know the cause?
MONTAGUE: I neither know it nor can learn of him.
BENVOLIO: Have you importuned him by any means?
MONTAGUE: Both by myself and many other friends. But he, his own affections' counsellor, is to himself. *[Enter Romeo]*
BENVOLIO: See, where he comes: so please you, step aside; I'll know his grievance, or be much denied.
MONTAGUE: I would thou wert so happy by thy stay to hear true shrift. Come, madam, let's away. *[Exeunt Montague and Lady]*
BENVOLIO: Good morrow, cousin.
ROMEO: Is the day so young?
BENVOLIO: But new struck nine.
ROMEO: Ay me! sad hours seem long. Was that my father that went hence so fast?
BENVOLIO: It was. What sadness lengthens Romeo's hours?
ROMEO: Not having that, which having makes them short.
BENVOLIO: In love?
ROMEO: Out--
BENVOLIO: Of love?
ROMEO: Out of her favour, where I am in love.
BENVOLIO: Alas, that love, so gentle in his view, should be so tyrannous and rough in proof!
ROMEO: Alas, that love, whose view is muffled still,
Should, without eyes, see pathways to his will!
BENVOLIO: I rather weep.

ROMEO: Good heart, at what?
BENVOLIO: At thy good heart's oppression.
ROMEO: Why, such is love's transgression.
Griefs of mine own lie heavy in my breast;
Which thou will propagate, to have it press'd
With more of thine: This love, that thou hast shown,
Doth add more grief to too much of mine own.
Farewell, my coz.
BENVOLIO: Soft! I will go along:
An if you leave me so, you do me wrong.
ROMEO: Tut, I have lost myself; I am not here;
This is not Romeo, he's some other where.
BENVOLIO: Tell me in sadness, who is that you love.
ROMEO: What, shall I groan, and tell thee?
BENVOLIO: Be ruled by me, forget to think of her.
ROMEO: O, teach me how I should forget to think.
BENVOLIO: By giving liberty unto thine eyes; examine other beauties.
ROMEO: 'Tis the way to call hers, exquisite, in question more:
Farewell: thou canst not teach me to forget.
BENVOLIO: I'll pay that doctrine, or else die in debt. [Exeunt] [Enter Capulet County Paris, and Servant]
CAPULET: But Montague is bound as well as I, in penalty alike; and 'tis not hard, I think for men so old as we to keep the peace.
PARIS: Of honourable reckoning are you both; and pity 'is you lived at odds so long. But now, my lord, what say you to my suit?
CAPULET: But saying o'er what I have said before:

My child is yet a stranger to the world,
She hath not seen the change of fourteen years;
Let two more summers wither in their pride
Ere we may think her ripe to be a bride.
PARIS: Younger than she are happy mothers made.
CAPULET: And too soon marr'd are those so early made. The earth hath swallow'd all my hopes but she, she is the hopeful lady of my earth:
But woo her, gentle Paris, get her heart, my will to her consent is but a part; An she agree, within her scope of choice lies my consent and fair-according voice. [to the Servant, giving him a paper] Go sirrah, trudge about through fair Verona; find those persons out whose names are written there, and to them say, my house and welcome on their pleasure stay. [Exit Capulet and Paris]
SERVANT: Find them out whose names are written here! It is written that the shoemaker should meddle with his yard, and the tailor with his last, the fisher with his pencil, and the   painter with his nets; but I am sent to find those persons whose names are here writ, and can never find what names the writing person hath here writ. I must to the learned:- in good time. [Enter Benvolio and Romeo]
SERVANT: God gi' god-den. I pray, sir, can you read?
ROMEO: Ay, mine own fortune in my misery. Stay, fellow; I can read. "Signior Martino and his wife and daughters; County Anselme and his beauteous sisters; the lady widow of Vitruvio; Signior Placentio and his lovely nieces; Mercutio and his brother Valentine; mine uncle Capulet, his wife, and daughters; my

fair niece Rosaline; Livia; Signior Valentio and his cousin Tybalt; Lucio and the lively Helena." A fair assembly: whither should they come?
SERVANT: To supper to our house.
ROMEO: Whose house?
SERVANT: My master's.
ROMEO: Indeed, I should have ask'd you that before.
SERVANT: Now I'll tell you without asking: my master is the great rich Capulet; and if you be not of the house of Montagues, I pray, come and crush a cup of wine. Rest you merry! *[Exit]*
BENVOLIO: At this same ancient feast of Capulet's sups the fair Rosaline whom thou so lovest; with all the admired beauties of Verona: Go thither; and, with unattainted eye, compare her face with some that I shall show, and I will make thee think thy swan a crow.
ROMEO: When the devout religion of mine eye maintains such falsehood, then turn tears to fires; And these, who, often drown'd, could never die.
BENVOLIO: Tut, you saw her fair, none else being by,
Herself poised with herself in either eye:
But in that crystal scales let there be weigh'd
Your lady-love against some other maid
ROMEO: I'll go along, no such sight to be shown,
But to rejoice in splendour of mine own. *[Exeunt]*

[A room in Capulet's house]
[Enter Lady Capulet and nurse]
LADY CAPULET: Nurse, where's my daughter? call her forth to me.
NURSE: God forbid! where's this girl? What, Juliet! *[Enter Juliet]*
JULIET: How now! who calls?

NURSE: Your mother.
ULIET: Madam, I am here, what is your will?
LADY CAPULET: This is the matter, nurse, give leave awhile, we must talk in secret: nurse, come back again; I have remember'd me, thou's hear our council. Thou know'st my daughter's of a pretty age.
NURSE: Faith, I can tell her age unto an hour.
LADY CAPULET: She's not fourteen.
NURSE: I'll lay fourteen of my teeth, and yet, to my teen be it spoken, I have but four, she's not fourteen. How long is it now to Lammas-tide?
LADY CAPULET: A fortnight and odd days.
NURSE: Even or odd, of all days in the year, come Lammas-eve at night shall she be fourteen.
LADY CAPULET: Enough of this; I pray thee, hold thy peace.
NURSE: Peace, I have done. God mark thee to His grace! Thou wast the prettiest babe that e'er I nursed; An I might live to see thee married once,I have my wish.
LADY CAPULET: Marry, that "marry" is the very theme I came to talk of:- tell me, daughter Juliet, how stands your disposition to be married?
JULIET: It is an honour that I dream not of.
LADY CAPULET: Well, think of marriage now; younger than you, here in Verona, ladies of esteem, are made already mothers: by my count,I was your mother much upon these years that you are now a maid. Thus, then, in brief; the valiant Paris seeks you for his love. Speak briefly, can you like of Paris' love?
JULIET: I'll look to like, if looking liking move. *[Enter a servant]*

SERVANT: Madam, the guests are come, supper served up, you call'd
LADY CAPULET: We follow thee. Juliet, the county stays.
NURSE: Go, girl, seek happy nights to happy days. *[Exeunt]*

[Verona. A street.]
[Enter Romeo, Mercutio, Benvolio, with five or six other Maskers, and Torch-Bearers]
ROMEO: Give me a torch, I am not for this ambling; being but heavy, I will bear the light.
MERCUTIO: Nay, gentle Romeo, we must have you dance.
ROMEO: Not I, believe me: you have dancing-shoes with nimble soles: I have a soul of lead,
MERCUTIO: You are a lover; borrow Cupid's wings,
ROMEO: I am too sore enpierced with his shaft, to soar with his light feathers.
MERCUTIO: Come, we burn daylight, ho!
ROMEO: Nay, that's not so.
MERCUTIO: I mean, sir, in delay We waste our lights in vain, like lamps by day.
Take our good meaning, for our judgement sits
Five times in that, ere once in our five wits.
ROMEO: And we mean well, in going to this mask; but 'tis no wit to go.
MERCUTIO: Why, may one ask?
ROMEO: I dreamt a dream to-night.
MERCUTIO: And so did I.
ROMEO: Well, what was yours?
MERCUTIO: That dreamers often lie.
ROMEO: In bed asleep, while they do dream things true.
BENVOLIO: Supper is done, and we shall come too late.
ROMEO: I fear, too early: for my mind misgives some consequence, yet hanging in the stars, shall bitterly begin his fearful date.

[A hall in Capulet's house] [Enter Capulet, Lady Capulet, Juliet, Tybalt, and others of the house among them, Romeo and Benvolio]
CAPULET: Welcome, gentlemen! ladies .
ROMEO: *[aside to servant]* What lady's that, which doth enrich the hand of yonder knight?
SERVANT: I know not, sir.
ROMEO: O, she doth teach the torches to burn bright!
Her beauty hangs upon the cheek of night
Like a rich jewel in an Ethiop's ear;
Beauty too rich for use, for earth too dear!
For I ne'er saw true beauty till this night.
TYBALT: This, by his voice, should be a Montague. Fetch me my rapier, boy: what, dares the slave come hither, cover'd with an antic face, to fleer and scorn at our solemnity?
CAPULET: Why, how now, kinsman! wherefore storm you so?
TYBALT: Uncle, this is a Montague, our foe;
A villain, that is hither come in spite, To scorn at our solemnity this night.
CAPULET: Young Romeo is it?
TYBALT: 'Tis he, that villain Romeo.
CAPULET: Content thee, gentle coz, let him alone.
TYBALT: It fits, when such a villain is a guest: I'll not endure him.
CAPULET: He shall be endured. What, goodman boy! I say, he shall; go to; Am I the master here, or you?
TYBALT: Why, uncle, 'tis a shame-
CAPULET: Go to, go to; You are a saucy boy
TYBALT: Patience perforce with wilful choler meeting

Makes my flesh tremble in their different greeting.
I will withdraw: but this intrusion shall,
Now seeming sweet, convert to bitter gall. *[Exit]*
ROMEO: *[to Juliet]* If I profane with my unworthiest hand
his holy shrine, the gentle fine is this,
My lips, two blushing pilgrims, ready stand
To smooth that rough touch with a tender kiss.
JULIET: Good pilgrim, you do wrong your hand too much,
Which mannerly devotion shows in this;
For saints have hands that pilgrims' hands do touch,
And palm to palm is holy palmers' kiss.
ROMEO: Have not saints lips, and holy palmers too?
JULIET: Ay, pilgrim, lips that they must use in prayer.
ROMEO: O, then, dear saint, let lips do what hands do;
They pray; grant thou, lest faith turn to despair.
JULIET: Saints do not move, though grant for prayers' sake.
ROMEO: Then move not, while my prayer's effect I take. Thus from my lips, by yours, my sin is purged. *[Kissing her]*
JULIET: Then have my lips the sin that they have took.
ROMEO: Sin from my lips? O trespass sweetly urged! Give me my sin again. *[Kissing her again]*
NURSE: Madam, your mother craves a word with you.
ROMEO: What is her mother?
NURSE: Marry, bachelor, her mother is the lady of the house.
ROMEO: Is she a Capulet? O dear account! my life is my foe's debt.
BENVOLIO: Away, be gone; the sport is at the best.

ROMEO: Ay, so I fear; the more is my unrest.
CAPULET: Nay, gentlemen, prepare not to be gone; We have a trifling foolish banquet towards.
JULIET: Come hither, nurse. What is yond gentleman?
NURSE: I know not.
JULIET: Go, ask his name: if he be married, my grave is like to be my wedding-bed.
NURSE: His name is Romeo, and Montague; the only son of your great enemy.
JULIET: My only love sprung from my only hate!
Too early seen unknown, and known too late!
Prodigious birth of love it is to me,
That I must love a loathed enemy.

PROLOGUE.
[Enter Chorus]
CHORUS.
Now old desire doth in his death-bed lie
And young affection gapes to be his heir;
That fair, for which love groan'd for, and would die,
With tender Juliet match'd, is now not fair.
Now Romeo is beloved, and loves again,
Alike bewitched by the charm of looks;
But to his foe supposed he must complain,
And she steal love's sweet bait from fearful hooks
Being held a foe, he may not have access
To breathe such vows as lovers use to swear;
And she as much in love, her means much less
To meet her new-beloved any where:
But passion lends them power, time means, to meet,

Tempering extremities with extreme sweet.   *[Exit]*

[A lane by the wall of Capulet's orchard] [Enter Romeo]
ROMEO: Can I go forward when my heart is here? *[Leaps the orchard wall]*
[Enter Benvolio with Mercutio]
BENVOLIO: Romeo! my cousin Romeo!
MERCUTIO: He is wise; and, on my life, hath stol'n him home to bed.
BENVOLIO: He ran this way, and leapt this orchard-wall. Go then, for 'tis vain to see him here that means not to be found.*[Exeunt]*
[Capulet's orchard][Romeo enters]
ROMEO: He jests at scars that never felt a wound. *[Juliet appears above at a window]* But, soft! what light through yonder window breaks? It is the east, and Juliet is the sun! Arise, fair sun, and kill the envious moon. It is my lady; O, it is my love! See, how she leans her cheek upon her hand! O, that I were a glove upon that hand, that I might touch that cheek!
JULIET: Ay me!
ROMEO: She speaks.
JULIET: O Romeo, Romeo! wherefore art thou Romeo? Deny thy father, and refuse thy name; or, if thou wilt not, be but sworn my love, and I'll no longer be a Capulet.
ROMEO: *[aside]* Shall I hear more, or shall I speak at this?
JULIET: 'Tis but thy name that is my enemy; thou art thyself though, not a Montague. What's Montague? it is nor hand, nor foot, nor arm, nor face, nor any other part belonging to a man. O, be some other name! What's in a name! that which we call a rose by any other name would smell as sweet; so Romeo would, were he not Romeo call'd, and for

that name, which is no part of thee, take all myself.
ROMEO: I take thee at thy word: Call me but love, and I'll be new baptized;
Henceforth I never will be Romeo.
JULIET: What man art thou, that, thus bescreen'd in night, so stumblest on my counsel?
ROMEO: By a name I know not how to tell thee who I am. My name, dear saint, is hateful to myself, because it is an enemy to thee; had I it written, I would tear the word.
JULIET: My ears have not yet drunk a hundred words of that tongue's utterance, yet I know the sound. Art thou not Romeo and a Montague?
ROMEO: Neither, fair saint, if either thee dislike.
JULIET: How camest thou hither, tell me, and wherefore? The orchard-walls are high and hard to climb; and the place death, considering who thou art, if any of my kinsmen find thee here.
ROMEO: With love's light wings did I o'er-perch these walls; for stony limits cannot hold love out.
JULIET: I would not for the world they saw thee here.
ROMEO: I have night's cloak to hide me from their sight; and but thou love me, let them find me here. My life were better ended by their hate than death prorogued, wanting of thy love.
JULIET: Thou know'st the mask of night is on my face, else would a maiden blush depaint my cheek for that which thou hast heard me speak to-night. Dost thou love me? I know thou wilt say "Ay"; and I will take thy word: yet, if thou swear'st, thou mayst prove false; at lovers' perjuries, they say, Jove laughs. O gentle Romeo, if thou dost love, pronounce it faithfully. Or if thou think'st I am too quickly won, I'll

frown, and be perverse, and say thee nay, so thou wilt woo; but else, not for the world. In truth, fair Montague, I am too fond; and therefore thou mayst think my haviour light. But trust me, gentleman, I'll prove more true than those that have more cunning to be strange. I should have been more strange, I must confess, but that thou overheard'st, ere I was ware, my true love's passion: therefore pardon me; and not impute this yielding to light love, which the dark night hath so discovered.

ROMEO: Lady, by yonder blessed moon I swear--

JULIET: O, swear not by the moon, th'inconstant moon, that monthly changes in her circled orb, lest that thy love prove likewise variable.

ROMEO: What shall I swear by?

JULIET: Do not swear at all; or, if thou wilt, swear by thy gracious self, which is the god of my idolatry, and I'll believe thee.

JULIET: Sweet, good night! This bud of love, by summer's ripening breath,

May prove a beauteous flower when next we meet.

Good night, good night! as sweet repose and rest

Come to thy heart as that within my breast!

ROMEO: O, wilt thou leave me so unsatisfied?

JULIET: What satisfaction canst thou have to-night?

ROMEO: Th'exchange of thy love's faithful vow for mine.

JULIET: I gave thee mine before thou didst request it. And yet I would it were to give again. My bounty is as boundless as the sea, my love as deep; the more I give to thee, the more I have, for both are infinite.

ROMEO: O blessed, blessed night! I am afeard, being in night, all this is but a dream, too flattering-sweet to be substantial. *[Reenter Juliet above]*

JULIET: Three words, dear Romeo, and good night indeed. If that thy bent of love be honourable, thy purpose marriage, send me word to-morrow, by one that I'll procure to come to thee, where and what time thou wilt perform the rite; and all my fortunes at thy foot I'll lay, and follow thee my lord throughout the world.

NURSE: *[within]* Madam!

JULIET: I come, anon. But if thou mean'st not well, I do beseech thee to cease thy suit, and leave me to my grief. To-morrow will I send.

ROMEO: So thrive my soul-

JULIET: A thousand times good night! Good night, good night! parting is such sweet sorrow, That I shall say good night till it be morrow. *[Exit]*

ROMEO: Sleep dwell upon thine eyes, peace in thy breast!-

Would I were sleep and peace, so sweet to rest!

Hence will I to my ghostly father's cell,

His help to crave, and my dear hap to tell. *[Exit]*

[Friar Laurence's cell] [Enter Friar Laurence and Romeo]

ROMEO: Good morrow, father.

FRIAR LAURENCE: What early tongue so sweet saluteth me?-

Young son, it argues a distemper'd head

So soon to bid good morrow to thy bed.

Or if not so, then here I hit it right,-

Our Romeo hath not been in bed to-night.

ROMEO: That last is true; the sweeter rest was mine.

FRIAR LAURENCE: God pardon sin! wast thou with Rosaline?

ROMEO: With Rosaline, my ghostly father? no;
I have forgot that name, and that name's woe.
FRIAR LAURENCE: That's my good son: but where hast thou been, then?
ROMEO: Then plainly know my heart's dear love is set
On the fair daughter of rich Capulet:
As mine on hers, so hers is set on mine;
And all combined, save what thou must combine
By holy marriage: when, and where, and how,
We met, we woo'd, and made exchange of vow,
I'll tell thee as we pass; but this I pray,
That thou consent to marry us to-day.
FRIAR LAURENCE: Holy Saint Francis, what a change is here!
Is Rosaline, whom thou didst love so dear,
So soon forsaken? young men's love, then, lies
Not truly in their hearts, but in their eyes.
ROMEO: Thou chidd'st me oft for loving Rosaline.
FRIAR LAURENCE: For doting, not for loving, pupil mine.
ROMEO: I pray thee, chide not: she whom I love now doth grace for grace and love for love allow. The other did not so.
FRIAR LAURENCE: O, she knew well thy love did read by rote, and could not spell. In one respect I'll thy assistant be; for this alliance may so happy prove, to turn your households' rancour to pure love.
ROMEO: O, let us hence; I stand on sudden haste.
FRIAR LAURENCE: Wisely, and slow; they stumble that run fast. *[Exeunt]*

[Capulet's orchard, Enter Juliet]
JULIET: The clock struck nine when I did send the nurse; In half an hour she promised to return.
[Enter Nurse] O honey nurse, what news? Hast thou met with him?
NURSE: I am a-weary, give me leave awhile: Fie, how my bones ache! what a jaunt have I had!
JULIET: I would thou hadst my bones, and I thy news. Nay, come, I pray thee, speak; good, good nurse, speak.
NURSE: Jesu, what haste? can you not stay awhile? Do you not see that I am out of breath?
JULIET: How art thou out of breath, when thou hast breath to say to me that thou art out of breath? What says he of our marriage? what of that?
NURSE: Your love says, like an honest gentleman, and a courteous, and a kind, and a handsome, and, I warrant, a virtuous,--Have you got leave to go to shrift to-day?
JULIET: I have.
NURSE: Then hie you hence to Friar Laurence' cell; There stays a husband to make you a wife. Hie you to church; I must another way, to fetch a ladder, by the which your love must climb a bird's-nest soon when it is dark.
JULIET: Hie to high fortune! Honest nurse, farewell.   *[Exeunt]*

[Friar Laurence's cell] [Enter Friar Laurence and Romeo]
FRIAR LAURENCE: So smile the heavens upon this holy act, that after-hours with sorrow chide us not! *[Enter Juliet, embraces Romeo]* Come, come with me, and we will make short work; For, by your leaves, you shall not stay alone till holy church incorporate two in one. *[Exeunt]*

[A public place] [Enter Mercutio, Benvolio, and Tybalt]

BENVOLIO: By my head, here come the Capulets.

MERCUTIO: By my heel, I care not.

TYBALT: Follow me close, for I will speak to them.

MERCUTIO: And but one word with one of us? couple it with something;

make it a word and a blow.

TYBALT: You shall find me apt enough to that, sir, an you will give me occasion.

MERCUTIO: Could you not take some occasion without giving?

TYBALT: Mercutio, thou consort'st with Romeo,--

MERCUTIO: Consort! what, dost thou make us minstrels?

TYBALT: Well, peace be with you, sir:- here comes my man. *[Enter Romeo]*

MERCUTIO: But I'll be hang'd, sir, if he wear your livery:

TYBALT: Romeo, the hate I bear thee can afford no better term than this,- thou art a villain.

ROMEO: Tybalt, the reason that I have to love thee doth much excuse the appertaining rage to such a greeting:- villain am I none. Therefore farewell; I see thou know'st me not.

TYBALT: Boy, this shall not excuse the injuries that thou hast done me; therefore turn, and draw.

ROMEO: I do protest I never injured thee; but love thee better than thou canst devise.

MERCUTIO:O calm, dishonourable, vile submission! *[Draws]* Tybalt, you rat-catcher, will you walk?

TYBALT: What wouldst thou have

ROMEO: Gentle Mercutio, put thy rapier up.

ROMEO: Draw, Benvolio; beat down their weapons. Gentlemen, for shame, forbear this outrage! Tybalt,- Mercutio,- the prince expressly hath forbidden bandying in Verona streets. *[Mercutio stabbed under Romeo's arm]*

MERCUTIO: I am hurt; A plague o' both your houses! I am sped.

BENVOLIO: What, art thou hurt?

MERCUTIO: Ay,ay, a scratch, a scratch; marry, 'tis enough. Where is my page? Go, villain, fetch a surgeon. *[Exit page]*

ROMEO: Courage, man; the hurt cannot be much.

MERCUTIO: No, 'tis not so deep as a well, nor so wide as a church door; but "is enough, 'twill serve: ask for me to-morrow, and you shall find me a grave man. Why, the devil, came you between us? I was hurt under your arm.

ROMEO: I thought all for the best.

MERCUTIO: Help me into some house, Benvolio, or I shall faint. They have made worms'-meat of me. *[Exit] [Enter Benvolio]*

BENVOLIO: O Romeo, Romeo, brave Mercutio's dead! *[Enter Tybalt]*

BENVOLIO: Here comes the furious Tybalt back again.

ROMEO: Alive, in triumph! and Mercutio slain! Now, Tybalt, take the "villain" back again that late thou gavest me; for Mercutio's soul is but a little way above our heads, staying for thine to keep him company.

TYBALT: Thou, wretched boy, that didst consort him here, shalt with him hence.

ROMEO: This shall determine that.

The citizens are up, and Tybalt slain:-
Stand not amazed; the prince will doom thee death, if thou art taken:-hence, be gone, away!
ROMEO: O, I am fortune's fool!
[Exit Romeo] [Enter Citizens and Officers]
FIRST OFFICER: Which way ran he that kill'd Mercutio? Tybalt, that murderer, which way ran he?
BENVOLIO: There lies that Tybalt.
[Enter Prince, old Montague, Capulet their Wives]
PRINCE ESCALUS: Where are the vile beginners of this fray?
BENVOLIO: O noble prince, I can discover all
The unlucky manage of this fatal brawl:
There lies the man, slain by young Romeo,
That slew thy kinsman, brave Mercutio.
LADY CAPULET: Tybalt, my cousin! O my brother's child!
PRINCE ESCALUS: Benvolio, who began this bloody fray?
BENVOLIO: Tybalt, here slain, whom Romeo's hand did slay; Romeo, that spoke him fair, bade him bethink how nice the quarrel was, and urged withal and to't they go like lightning; for, ere I could draw to part them, was stout Tybalt slain; And, as he fell, did Romeo turn and fly. This is the truth, or let Benvolio die.
LADY CAPULET: He is a kinsman to the Montague,
Affection makes him false, he speaks not true:
PRINCE ESCALUS: Romeo slew him, he slew Mercutio;
Who now the price of his dear blood doth owe?
MONTAGUE: Not Romeo, prince, he was Mercutio's friend;

His fault concludes but what the law should end,
The life of Tybalt.
PRINCE ESCALUS: And for that offence immediately we do exile him hence. *[Capulet's orchard, enter Juliet]*
JULIET: Give me my Romeo; and, when he shall die, take him and cut him out in little stars, and he will make the face of heaven so fine, that all the world will be in love with night. Now, nurse, what news? What hast thou there? the cords that Romeo bid thee fetch? *[enter nurse]*
NURSE: Ah, well-a-day! he's dead, he's dead, he's dead! We are undone, lady, we are undone!-Alack the day!-he's gone, he's kill'd, he's dead!
JULIET: Can heaven be so envious?
NURSE: Romeo can, though heaven cannot:-O Romeo, Romeo!
JULIET: What devil art thou, that dost torment me thus? This torture should be roar'd in dismal hell. Hath Romeo slain himself? say thou but "ay."
NURSE: O Tybalt, Tybalt, the best friend I had! O courteous Tybalt! honest gentleman! That ever I should live to see thee dead!
JULIET: What storm is this that blows so contrary? Is Romeo slaughter'd, and is Tybalt dead?
NURSE: Tybalt is gone, and Romeo banished; Romeo that kill'd him, he is banished.
JULIET: Blister'd be thy tongue for such a wish! he was not born to shame: Upon his brow shame is ashamed to sit; For 'tis a throne where honour may be crown'd sole monarch of the universal earth. O, what a beast was I to chide at him!
NURSE: Will you speak well of him that kill'd your cousin?
JULIET: Shall I speak ill of him that is my husband? Ah, poor my lord, what tongue shall smooth thy name,

when I, thy three-hours wife, have mangled it? But wherefore, villain, didst thou kill my cousin? That villain cousin would have kill'd my husband.

NURSE: Weeping and wailing over Tybalt's corse. Will you go to them? I will bring you thither.

JULIET: Wash they his wounds with tears: mine shall be spent,
When theirs are dry, for Romeo's banishment.
Take up those cords:--poor ropes, you are beguiled,
Both you and I; for Romeo is exiled:
He made you for a highway to my bed;
But I, a maid, die maiden-widowed.
Come, cords; come, nurse; I'll to my wedding-bed;
And death, not Romeo, take my maidenhead!

NURSE: Hie to your chamber: I'll find Romeo to comfort you.

JULIET: O, find him! give this ring to my true knight and bid him come to take his last farewell. *[Exeunt]*

[Friar Laurence's cell] [Enter Friar Laurence]

FRIAR LAURENCE: Romeo, come forth; come forth, thou fearful man. *[Enter Romeo]*

ROMEO: Father, what news? what is the prince's doom?

FRIAR LAURENCE: Too familiar is my dear son with such sour company. I bring thee tidings of the prince's doom. A gentler judgement-"banish'd" from his lips; Not body's death, but body's banishment. Hence from Verona art thou banished. Be patient, for the world is broad and wide.

ROMEO: There is no world without Verona walls, but purgatory, torture, hell itself.

FRIAR LAURENCE: O deadly sin! O rude unthankfulness!

ROMEO: 'Tis torture, and not mercy: heaven is here, where Juliet lives. *[Nurse knocks]*

FRIAR LAURENCE: Arise; one knocks; good Romeo, hide thyself. Who's there?

NURSE: Let me come in, and you shall know my errand. I come from Lady Juliet.

FRIAR LAURENCE: Welcome, then. *[Enter Nurse]*

NURSE: O holy friar, O, tell me, holy friar, where is my lady's lord, where's Romeo?

FRIAR LAURENCE: There on the ground, with his own tears made drunk.

NURSE: O, he is even in my mistress' case.

ROMEO: Spakest thou of Juliet? how is it with her? Doth she not think me an old murderer.

NURSE: O, she says nothing, sir, but weeps and weeps; and now falls on her bed; and then starts up, and Tybalt calls; and then on Romeo cries, and then down falls again. *[Romeo threatens suicide]*

FRIAR LAURENCE: Hold thy desperate hand! Art thou a man? thy form cries out thou art. Thy tears are womanish; thy wild acts denote the unreasonable fury of a beast. Unseemly woman in a seeming man! Hast thou slain Tybalt? wilt thou slay thyself? And slay thy lady that in thy life lives, by doing damned hate upon thyself?

NURSE: Here is a ring, sir, that she bade me give you. Hie you, make haste, for it grows very late. *[Exit]*

FRIAR LAURENCE: Go hence; good night; and here stands all your state. Either be gone before the watch be set, or by the break of day disguised from hence. Sojourn in Mantua; I'll find out your man and he shall signify from time to time every good hap to you that chances here.   Give me thy hand; 'tis late: farewell; good night.

ROMEO: But that a joy past joy calls out on me, it were a grief so brief to part with thee. Farewell. *[Exeunt]*

[A room in Capulet's house] [Enter old Capulet, Lady Capulet, and County Paris]

PARIS: These times of woe afford no time to woo. Madam, good night: commend me to your daughter.

LADY CAPULET: I will, and know her mind early to-morrow; To-night she's mew'd up to her heaviness.

CAPULET: Sir Paris, I will make a desperate tender of my child's love: I think she will be ruled in all respects by me; nay, more, I doubt it not. Wife, go you to her ere you go to bed; acquaint her here of my son Paris' love; and bid her, mark you me, on Wednesday next- But, soft! what day is this?

PARIS: Monday, my lord.

CAPULET: Monday! ha, ha! Well, Wednesday is too soon, O' Thursday let it be:- o' Thursday, tell her, she shall be married to this noble earl.

PARIS: My lord, I would that Thursday were to-morrow. *[Exeunt]*

[Juliet's chamber with Romeo preparing to leave]

JULIET: Wilt thou be gone? it is not yet near day. t was the nightingale, and not the lark, that pierced the fearful hollow of thine ear; nightly she sings on yond pomegranate-tree. Believe me, love, it was the nightingale.

ROMEO: It was the lark, the herald of the morn no nightingale. I must be gone and live, or stay and die.

JULIET: Yond light is not day-light, I know it, I. It is some meteor that the sun exhales, to be to thee this night a torch-bearer, and light thee on thy way to Mantua Therefore stay yet, thou need'st not to be gone.

ROMEO: Let me be ta'en, let me be put to death; I am content, so thou wilt have it so.

JULIET: Hie hence, be gone, away! It is the lark that sings so out of tune, straining harsh discords and unpleasing sharps. *[Enter Nurse]*

NURSE: Madam, your lady mother is coming to your chamber. The day is broke; be wary, look about. *[Exit]*

JULIET: Then, window, let day in, and let life out.

ROMEO: Farewell, farewell! one kiss, and I'll descend.

JULIET: O, think'st thou we shall ever meet again?

ROMEO: I doubt it not; and all these woes shall serve for sweet discourses in our time to come.

JULIET: O God, I have an ill-divining soul! Methinks I see thee, now thou art below, as one dead in the bottom of a tomb. Either my eyesight fails, or thou look'st pale.

ROMEO: And trust me, love, in my eye so do you. Dry sorrow drinks our blood. Adieu, adieu! *[Exit]*

LADY CAPULET: Ho, daughter! are you up?

JULIET: Who is't that calls? is it my lady mother?[Enter Lady Capulet]

LADY CAPULET: Evermore weeping for your cousin's death?

JULIET: Ay, madam, from the reach of these my hands. Would none but I might venge my cousin's death!

LADY CAPULET: But now I'll tell thee joyful tidings, girl. Marry, my child, early next Thursday morn, the gallant, young, and noble gentleman, the County Paris, at Saint Peter's Church, shall happily make thee there a joyful bride.

JULIET: Now, by Saint Peter's Church, and Peter too, he shall not make me there a joyful bride.

LADY CAPULET: Here comes your father; tell him so yourself, and see how he will take it at your hands.

[Enter Capulet]

CAPULET: When the sun sets, the air doth drizzle dew; but for the sunset of my brother's son it rains downright.

LADY CAPULET: Ay, sir; but she will none, she gives you thanks. I would the fool were married to her grave!

CAPULET: How! will she none? doth she not give us thanks? Is she not proud? doth she not count her bless'd unworthy as she is, that we have wrought so worthy a gentleman to be her bridegroom?

JULIET: Not proud, you have; but thankful, that you have. Proud can I never be of what I hate; but thankful even for hate, that is meant love.

CAPULET: But fettle your fine joints 'gainst Thursday next, to go with Paris to Saint Peter's Church, or I will drag thee on a hurdle thither. Out, you green-sickness carrion! out, you baggage! You tallow-face!

JULIET: Good father, I beseech you on my knees, hear me with patience but to speak a word.

CAPULET: Hang thee, young baggage! disobedient wretch! I tell thee what, get thee to church o' Thursday, or never after look me in the face.

LADY CAPULET: Talk not to me, for I'll not speak a word. Do as thou wilt, for I have done with thee.

[Exeunt]

JULIET: O God! O nurse, how shall this be prevented?

NURSE: Faith, here it is. Romeo is banished; and all the world to nothing, that he dares ne'er come back to challenge you. I think it best

you married with the county. O, he's a lovely gentleman! Romeo's a dishclout to him. I think you are happy in this second match, for it excels your first; or if it did not, your first is dead; or 'twere as good he were, as living here, and you no use of him.

JULIET: Speakest thou from thy heart?

NURSE: And from my soul too.

JULIET: Go in; and tell my lady I am gone, having displeased my father, to Laurence' cell, to make confession, and to be absolved.

NURSE: Marry, I will; and this is wisely done. *[Exit]*

JULIET: Ancient damnation! O most cursed fiend! Go, counsellor. Thou and my bosom henceforth shall be twain. I'll to the friar, to know his remedy. If all else fail, myself have power to die. *[Exit]*

[Friar Laurence's cell] [Enter Friar Laurence and Paris]

FRIAR LAURENCE: On Thursday, sir? the time is very short.

PARIS: My father Capulet will have it so; and I am nothing slow to slack his haste.

FRIAR LAURENCE: Look, sir, here comes the lady toward my cell.

[Enter Juliet]

PARIS: Happily met, my lady and my wife!

JULIET: That may be, sir, when I may be a wife.

PARIS: That may be must be, love, on Thursday next.

FRIAR LAURENCE: My leisure serves me, pensive daughter, now. My lord, we must entreat the time alone.

PARIS: God shield I should disturb devotion! Juliet, on Thursday early will I rouse ye. Till then, adieu; and keep this holy kiss. *[Exit]*

JULIET: O, shut the door! and when thou hast done so, come weep with me; past hope, past cure, past help! Tell me not, friar, that thou hear'st of this, unless thou tell me how I may prevent it. God join'd my heart and Romeo's, thou our hands; and ere this hand, by thee to Romeo seal'd, shall be the label to another deed, or my true heart with treacherous revolt turn to another, this shall slay them both. Give me some present counsel; or, behold, 'twixt my extremes and me this bloody knife shall play the umpire. Be not so long to speak; I long to die, if what thou speak'st speak not of remedy.

FRIAR LAURENCE: If, rather than to marry County Paris,
Thou hast the strength of will to slay thyself,
Then is it likely thou wilt undertake
A thing like death to chide away this shame,
That copest with death himself to scape from it;
And, if thou darest, I'll give thee remedy.

JULIET: O, bid me leap, rather than marry Paris, from off the battlements of yonder tower.

FRIAR LAURENCE: Hold, then; go home, be merry, give consent you marry Paris. To-morrow night look that thou lie alone, let not thy nurse lie with thee in thy chamber. Take thou this vial, being then in bed, and this distilled liquor drink thou off. When, presently, through all thy veins shall run a cold and drowsy humour; for no pulse shall keep his native progress, but surcease. No warmth, no breath, shall testify thou livest. he roses in thy lips and cheeks shall fade to paly ashes; thy eyes' windows fall, like death, when he shuts up the day of life. Each part, deprived of supple government, shall, stiff and stark and cold, appear like death. And in this borrow'd likeness of shrunk death thou shalt continue two-and-forty hours, and then awake as from a pleasant sleep. Thou shalt be borne to that same ancient vault where all the kindred of the Capulets lie. In the mean time, against thou shalt awake, shall Romeo by my letters know our drift; and hither shall he come: and he and I will watch thy waking, and that very night shall Romeo bear thee hence to Mantua.

JULIET: Give me, give me! O, tell not me of fear!

FRIAR LAURENCE: Hold; get you gone, be strong and prosperous in this resolve: I'll send a friar with speed to Mantua, with my letters to thy lord.

JULIET: Love give me strength! and strength shall help afford.Farewell, dear father!   *[Exeunt]*

[Juliet's chamber] [Enter Juliet and Nurse]
JULIET: Gentle nurse, I pray thee, leave me to myself to-night. *[Enter Lady Capulet]*
LADY CAPULET: Good night:
Get thee to bed, and rest; for thou hast need.   *[Exeunt]*
JULIET: Farewell! God knows when we shall meet again. Come, vial. What if this mixture do not work at all? Must I of force be married to the county? No, no; this shall forbid it:- lie thou there.*[Laying down her dagger]* Romeo, I come! this do I drink to thee. *[Falls upon her bed] [Enter Nurse]*
NURSE: Mistress!- what, mistress!- Juliet!- fast, I warrant her, you slug-a-bed! Help, help! my lady's dead!- O, well-a-day, that ever I was born! My lord! my lady! *[Enter Lady Capulet]*
LADY CAPULET: What is the matter? O me, O me! My child, my

only life, envive, look up, or I will die with thee! Help, help!- call help.
[Enter Capulet]
CAPULET: For shame, bring Juliet forth; her lord is come.
NURSE: She's dead, deceased, she's dead; alack the day!
CAPULET: Let me see her. Her blood is settled, and her joints are stiff. Life and these lips have long been separated. Death lies on her like an untimely frost upon the sweetest flower of all the field. *[Enter Friar Laurence and Paris]*
FRIAR LAURENCE: Come, is the bride ready to go to church?
CAPULET: Ready to go, but never to return. O son, the night before thy wedding-day hath Death lain with thy wife: see there she lies, flower as she was, deflowered by him Death is my son-in-law, Death is my heir; my daughter he hath wedded: I will die, and leave him all; life, living, all is Death's.
PARIS:Beguiled, divorced, wronged, spited, slain! Most detestable Death, by thee beguiled, by cruel cruel thee quite overthrown! O love! O life! not life, but love in death!
CAPULET: All things that we ordained festival turn from their office to black funeral. Our instruments to melancholy bells; our wedding cheer to a sad burial feast; our solemn hymns to sullen dirges change; our bridal flowers serve for a burial corse; and all things change them to the contrary.*[Exeunt]*

[Mantua] [Enter Romeo]
ROMEO: I dreamt my lady came and found me dead, strange dream, that gives a dead man leave to think! And breathed such life with kisses in my lips, that I revived, and was an emperor.*[Enter Balthasar]* News from Verona! Dost thou not bring me letters from the friar? How doth my lady?
BALTHASAR: Then she is well, and nothing can be ill. Her body sleeps in Capels' monument, and her immortal part with angels lives.
ROMEO: Leave me, and do the thing I bid thee do. Hast thou no letters to me from the friar?
BALTHASAR: No, my good lord.
ROMEO: Well, Juliet, I will lie with thee to-night. Let's see for means. What, ho! apothecary! *[Enter Apothecary]*
APOTHECARY: Who calls so loud?
ROMEO: Come hither, man. Let me have a dram of poison as will disperse itself through all the veins.
APOTHECARY: Such mortal drugs I have. Put this in any liquid thing you will, and drink it off; and, if you had the strength of twenty men, it would dispatch you straight. *[Exeunt]*

[Friar Laurence's cell] [Enter Friar John]
FRIAR LAURENCE: Welcome from Mantua: what says Romeo? Or, if his mind be writ, give me his letter. Who bare my letter to Romeo?
FRIAR JOHN: I could not send it, here it is again.
FRIAR LAURENCE: Now must I to the monument alone. Within this three hours will fair Juliet wake. *[Exeunt]*

[A churchyard] [Enter County Paris]
PARIS: Sweet flower, with flowers thy bridal bed I strew.*[Enter Romeo]* This is that banish'd haughty Montague that murder'd my love's cousin,with which grief, it is supposed, the fair creature died. Condemned villain, I do apprehend

thee. Obey, and go with me; for thou must die.

ROMEO: I must indeed; and therefore came I hither. Good gentle youth, tempt not a desperate man. Wilt thou provoke me? then have at thee, boy! *[Paris falls]*

ROMEO: *[Enters tomb]* Eyes, look your last! Arms, take your last embrace! and, lips, O you the doors of breath, seal with a righteous kiss a dateless bargain to engrossing death! Come, bitter conduct, come, unsavoury guide! Thou desperate pilot, now at once run on the dashing rocks thy sea-sick weary bark! Here's to my love! O true apothecary! Thy drugs are quick. Thus with a kiss I die. *[Enter Friar Laurence]*

FRIAR LAURENCE: Romeo! O, pale! Who else? what, Paris too? The lady stirs. *[Juliet wakens]*

JULIET: O comfortable friar! where is my lord? I do remember well where I should be, and there I am: where is my Romeo?

FRIAR LAURENCE: I hear some noise. Lady, come from that nest of death, contagion, and unnatural sleep. A greater power than we can contradict hath thwarted our intents. Thy husband in thy bosom there lies dead. Come, I'll dispose of thee among a sisterhood of holy nuns. Come, good Juliet; I dare no longer stay. *[Exit]*

JULIET: Go, get thee hence, for I will not away. What's here? a cup, closed in my true love's hand? Poison, I see, hath been his timeless end. O churl! drunk all, and left no friendly drop to help me after? I will kiss thy lips. Haply some poison yet doth hang on them, to make me die with a restorative. Thy lips are warm! Yea, noise? Then I'll be brief. O happy dagger! *[Uses Romeo's dagger]* This is thy sheath; there

rust, and let me die. *[She stabs herself and falls] [Enter Watch]*

FIRST WATCHMAN: Go tell the prince, run to the Capulets, raise up the Montagues. *[Enter the Prince]*

PRINCE ESCALUS: What misadventure is so early up, that calls our person from our morning rest? *[Enter old Capulet, Lady Capulet]*

CAPULET: What should it be, that they so shriek abroad?

LADY CAPULET: The people in the street cry "Romeo," some "Juliet," and some "Paris;" and all run, with open outcry, toward our monument.

FIRST WATCHMAN: Sovereign, here lies the County Paris slain; and Romeo dead; and Juliet, dead before, Warm, and new kill'd.

PRINCE ESCALUS: Search, seek, and know how this foul murder comes.

LADY CAPULET: O me! this sight of death is as a bell, that warns my old age to a sepulchre. *[Enter old Montague]*

PRINCE ESCALUS: Come, Montague for thou art early up, to see thy son and heir more early down.

MONTAGUE: Alas, my liege, my wife is dead to-night. Grief of my son's exile hath stopp'd her breath. What further woe conspires against mine age?

PRINCE ESCALUS: Look, and thou shalt see.

FRIAR LAURENCE: I am the greatest, able to do least, yet most suspected, as the time and place doth make against me, of this direful murder; And here I stand, both to impeach and purge myself condemned and myself excused.

PRINCE ESCALUS: See, what a scourge is laid upon your hate, that heaven finds means to kill your joys

with love! And I, for winking at your
discords too, have lost a brace of
kinsmen: all are punish'd.
CAPULET: O brother Montague,
give me thy hand.This is my
daughter's jointure, for no more can I
demand.
MONTAGUE: But I can give thee
more. For I will raise her statue in
pure gold; That while Verona by that
name is known, there shall no figure
at such rate be set as that of true and
faithful Juliet.
PRINCE ESCALUS: A glooming
peace this morning with it brings;
The sun, for sorrow, will not show
his head:
Go hence, to have more talk of these
sad things;
Some shall be pardon'd, and some
punished:
For never was a story of more woe
Than this of Juliet and her Romeo.
[Exeunt]

Norman windows in Westminister Abbey, the burial site of Mary I and Elizabeth I

15. *THE TWO GENTLEMEN OF VERONA*

<u>The play</u>

Another of Shakespeare's early plays dealing with love, the confusion of identity, and the relationship between men and women and men and men is *The Two Gentlemen of Verona* in which two good friends, Valentine and Proteus, separate company in order to achieve two different goals; one is to develop in the ways of the world by experiencing life in Milan, while the other is to woo and marry a young lady. In this play the relationship between men and women is of less importance than the male bonding which occurs, a fairly common notion in a late Middle Ages and early Renaissance society in which women are at best second class citizens and the property of first their fathers and then their husbands.

As the play opens, the lover Proteus sends his friend's manservant to deliver a note to his beloved Julia. The manservant returns much taken aback that Julia has not rewarded him for delivering the note with even so much as a small tip. The manservant, Speed, warns Proteus that Julia is cold and unapproachable and will probably be difficult to win. However, Proteus feels that the failure lies, not in the wooing, but in the delivery of the words of love and goes off to find a better delivery method. Neither appears to realize that Julia is playing coy and hard-to-get as is the custom of young women.

In the meantime, Julia seeks advice on love from her maid-servant, Lucetta. Julia is still fairly young and innocent about the game of love; she is even unsure of which suitor to favor with her affections. However, when Lucetta produces Proteus' freshly delivered letter which she received for Julia over her protests, Julia quickly but furtively shows interest in Proteus. Julia is aware of the proper behavior for a sweet, young woman encountering her first love and does not want to appear too eager to receive love tokens from Proteus. Julia, therefore, refuses to read the letter as she orders it removed from her sight. Lucetta, being privy to the customs of the upperclass, understand that Julia must outwardly follow the customary and expected behavior of the times and pretends to remove the letter in order to return it with her mistress' regrets. In actuality, the offending love letter is left on the table within easy view of Julia who guiltily reads it, being relieved to find that the letter has been left behind. Now, unfortunately, proper etiquette demands that Julia make a great show of destroying the offensive but beautifully written epistle of love. She orders Lucetta to destroy the letter by tearing it into small pieces. Lucetta is aware of the cat-and-mouse game being played by her young mistress and mockingly says that Julia "would be best pleased/To be so ang'red with another letter."(Act I, sc ii)

Proteus' father has other expectations for his love-lorn son as he makes immediate plans to send Proteus to spend time away from home in order to be a properly trained gentleman. Upon hearing of his departure the next day, Proteus asks for more time thinking that he can win Julia with a few more days' effort. However, the extension is denied by his father and the journey is set to begin. Proteus takes full advantage of the time remaining before his departure to aggressively press and win his suit before leaving for Milan after exchanging rings and promises of constancy with Julia. Unfortunately, as soon as Proteus arrives in Milan and meets Silvia, daughter of the Duke of Milan and love of his friend Valentine, he falls in love with her and begins to plot a method by which to gain her love. Julia is forgotten and left pining away in Verona.

The scene changes from Verona to Milan where the reader finds Valentine and Speed, his man-servant, discussing the letter which Valentine has composed for Silvia. When Valentine tries to deliver the letter which he has written at Silvia's request, she rejects it saying that if the letter does not please him as its author, it could not possibly be sufficiently well written for her to send or receive although she admits that it contains some well stated points. Speed does not see Silvia's rejection of the letter as a dismissal of Valentine's writing ability but as Silvia's way of saying that she agrees with the sentiments expressed and wants the letter delivered to its proper recipient, Valentine, without actually expressing her feelings. Valentine is so love-sick after this exchange which he perceives as rejection by the object of his affection that he refuses dinner.

Meanwhile the love-sick Julia begins to formulate a plan which will take her to Milan to be with Proteus not knowing that she is but a distant memory. Understanding that the trip is arduous and unseemly for a woman, she decides to travel in the disguise of a page in search of employment. She is warned by Lucetta that Proteus' affection might have cooled since his departure; however, Julia has the utmost confidence in the constancy of his love and continues her preparations believing that the ever-faithful Proteus will rejoice upon seeing her again.

Proteus, despite his friendship with Valentine, decides that the easiest way to clear the path to Silvia is by telling her father about the elopement plans made by Valentine and Silvia for that same night, knowing that the Duke of Milan objects to the union of Valentine and Silvia. The Duke reacts as predicted as he begins to develop a plan by which to uncover Valentine's feelings for Silvia. The Duke pretends to himself be in love with a woman who will not accept his attentions and asks Valentine to suggest the proper way in which to press his suit. Valentine tells the Duke all of the things to do and unknowingly divulges his own plans regarding the conquest of Silvia. The Duke tries on Valentine's cloak concealed in which is a love letter to Silvia which is all that the Duke requires as proof of Valentine's plans for his daughter. He banishes Valentine from his court forever. Poor Valentine would rather be dead than never to see Silvia again. Valentine's concerned friend, Proteus, offers to be the go-between for the delivery of his letters to Silvia. The trusting, naive Valentine agrees to the arrangement and entrusts his beloved into the hands of his best friend.

Thurio, another of Silvia's intended suitors and the Duke of Milan's favorite, is reassured by the Duke that Silvia will surely be more receptive to his affections now that Valentine is banished. The ever helpful Proteus offer his assistance also as the go-between for Thurio in order to disparage Valentine. The men do not suspect Proteus' ulterior motive which is to position himself with Silvia and to double cross the Duke of Milan, Valentine, and Thurio. Silvia, however without appearing overly offended by the duplicity of Proteus, rejects his words of love reminding Proteus of his friendship for Valentine.

Unknown to either Proteus or Silvia, Julia has arrived in Milan and has overheard the conversation in which Proteus tries to discredit his friend and make himself the object of Silvia's affections. Later that day, Julia begins her own plan to regain her position with Proteus as she is introduced to Proteus as the page Sebastian. Proteus employs Julia to give the ring once given to him by her as a love token to Silvia. Silvia refuses to accept the ring knowing that it is a woman's ring and was once given to Proteus as a token of affection by a forgotten lover.

Later, Silvia runs away to find the banished Valentine with the help of her agent of escape Eglamour. However, her disappearance is quickly discovered by the Duke of Milan, Thurio, and Proteus who follow her. Julia, of course, follows Proteus to prevent him from winning Silvia for himself. They find Silvia hiding in an outlaw's cave in which, unknown to her, Valentine is also hiding. Silvia scolds Proteus for swearing his love to her when he is loved by another and for betraying his friendship with Valentine to which he replies, "In love/Who respects friends?" As Proteus tries to force Silvia to accept his affections, Valentine appears out of the recesses of the cave to stop him.

The play ends with Valentine accepting Proteus' apology for his poor
conduct, Julia unmasking herself by showing Proteus the ring given to her by him,
Thurio denouncing any interest in Silvia if he must fight for her, the Duke of
Milan allowing Valentine to marry his daughter, and the couples planning a
double wedding with the men having forgotten their rivalry for the same woman.

<u>Julia</u>

Shakespeare's Julia is a young woman who, in the beginning of the play,
is torn between convention and the desire to respond to the affections of a young
man whom she finds attractive. She knows that custom requires her to reject his
letters repeatedly before reluctantly and with resignation opening them. She,
however, is tricked by her maid-servant into reading Proteus' letters when they
are first offered. Julia does not regret this breach of custom for very long as she
begins to encourage Proteus' affections. An example of her torment over the
disposition of the letter occurs in Act I, scene ii in which Julia chides herself for
her lack of resolve in reading the letter.

> Nay, would I were so ang'red with the same!
> O hateful hands, to tear such loving words!
> Injurious wasps, to feed on such sweet honey,
> And kill the bees that yield it with your stings!
> I'll kiss each several paper for amends.
> Look, here is writ 'Kind Julia,' Unkind Julia!
> As in revenge of thy ingratitude,
> I will throw thy name against the bruising stones,
> Trampling contemptuously on thy disdain.
> And here is writ 'Love-wounded Proteus.'
> Poor wounded name! My bosom as a bed
> Shall lodge thee til thy wound be thoroughly healed,
> And thus I search it with a sovereign kiss.
> But twice or thrice was 'Proteus' written down-
> Becalm good wind, blow not a word away
> Til I have found each letter in the letter.

Once they fall in love, Julia firmly believes in the teachings of society
which encourages people to be monogamous. Little does she suspect that the
object of her affection will deny her existence and fall for another woman.

Julia, perhaps reflecting the new Renaissance woman's desire for freedom
of choice and expression, follows Proteus to Milan where she discovers his
infidelity first hand. Dressed as a young page boy, Julia has the opportunity to

eaves-drop on Proteus' conversations and to play a role in her own deception. However, she does not rage at Proteus but accepts his apology when his deceit is unmasked. She and his friend, Valentine, appear to accept Proteus' lack of constancy to both of them as natural and expected of a young man newly sent out on his own. After all, it is not possible for Julia to react too strongly when Valentine, whose beloved is wooed by his best friend while he is in exile, accepts the deed as natural. Even Silvia who is passed from one man to another for safe keeping is not offended by such treatment. The camaraderie between men allows for this type of transgression and that camaraderie is stronger than the fidelity that a man owes to a girlfriend.

Shakespeare has tried to show in *The Two Gentlemen of Verona* that the relationship between two buddies supersedes the relationship between a man and a woman. Proteus is quickly forgiven his transgressions by Valentine, the women understand the camaraderie between the men, and both couples plan to be fast friends forever, even sharing a wedding day. However liberated and free-spirited Julia may appear in her decision to follow her love to Milan, her relationship with and understanding of Proteus is not as important as Proteus' relationship with Valentine. The relationship of male bonding is more important in that society than the relationship between man and woman.

Shakespeare echoes this feeling in his sonnets in which he writes to the other man about the unworthy woman for whom they both have an interest. Shakespeare does not try in his sonnets to convince the woman that the other man is not worthy of her, he tries to convince the other man that the woman is not worthy of his attentions. In *The Two Gentlemen of Verona* the love relationship with the women is secondary to the understanding shared by Valentine and Proteus that man's affections and loyalties will be, at times, inconstant but will always be understood and forgiven in the brotherhood of men.

Bibliography

Bate, Walter Johnson, *From Classic to Romantic*: *Premises of Taste in Eighteenth Century England*. New York: Harper Torchbooks, 1961.

Bergeron, David and Desousa, Gerald U., *William Shakespeare: A Study and Research Guide*. Kansas: University Press of Kansas, 1987.

Bindoff, S. T., *Tudor England*. New York, Penquin Books, 1983.

Black, J. B. *The Reign of Elizabeth 1558-1603*. Oxford. Oxford University Press, 1987.

Bradbury, Jim, *William Shakespeare and His Theatre*. England: Longman Group Limited, 1975.

Burrell, Sidney A., ed., *The Role Religion in Modern European History*. New York: The Macmillan Company, 1964.

Brye, M. St. Clare, *Elizabethan Life in Town and Country*. London: University Paperback, 1961.

Chute, Marchette, *William Shakespeare of London*. New York: E. P. Dutton and Company, Inc., 1974.

___, *An Introduction to William Shakespeare*. New York: E. P. Dutton and Company, Inc., 1974.

Day, Martin S., *History of English Literature to 1660*. New York: Doubleday and Co., Inc., 1973.

Dean, Leonard, ed., *William Shakespeare: Modern Essays in Criticism*. Oxford: Oxford University Press, 1967.

Eastman, Arthur M., *A Short History of Shakespearean Criticism*. Washington, D. C.: University Press of America, Inc., 1965.

Eliot, T. S., *Essays on Elizabethan Drama*. New York: Harcourt, Brace and World, Inc. 1932.

Evans, Gareth Lloyd, *The Upstart Crow: An Introduction to Shakespeare's Plays*. London: J.M. Demont and Sons, LTD, 1982.

Frader, Russell, *Young William Shakespeare*. New York: Columbia University Press, 1988.

Frankenberg, Lloyd, ed., *Poems of William Shakespeare*. New York: Thomas Y. Crowell Company, 1966.

Frye, Northrop, *Northrop Frye on William Shakespeare*. Ontario: Fitshenry and Whiteside, 1986.

Goddard, Harold C. , *The Meaning of William Shakespeare*. Illinois: University of Chicago Press, 1951.

Harbage. Alfred, ed., *William Shakespeare: The Complete Works*. Maryland: Penquin Books, 1969.

Holmes, Martin, *Elizabethan London*. New York: Frederick A. Praeger, Inc., 1969.

Hill, Christopher, *The Century of Revolution: 1603-1714*. New York: W.W. Norton and Company, Inc., 1961.

Halliday, R. E., *William Shakespeare*. New York; Thames and Hudson, 1956.

Jones, Ernest, *Hamlet and Oedipus*. New York: W. W. Norton and Company, Inc., 1954.

Kaufman, Ralph, J., ed., *Elizabethan Drama: Modern Essays in Criticism*. Oxford: Oxford University Press, 1961.

Kenan, Alvin B., ed., *Modern Shakespearean Criticism*. New York: Harcourt, Brace and World, Inc., 1970.

Knight, G. Wilson, *Shakespeare's Dramatic Challenge*. Washington, E. D.: University Press of America, 1981.

Levi, Peter, *The Life and Times of William William Shakespeare*. New York: Henry Holt and Company, 1988.

Magill, Frank N. ed., *English Literature: William Shakespeare*. California: Salem Press Inc., 1988.

McCartry, Jo, *Understanding Shakespeare's England: A Companion for the American Reader*. Connecticut: Archon Book, 1989.

Neale, J. E., *Elizabeth and her Parliament*. New York: W. W. Norton and Company, Inc., 1958.

Plowden, Alison, *Tudor Women: Queen and Commoners*. London: Butler and Tanner, Inc., 1979.

Pohl, Frederick J., Like to the Lark: *The Early Years of William Shakespeare*. New York: Clarkson N. Potter, Inc., 1972.

Read, Conyers, *The Tudors*. New York: Holt, Rinehart and Winston, Inc., 1963.

Read, Rover Rentoul, Jr., *The Occult of the Tudor and Stuart Stage*. Massachusettes: The Christopher Publishing House, 1965,

Righter, Anne, *William Shakespeare and the Idea of the Play*. New York: Penquin Book LTD, 1967.

Rowse, A. L., *The Elizabethan Renaissance: The Cultural Achievement*. New York: Charles Scribner's Sons, 1972.

___, *The Elizabethan Renaissance: The Life of Society*. New York: Charles Scribner's Sons, 1971.

___, *The England of Elizabeth*. New York: Macmillan Company, 1950.

___, *William Shakespeare: The Man*. London: Macmillan Press LTD, 1988.

Saccio, Peter, *Shakespeare's English Kings*. Oxford: Oxford University Press, 1977.

Santwood, George Van, ed., *The Merry Wives of Windsor*. Connecticut: Yale University Press, 1922.

Scott, A. F., *The Tudor Age*. New York: Thomas Crowell Co., 1976.

Spurgeon, Caroline F. E., *Shakespeare's Imagery and What It Tells Us*. Massachusettes: Beacon Press, 1961.

Tillyard, E. M. W., *The Elizabethan World Picture*. New York: Vantage Books, ?.

Wells, Stanley, ed., *The Cambridge Companion to William Shakespeare Studies*. Cambridge: Cambridge University Press, 1986.

A Note about the Author

Courtni Crump Wright is a teacher of English at The National Cathedral School in Washington, D. C. She is a Council for Basic Education and The National Endowment for the Humanities Independent Study in the Humanities Fellow (1990). She was awarded a Master of Education degree from Johns Hopkins University in 1980. Born in Washington, D. C in 1950, she was graduated from Trinity College (D.C.) in 1972 with an undergraduate degree in English and a minor in History. She is currently researching and writing children's books on the African-American theme.